Pop Stars on Film

Pop Stars on Film

Popular Culture in a Global Market

Edited by
Kirsty Fairclough and Jason Wood

BLOOMSBURY ACADEMIC
NEW YORK · LONDON · OXFORD · NEW DELHI · SYDNEY

BLOOMSBURY ACADEMIC
Bloomsbury Publishing Inc
1385 Broadway, New York, NY 10018, USA
50 Bedford Square, London, WC1B 3DP, UK
29 Earlsfort Terrace, Dublin 2, Ireland

BLOOMSBURY, BLOOMSBURY ACADEMIC and the Diana logo are trademarks of
Bloomsbury Publishing Plc

First published in the United States of America 2023
Paperback edition published 2024

Copyright © Kirsty Fairclough and Jason Wood, 2023

Each chapter copyright by the contributor, 2023

For legal purposes the Acknowledgements on p. viii constitute an extension
of this copyright page.

Cover design: Louise Dugdale
Cover image courtesy of HOME

All rights reserved. No part of this publication may be reproduced or transmitted
in any form or by any means, electronic or mechanical, including photocopying,
recording or any information storage or retrieval system, without prior
permission in writing from the publishers.

Bloomsbury Publishing Inc does not have any control over, or responsibility for, any
third-party websites referred to or in this book. All internet addresses given in this
book were correct at the time of going to press. The author and publisher regret any
inconvenience caused if addresses have changed or sites have ceased to exist, but can
accept no responsibility for any such changes.

A catalog record for this book is available from the Library of Congress

ISBN: HB: 978-1-5013-7251-3
PB: 978-1-5013-7255-1
ePDF: 978-1-5013-7253-7
eBook: 978-1-5013-7252-0

Typeset by Newgen KnowledgeWorks Pvt. Ltd., Chennai, India

To find out more about our authors and books visit www.bloomsbury.com
and sign up for our newsletters.

Contents

List of Figures	vii
Acknowledgements	viii
Notes on Contributors	ix
Foreword	xii

Introduction 1
Kirsty Fairclough and Jason Wood

1 The boy can't help it: Little Richard's disruption and reconstruction of Black male screen performativity 11
   Tom Attah

2 There's always gonna be queens on the rag: Madonna and queer intertextuality 31
   Sarah Perks

3 Prince's fashion during the *Batman* era: Symbols, silhouettes and the return of purple 47
   Karen Turman

4 'Meet the long-lost Phillip Jeffries': The elusive cinema of David Bowie 63
   James King

5 Where the popular meets the esoteric: *Videodrome* (1983) and *Holy Motors* (2012) 81
   Ellen Smith

6 Translating personas: French singers on film 95
   Andy Willis

7 Adam Ant, John Lydon and Jordan: Punk stars on film 111
   Rachel Hayward

8 From the street to the dance floor: Political imaginings of the pop star in popular Indian cinema 131
   Omar Ahmed

9	'... and presenting JUANITA MOORE as Annie Johnson and MAHALIA JACKSON as Choir Soloist' ... singing 'Trouble of the World' in *Imitation of Life* *Benjamin Halligan*	147
10	Cinema, jazz and representation *Daniel Graham*	167
11	Ryuichi Sakamoto: Behind the mask *Jason Wood*	181
12	Reframing time and space in *Dogs in Space* *Kristy Matheson*	195

Index 211

Figures

9.1 Details from three opening credit titles, from *Imitation of Life* (1959) — 152
9.2 Sirk juxtaposes open gazes of desire from free white men with a hidden gaze of horror, for which bars cage the face of the on-looking African American: Sarah Jane's performance of 'Empty Arms' in Harry's Club — 158
9.3 Unfamiliarity, jarringly, crowds the frame – unknowns and, outlandishly, a bit-part player, indicate that another life was lived, as Mahalia Jackson sings at Annie's funeral — 161
9.4 The crowd shots from the 1959 newsreel '"*Imitation of Life*" Has Gala Preview' — 163
11.1 Ryuichi Sakamoto — 182

Acknowledgements

The editors are grateful to all the writers who generously contributed as well as the following individuals and organisations for their assistance during the completion of this book: Barry Adamson, Leah, Amy and Rachel at Bloomsbury New York, Kat Harrison-Dibbits, HOME, Steve Jenkins, Andy Starke, Bob Stanley and Peter Strickland.

Notes on Contributors

Barry Adamson is a self-taught musician who rose to prominence as the bass player in Magazine and toured extensively. His establishment as a solo artist came after a three-year stint with Nick Cave and the Bad Seeds and heralded the release of his seminal first solo album, *Moss Side Story*. Critically acclaimed, it raised Adamson's name as a composer of diverse complexity, working with the film industry's most intriguing mavericks including Derek Jarman, David Lynch and Oliver Stone. In 2021, Adamson published his memoir *Up Above the City, Down Beneath the Stars* – written in his own distinctive, cinematic-noir style and shining a probing light into his own heart of darkness. Having released nine studio albums, including the 1992 Mercury Music Prize–nominated *Soul Murder*, Adamson continues an esteemed career, with his talents being in as much demand by new generations of artists, as he was after his first solo release.

Omar Ahmed is a freelance film scholar and international film curator. He has a PhD in Screen Studies (funded by the AHRC) from the University of Manchester, specialising in alternative South Asian cinema. Omar taught Media and Film Studies in Further & Higher Education for over fifteen years. He also co-curates 'Not Just Bollywood' for HOME in Manchester. He has published widely particularly on Indian cinema and most recently co-curated a major strand on Indian Parallel Cinema for 'Il Cinema Ritrovato' in Bologna, Italy. He lives in Manchester with his wife and two children, writes regularly on Indian cinema for his film site 'Movie Mahal' and is currently researching and writing a book on Indian Parallel Cinema.

Tom Attah is a musician, teacher and published author who leads the BMus (Hons) Popular Music Performance degree at Leeds Arts University. His research and writing focusses on the effects of technology on popular music and culture, particularly the blues. As a guitarist and singer, Tom performs solo, with acoustic duos and as leader of an electric band. Tom's solo acoustic work includes his own original blues compositions and has led to international theatre tours and performances at major music festivals. Tom's media appearances as a subject matter expert in blues include multiple performances and documentaries for BBC Radio and Sky Arts.

Kirsty Fairclough is Professor of Screen Studies and Head of Research and Innovation at the School of Digitals Arts at Manchester Metropolitan University, UK. She is the co-editor of *Prince and Popular Culture* (2020), *The*

Music Documentary: Acid Rock to Electropop (2013), *The Arena Concert: Music, Media and Mass Entertainment* (2015), *The Legacy of Mad Men: Cultural History, Intermediality and American Television* (2019), *Music/Video: Forms, Aesthetics, Media* (2017) and author of the forthcoming *Beyoncé: Celebrity Feminism and Popular Culture*. She is the curator of 'Sound and Vision: Pop Stars on Film' and 'In Her View: Women Documentary Filmmakers' film seasons at HOME, Manchester, and chair of Manchester Jazz Festival.

Daniel Graham has worked in film exhibition, distribution and journalism and has written and directed short films in Australia and France. In 2011 Graham worked for Mexican auteur Carlos Reygadas as line producer on *Post Tenebras Lux*, which won Best Director at the 2012 Cannes Film Festival. This formative encounter with Reygadas led directly to Graham's first feature film as writer/director, Opus Zero (2012, UK/Mexico, Willem Dafoe). Influenced by the work of Theo Angelopoulos and Michelangelo Antonioni, *Opus Zero* was released in the UK by New Wave Films and led to Daniel's second feature film *The Obscure Life of the Grand Duke of Corsica*, starring Timothy Spall and Peter Stormare. Summer 2022 will see the release of Graham's third film *Prizefighter*, a period film boxing drama starring Russell Crowe and Ray Winstone. Daniel has periodically written on jazz for www.allaboutjazz.com, including a career profile on free jazz trumpet player Bobby Bradford.

Benjamin Halligan is Director of the Doctoral College for the University of Wolverhampton. Publications include the monographs *Michael Reeves* (Manchester University Press), *Desires for Reality: Radicalism and Revolution in Western European Film* (Berghahn) and *Hotbeds of Licentiousness: The British Glamour Film and the Permissive Age* (Berghahn), and the co-edited collections *Diva: Feminism and Fierceness from Pop to Hip Hop* (Bloombury), *Adult Themes: British Cinema and the "X" Certificate in the Long 1960s* (Bloombury), *Politics of the Many: Contemporary Radical Thought and the Crisis of Agency* (Bloomsbury), David Sanjek's *Stories We Could Tell: Putting Words to American Popular Music* (Routledge), *The Arena Concert: Music, Media and Mass Entertainment* (Bloomsbury), *Resonances: Noise and Contemporary Music* (Bloomsbury), *Reverberations: The Philosophy, Aesthetics and Politics of Noise* (Bloomsbury), *The Music Documentary: Acid Rock to Electropop* (Routledge) and *Mark E. Smith and The Fall: Art, Music and Politics* (Ashgate). www.BenjaminHalligan.com.

Rachel Hayward is Head of Film at HOME, Manchester. She has a long history working in cinema-based film exhibition and engagement and is the director of '¡Viva!' Spanish and Latin American Festival, a curator of Indian independent cinema and a founder member of the Chinese Film Forum, UK. Rachel is a curator of film seasons, including 'Jarman' at HOME, 'Poet Slash Artist' and the thirteen-month programme 'Celebrating Women in Global Cinema'. Alongside her work at HOME, Rachel lectures on film and culture, specialising in the academic exploration of cinema exhibition. She has published work on European thrillers.

James King is a writer, curator and film distributor based in the UK. After studying film at King's College London and the University of California, Berkeley, he went on to work for organisations such as the Institute of Contemporary Arts, the British Film Institute and Curzon Artificial Eye. He is currently making his own mistakes at Koenig Pictures.

Kristy Matheson is the Creative Director of 'Edinburgh International Film Festival'. She is the former director of Film at ACMI, Australia's national museum of screen culture, a member of Screen Australia's Gender Matters Taskforce and a recipient of the 2017 Natalie Miller Fellowship.

Karen Turman is a Preceptor of French in the Department of Romance Languages and Literatures at Harvard University. She earned her MA (2008) and PhD (2013) in French Literature with an emphasis on Applied Linguistics at the University of California, Santa Barbara. Her interdisciplinary research interests include nineteenth-century Bohemian Paris, music and dance during the Jazz Age, fashion and popular culture studies, community engagement scholarship, and topics of social justice and sustainability in the language classroom. Turman's publications on Prince include an essay on Josephine Baker, Claude McKay and Prince titled 'Banana Skirts and Cherry Moons: Utopic French Myths in Prince's Under the Cherry Moon', 'Prettyman in the Mirror: Dandyism in Prince's Minneapolis' and a forthcoming publication titled 'Zoot Suits and New Jack Swing: Morris Day's Dandyism'.

Andy Willis is Professor of Film Studies at the University of Salford and Senior Visiting Curator for Film at HOME, Manchester. He is the co-author of *The Cinema of Alex de la Iglesia* (with Peter Buse and Nuria Triana), editor of *Film Stars: Hollywood and Beyond*, and co-editor of *DVD, Blu-ray and Beyond: Navigating Formats and Platforms within Media Consumption* (with Jonathon Wroot), *Cult Media: Re-packaged, Re-released and Restored* (with Jonathon Wroot), *Chinese Cinemas, International Perspectives* (with Felicia Chan), *East Asian Film Stars* (with Wing Fai-Leung), *Spanish Popular Cinema* (with Antonio Lazaro-Reboll) and *Cult Movies: The Cultural Politics of Oppositional Taste* (with Mark Jancovich, Julian Stringer and Antonio Lazaro-Reboll).

Jason Wood, the former director of Film and Culture at HOME, is currently Executive Director of Public Programmes and Audiences at the British Film Institute. The author of numerous books on film and popular culture, Wood is also the co-director of a number of documentary features and short experimental works.

Foreword

Barry Adamson

All Pop stars are actors because being a pop star is an act.
– Nicolas Roeg

Pop stars saunter across the stage, larger than life. They are the ultimate in charisma, projecting onto us everything that we ourselves would want to be. Bold, confident and alluring, they seemingly sling two fingers up to the world of convention, flaunting the law, right before our eyes. They are the biggest brightest thing on the planet.

We love them for their rebelliousness and we need them to pull us out of the everyday. Charged with sexualised desire, they can have their cake and eat it right in front of us as far as we're concerned. They do our bidding for us and in return we get to fixate, love, idolise and adore them.

A mere mortal would shudder to dare let themselves believe or even think that they could be that person, allow themselves to follow a trajectory to stardom and indeed, the stars. Pop stars know that it was an intention they were born into, and with that birthright comes the quest: to be the biggest, brightest star on the planet. And each star that comes along demands to shine brighter and bigger than the last and we can't get enough of their lascivious nature, their 'fuck you' to everyone and the sheer exuberance they bring to our everyday lives. They give us the permission to be like them, whether in our bedrooms, gazing lovingly at images of them, or when we stand in front of our own audience at a karaoke night, and there we are, finding the bottle to pretend to be them.

Their star cannot shine bright enough for us. The bigger the better, and there is no bigger projection than that of the silver screen.

Introduction

Kirsty Fairclough and Jason Wood

From the relatively early days of cinema, figures from the world of music performance have made forays into acting and appeared on screen. The reasons are legion and run from a desire to maximise and amplify their brand, to a drive to capitalise on a specific audience demographic (social, racial, economic, sexuality or age), to an actual ability to act. The latter is in some instances very much an afterthought. *Pop Stars on Film: Popular Culture in a Global Market* offers a collection of essays on influential international performances from a diverse range of cultural musical icons. The aim of the collection is to consider issues relating to industry shifts, to investigate notions of access, diversity and cultural appropriation and to ruminate on issues around satisfying audience appeal in different global markets. Perhaps most importantly, the publication will look at what happens when popular culture collides and coalesces.

The impetus for this publication was a 2019 film season at HOME Manchester, titled *Pop Stars on Film*. Generously sponsored by MUBI, the season was an eclectic compilation of sixteen films and talks that celebrated the phenomenon of casting pop stars in acting roles. Curated by the editors of this book, the season offered a showcase of some of the most influential performances from a diverse range of musical icons – Elvis Presley to Cher – exploring some of the cultural and commercial factors that contributed to their casting.

The season opened with a celebration of Prince and a sold-out screening of *Purple Rain* (1984), the film that launched Prince's cinema career and propelled him into the mainstream alongside the worldwide hit soundtrack, a disc that sold 1.5 million copies in the United States in its first week alone. Other breakthrough acting roles from major artists featured in the season included Madonna in *Desperately Seeking Susan* (1985), Queen Latifah in *Set It Off* (1996) and Tupac Shakur in *Juice* (1992).

The pop star on screen

From the 1950s onwards, an industry trend developed for pop stars to take leading roles in vehicles specifically created to exploit their appeal and capture their spirit of rebellion. The season included Elvis Presley's magnetic performance in *King Creole* (1958), Mick Jagger's role as Turner, a washed-up singer with a personality crisis and identity issues in Donald Cammell and Nicolas Roeg's 1970 counter-culture classic *Performance* (featuring Jagger's immortal line, 'I know a thing or two about performing my boy, I can tell you') and reggae superstar Jimmy Cliff's renegade songwriter character in rudeboy classic *The Harder They Come* (1972), credited as the first Jamaican film and the film that allowed Jamaicans to see themselves depicted with authenticity on screen. A highly creditable account of the Jamaican music industry (and featuring cameo performances from other Jamaican recording artists), the film's score, to which Cliff contributed, has achieved heritage status, with the film helping to set the gold standard for youth and music orientated features.

The programme also included the work of high-profile pop stars who have pursued successful parallel acting careers – such as Cher (*Come Back to the 5 and Dime, Jimmy Dean, Jimmy Dean* 1982), Debbie Harry (*Hairspray* 1988 and *Videodrome* 1983) and Jennifer Lopez (*Out of Sight* 1998). David Bowie, alongside Tom Waits, arguably the pop star to have sustained the most sterling acting career (if we ignore *The Linguini Incident* 1991, and *Everybody Loves Sunshine* 1999), featured no less than three times with *Merry Christmas Mr. Lawrence* (1983), *Absolute Beginners* (1986) – also featuring Ray Davies, Sade Adu, Patsy Kensit and Smiley Culture – and David Lynch's *Twin Peaks: Fire Walk with Me* (1992). Bowie would also work with Martin Scorsese (*The Last Temptation of Christ* 1998) and Christopher Nolan (*The Prestige* 2006). Not many can claim such an impressive curriculum vitae. Rounding out the season were films featuring Mariah Carey and Lenny Kravitz (*Precious* 2009) and Bowie-influencing actor and singer Anthony Newley in the Soho-set *The Small World of Sammy Lee* (1963). The latter was introduced by an actual pop star, Saint Etienne's Bob Stanley.

Pop Stars on Film proved a success on a number of levels. Over a thousand tickets were sold for twenty-two screenings, and the cinema screens often felt more like concert venues, with incredibly diverse audiences grabbing the chance to witness a piece of cinematic history or to simply see their favourite pop star doing their thing in 7.1 surround sound through a 4K projector on a huge cinema screen. From the season, the idea of a collection of essays drawing on international contributors was born in which some of the findings of the retrospective and some of the factors determining the synergy, sometimes harmonious and sometimes less so, between pop stars and pop stars acting in fictional roles, could be interrogated.[1]

---

[1] As ever, with any curated film season, there were a number of titles that we wanted to screen but had to discount for numerous reasons (rights issues/materials availability/titles that had recently played at the venue of part of another season). However, to demonstrate how wide we cast our net and to give an indication of the plethora of pop stars that have been cast in dramatic roles, we reproduce here our initial list of titles.

Early
Al Jolson, *The Jazz Singer*, Alan Crosland, 1927
Bessie Smith – *St. Louis Blues*, Dudley Murphy, 1928
Bing Crosby, *Holiday Inn*, Mark Sandrich (and Robert Allen, uncredited) 1942
Cab Calloway – *Stormy Weather*, Andrew Stone, 1943

1950s
Frank Sinatra – *Suddenly*, Lewis Allen, 1954
Ella Fitzgerald – *Pete Kelly's Blues*, Jack Webb, 1955
Dean Martin + Ricky Nelson – *Rio Bravo*, Howard Hawks, 1959
Harry Belafonte – *Odds Against Tomorrow*, Robert Wise, 1959
Cliff Richard – *Expresso Bongo*, Val Guest, 1959

1960s and 1970s
Nico/Serge Gainsbourg – *Strip-Tease*, Jacques Pointrenaud, 1963
John Lennon – *How I Won the War*, Richard Lester, 1967
Marianne Faithful – *Girl on a Motorcycle*, Jack Cardiff, 1968
Johnny Cash – *A Gunfight*, Lamont Johnson, 1971
Dennis Wilson/James Taylor – *Two-Lane Blacktop*, Monte Hellman, 1971
Diana Ross – *Lady Sings the Blues*, Sidney J. Furie, 1972
David Essex/Ringo Starr – *That'll Be the Day*, Claude Watham, 1973
Amitabh Bachchan – *Abhimaan*, Hrishikesh Mukherjee, 1973
Kris Kristofferson/Bob Dylan – *Pat Garrett and Billy the Kid*, Sam Peckinpah, 1973
Tina Turner – *Tommy*, Ken Russell, 1975
David Bowie – *The Man Who Fell to Earth*, Nicolas Roeg, 1976
Sam Hui – *The Private Eyes*, Michael Hui, 1976
Sting – *Radio On*, Chris Petit, 1979

1980s
Hazel O'Connor – *Breaking Glass*, Brian Gibson, 1980
John Lurie – *Permanent Vacation*, Jim Jarmusch, 1980
Nazia Hassan – *Star*, Vinod Pande, 1982
John Lydon – *Order of Death*, Roberto Faenza, 1983
Charlotte Gainsbourg – *The Cement Garden*, Andrew Birkin, 1983
George Lam/Teddy Rodin – *Banana Cop*, Po Chih Leong, 1984
Grace Jones – *Vamp*, Richard Wenk, 1986
Michael Hutchence – *Dogs in Space*, Richard Lowenstein, 1986
Alice Cooper – *Prince of Darkness*, John Carpenter, 1987

Having described some of the things that we hope that this book is, so as to temper expectations, here are a number of things that it is not. This book is not about the use of pop music in film per se and films that use a cleverly curated playlist, a celluloid jukebox tradition that can arguably be tracked back to the use of Bill Haley in the Richard Brooks directed *Blackboard Jungle* (1955). However, that film is undeniably of import because it was amongst the first to attract the youth market, a concept that is intrinsic to this project, especially in terms of considering different national and international markets.

Nor is this collection of essays concerned with films in the documentary format – factual or fictional – about pop figures or bands and climactic concerts, performances or career trajectories. This collection is also less about that genre of films that tell stories about pop music figures, real or imagined (so

Tom Waits/Joe Strummer/Dr. John/Arto Lindsay, Mary Margaret O'Hara/David Johannson – *Candy Mountain*, Robert Frank, 1988
Nick Cave – *Ghosts of the Civil Dead*, John Hillcoat, 1988

1990s
Lydia Lunch/Henry Rollins – *Kiss Napoleon Goodbye*, Babeth Mondini, 1990
Jacques Dutronc – *Van Gogh*, Maurice Pialat, 1991
Ice Cube/Ice T – *Trespass*, Walter Hill, 1992
Faye Wong – *Chungking Express*, Wong Kar Wai, 1994
Iggy Pop – *Dead Man*, Jim Jarmusch, 1995
Evan Dando/Deborah Harry – *Heavy*, James Mangold, 1995
Tricky – *The Fifth Element*, Luc Besson, 1997
Meat Loaf – *Fight Club*, David Fincher, 1999
Vanessa Paradis – *The Girl on the Bridge*, Patrice Leconte, 1999

2000s
Bjork – *Dancer in the Dark*, Lars von Trier, 2000
Sammi Cheng/Andy Lau – *Needing You*, Johnnie To, 2000
P. J. Harvey – *The Book of Life*, Hal Hartley, 2000
Johnny Hallyday – *The Man on the Train*, Patrice Leconte, 2002
Eminem – *8 Mile*, Curtis Hanson, 2002
Ashley Walters – *Bullet Boy*, Saul Dibb, 2004
Mos Def – *The Woodsman*, Nicole Kassell, 2004
Kim Gordon – *Last Days*, Gus Van Sant, 2005
Will Oldham – *Old Joy*, Kelly Reichardt, 2006
Beyonce/Jennifer Hudson – *Dreamgirls*, Bill Condon, 2006
Miriam Yeung – *Hooked on You*, Johnnie To, 2007
Kylie Minogue – *Holy Motors*, Leos Carax, 2012
Selina Gomez – *Spring Breakers*, Harmony Korine, 2012
Justin Timberlake – *Inside Llewyn Davies*, Coen Bros, 2013
Janelle Monae – *Moonlight*, Barry Jenkins, 2016
Adam Horovitz – *Golden Exits*, Alex Ross Perry, 2017
Takuya Kimura – *Blade of the Immortal*, Takashi Miike, 2017
Barry Adamson – *In Fabric*, Peter Strickland, 2018

no biopics), as it is more specifically engaged with the tradition of pop stars or figures from the discipline of music appearing on screen in an acting role as a fictional character, and thus someone other than themselves. Sadly, this also closes that long and winding avenue of cameo appearances, which could have formed a bizarre but nonetheless interesting chapter in its own right. There is, however, space within these pages to consider instances where musicians appear in protracted appearances on screen. Little Richard is one such example and is emblematic of a Black performer who had their work exposed to a wider public through the medium of film having had their hits banned from predominantly white-owned radio stations.

Film and popular music are largely equated with the 1950s and the emergence of rock and roll, but it actually goes back far earlier and to the emergence of sound or synchronised cinema. The Dudley Murphy sixteen-minute short film *St. Louis Blues* (1929) features Bessie Smith, 'the empress of the blues', in her sole screen role as the wife of a violent spouse. The film builds a narrative around the performance of the titular song, but the wider context of the film involves misogyny, patriarchy and race. The film was also influential in the development of film grammar, with close-ups and tracking shots capturing the spiritual ecstasy of performance and the communal and reverential act of listening. We see the techniques pioneered in *St. Louis Blues* continuing to reverberate many years later. Criminally, in terms of race and on-screen representation, its influence took far longer to become established, and for an uncomfortably long intervening period, jazz and blues in Hollywood productions would often be performed by white performers, an example of the institutionalised racism at the foundations of the industry and of society in general. From time to time, Black performers would find themselves on screen – for example, Cab Calloway and his Cotton Club Orchestra appearing alongside Lena Horne and Bill Robinson in Andrew Stone's *Stormy Weather* (1943).

The pre–rock and roll era was becoming increasingly benevolent in terms of showcasing popular crooner figures such as Bing Crosby and Frank Sinatra, but the levees truly broke with the emergence of Elvis Presley in Robert D. Webb's Western/musical hybrid, *Love me Tender* (1956). The Presley films that followed in relatively quick succession to capture an insatiable, largely teenage, thirst for a genuine cultural phenomenon had a charm and an innocence, despite their money-making objectives, and they would prove as successful and lucrative as any concert tour in showcasing and maximising the Presley brand.

A huge admirer of Marlon Brando, Presley's early features signified a performer possessed of an ability to be at least competent as a big screen figure with an acting range that went beyond merely hitching a guitar to his side and strumming it surrounded by exotic backdrops – a sort of James Bond, minus the killing and the overt racism. Presley's film career can be divided into two sections: pre- and post-conscription to the US army. The post-conscription works are largely dead behind the eyes, joyless cash-ins, made at the behest of his unscrupulous manager, Colonel Tom Parker. Presley's popularity remained undiminished, but the later films became a shorthand for unremarkable pop star vehicles, the most damning verdict coming from Bowie when after having witnessed for the first time a completed cut of *Just a Gigolo* (David Hemmings 1978) he described it to the assembled press as '32 Elvis Presley movies rolled into one' (MacKinnon 1980).

The Beatles took the pop star vehicle and ran with it in *A Hard Day's Night* (1964), spawning a number of equally successful follow-ups that helped sustain their affections in the hearts of their rapacious fans long after they had ceased touring, or even communicating with each other. Intelligently and bracingly directed by American-born Anglophile filmmaker Richard Lester (who would cast Lennon as a non-Beatle in *How I Won the War* 1967) with references aplenty to the French nouvelle vague and other modern film-making techniques, the pop star vehicle, which has seen some incredible highs – The Monkees in *Head* (Bob Rafelson 1968), Slade in *Slade in Flame* (Richard Loncraine 1975) – and some fascinating zeitgeist-surfing casualties (*It Couldn't Happen Here*, Jack Bond 1997, and *Spice World*, Bob Spiers 1987) remains of significance as a peek behind the curtain. Such films detail Svengali-like figures, pinpoint the perils of fame and, in their representation of hype, fandom and marketing, are often sometimes self-sabotaging exercises in deconstructivism.

Such vehicles veer more sharply into focus for the collection of writers assembled between these covers when the conduit takes the persona of the pop star and weaves a fictional web from it, blurring the boundaries between genius, artifice and construction. So although conventional and often enjoyable and well-received rock biopics such as *The Buddy Holly Story* (Steve Rash 1978), *Coal Miner's Daughter* (Michael Apted 1980), *Sid and Nancy* (1986), *Great Balls of Fire!* (Jim McBride 1989) and *What's Love Got to Do with It* (Brian Gibson 1993) provide sustenance for fans and good parts for actors with a strong vocal ability, a consideration of such films is not to be found in these pages in anything other than despatches. Their popularity and success are, however, unquestionable, again reaffirming the cultural and commercial power of the popular performer.

The last two decades have reinforced this with pictures, including *Walk the Line* (James Mangold 2005), *Control* (Anton Corbijn 2007), *Love and Mercy* (Bill Pohlad 2014), *Miles Ahead* (Don Cheadle 2015), *Get on Up* (Tate Taylor 2014, featuring the late Chadwick Boseman), *Bohemian Rhapsody* (Bryan Singer 2018) and *Rocketman* (Dexter Fletcher 2019). Another entry, F. Gary Gray's *Straight Outta Compton* (2015) is a biopic example that stands out for a number of key reasons. It illustrates an increase in the number of films being made about Black musicians, offering perhaps an indication that in the American film industry, and beyond, things may be changing in terms of opportunity and representation and what type of culture is valued as being of significance and worthy of documentation.

A moment in which hip-hop and Black African American culture was invited (or co-opted) into the corporate mainstream (the film was produced by Universal and Legendary Pictures), at the heart of *Straight Outta Compton* is a standout performance by O' Shea Jackson, playing his own father and key NWA member, Ice Cube. Ice Cube is another performer from the world of music who has sustained a parallel acting career, delivering a particularly compelling performance in John Singleton's *Boyz n the Hood* (1991). *Straight Outta Compton* also speaks to the subject of 'Afrofuturism', a term first coined by writer Mark Dery in an influential 1994 essay titled *Black to the Future* (Dery 1994). A desire to address black themes through science fiction and technoculture lenses and partly inspired by the work of legendary musician Sun Ra, Afrofuturism and the discourse around it, recently rose very prominently to the fore in Ryan Coogler's *Black Panther* (2018) but can also be found in the work and spirit of Janelle Monáe's trilogy of albums beginning with *The ArchAndroid* (2010). Monae has of course now firmly established herself as an actor of some repute, with screen credits including *Moonlight* (Barry Jenkins 2016) and *Harriet* (Kasi Lemmons 2019). Early signs are that like Bowie, Barbara Streisand, Kris Kristofferson and Frank Sinatra, Monae will be a very capable actor. Others, such as Bob Dylan, Mick Jagger (though Herzog described him as the best actor he ever worked with[2]) and Ryuichi Sakamoto (superb alongside

---

[2] Jagger was originally cast in the role of Wilbur, Fitzcarraldo's English sidekick in *Fitzcarraldo* (1982). The role had to be later cut when production difficulties on the film conflicted with a Rolling Stones tour. Herzog cut the role, believing that nobody but Jagger could play it. 'I liked him so much as a performer. Jagger is a truly great actor, something very few people have noticed' (Cronin and Herzog 2014, 186). Herzog seems to share some of Roeg's philosophy in regard to rock stars acting, believing that an ability to perform in front of an audience of thousands more than equips them to deliver lines and assume a role.

Bowie in Oshima's *Merry Christmas Mr. Lawrence* 1983, and an example of one of the originators of pop stars in Asia crossing over into cinema), are very much likely to remain one-screen wonders.

Sometimes, of course, music biographies do provide musical artists with the chance to shine, sometimes even the chance to emulate and immortalise their heroes and heroines: witness Diana Ross as Billie Holiday in *Lady Sings the Blues* (Sidney J. Furie 1972), or Dexter Gordon as a conflation of Bud Powell and Lester Young in Bertrand Tavernier's exemplary *'Round Midnight* (1986), which also features other real-life jazz players such as Herbie Hancock, Bobby Hutcherson, Freddie Hubbard and Cedar Walton.

'Vehicles' featuring the likes of Prince and Madonna, who arguably never managed to improve upon her engaging and whip smart debut feature *Desperately Seeking Susan* (Susan Seidelman 1985) and ditto Prince and *Purple Rain* (Albert Magnoli 1984), are very much offered deeper consideration here. Both – and Eminem in *8 Mile* (Curtis Hanson 2002) is another example – appear as fictional or inflated versions of themselves, creating both easily relatable meta-texts and a genuine necessity for fans to buy a cinema ticket/Blu-Ray/soundtrack/ download. The underground New York music scene of John Lurie, Richard Hell and Arto Lindsay is the backdrop for Seidelman's film, but it's Madonna's *Into the Groove* that closes it. *Desperately Seeking Susan* was a critical success; *Purple Rain* was a colossal commercial one.

Compensating for its undoubted flaws and status as pure hagiography (charges that could also be levelled at the Whitney Houston megahit, *The Bodyguard* 1992, and certainly at Prince's largely moribund future features), the film had a genuine dramatic arc and wisely folded actual musical performances into the plot, with Prince being required to act just enough to not extinguish the brio and energy of the live concert footage. It also helped, of course, that the songs were first-rate, with *Let's Go Crazy* and *When Doves Cry* being registered as instant classics and topping the Billboard singles chart. The soundtrack album, and Prince's first record to feature 'The Revolution' on the cover billing, would go on to sell over 25 million copies. Made on a budget of approximately $7.2 million, the film would gross $68 million at the US box office and over $80 million worldwide. At the 1985 Academy Awards, *Purple Rain* won Best Soundtrack and remains amongst the biggest selling soundtracks of all time. *Purple Rain* proved that Prince was able to be a star in the music studio, on the performing stage and on the cinema screen. Other acts and studios would want a piece of that action.

Not all artists can be as successful as Prince in their switch between forms, and the following essays explore the oscillation between pop star and film star, with varying outcomes and impact upon the brand and image of the artist.

References

Cronin, Paul, and Werner Herzog (2014), *A Guide for the Perplexed*, London: Faber & Faber.

Dery, Mark, ed. (1994), 'Black to the Future: Interviews with Samuel R. Delany, Greg Tate, and Tricia Rose', in *Flame Wars: The Discourse of Cyberculture*, Durham, NC: Duke University Press.

MacKinnon, Angus (1980), 'The Future Isn't What It Used to Be', *New Musical Express*, 13 September: 32–7.

1

The boy can't help it: Little Richard's disruption and reconstruction of Black male screen performativity

Tom Attah

> Little Richard was a rocker, and this is one way you can tell: rockers don't sublimate their idiosyncrasies, they exaggerate them, revel in them.
> – Palmer 1995, 140–1

> and the best new artist is – ME. I have never received nothing. [hand on hip] Y'all ain't never gave me no Grammy, and I've been singing for YEARS. I AM THE ARCHITECT OF ROCK & ROLL, you ain't never gave me nothing. [10-second standing ovation] I am the ORIGINATOR, and I still say WOOOOH!
> – Grein, 2020

As both 'the architect of rock and roll' and the archetypal rock and roller, Little Richard's genre-defining performance of sound and self in the studio, on stage and on screen, repeatedly sets and transgresses the boundaries of performativity within popular music and popular culture. In film appearances which include lip- and finger-syncing to his music in *The Girl Can't Help It* (Tashlin 1956), portraying a slowly exploding music producer in *Down and Out in Beverley Hills* (Mazursky 1986) and voicing his own cartoon cameo for television's 'Special Edna', *The Simpsons* (Anderson 2003), Little Richard's screen performance collapses performer, persona and protagonist into an expressive mode which draws on, defies and so redefines our understanding of pop stars as actors.

This essay examines the cultural impact of Little Richard as a multimedia stylistic originator and disruptor, with a specific focus on screen-based dimensions of his musical influence and performance legacy. Through the presentation and discussion of illustrative examples underpinned by a theoretical framework informed by performance theory, film theory and cultural studies, this essay argues that Little Richard (1) extended the range of cultural characters available to Black performers depicted in electrical media to include new 'outside' archetypes, (2) was a catalytic and political artistic presence in cinematic media at a time when the music of African Americans was increasingly *heard* but not *seen* and (3) consolidated his own performative legacy through an expressive coherence of gesture, text and context sustained over six decades.

Racism, homophobia and rock and roll characterise the two folk devils and one moral panic which intersected in the character of Little Richard during his rise to stardom through electrical media in the mid-1950s (Cohen 2002). That he was Black stoked fears of a hypersexualised, almond-eyed and unblinking savage whose pounding, hypnotic rhythms and undeniable charisma were being deployed to steal the innocence of America's daughters (Palmer 1995, 139); that he was an openly bisexual former drag queen with a criminal conviction for voyeurism meant that he may also distract, delight and consume its unwary sons (Hamilton 1998, 174); and that he was both riding and powering the beat-driven youth culture that threatened to engulf the increasingly unstable structures of post-war segregation meant that 'the originator, the architect of rock & roll' (Grein 2020) should have been a prime target for the type of victimisation, violence and horror that characterised the lives of many black people in the rapidly evolving sociocultural landscape of 1950s America. A thorough practical grounding in African American performance traditions allied to an undeniable vocal and performance talent meant that, exactly as an architect does, Little Richard was able to perceive the way that individuals inhabit specific worlds and establish an evolving structure to sustain himself in a culturally dynamic and potentially hostile environment (Crawley 2020).

There are three important contextual points to note. The first is the prevalence of pejorative Black performance stereotypes in cinematic and other media at this time, descended from the nineteenth-century minstrel show and vaudeville (Lott 1992). This range of characters, which Bogle (2001) lists as 'Toms, Coons, Mulattoes, Mammies and Bucks', were the basis of almost all African American screen representations in the early twentieth century. Occasionally known by other names including 'Sambo', 'Aunt Jemimah' and 'Sapphire', in order, the tropes represented by these characters were (and continue to be) servile and deferent male slaves who would turn against other Blacks in favour of their white masters;

wisecracking buffoons given to pomp and dandyism; tragic characters (most often female) who wished to pass for white; asexual matrons who prefigured the modern 'magical negro', who were occasionally able to speak truth to [white] power; and hypersexualised males who also represented the unruly and savage 'bad nigger'. This last stereotype had a female equivalent in the 'Jezebel[le]', a similarly hypersexualised female whose main role was to 'absolve white males of responsibility in the sexual abuse and rape of African American women. Black women in such cases were said to be "…askin' for it"' (Gilmore 1975, 13; Glenn and Cunningham 2009; Goings 1994, 67; Green 1998).

Secondly, missing from this list in the 1950s is an African American stereotype familiar to late twentieth-century cinema and media audiences, partially midwifed into mainstream media prominence by Little Richard: the drag queen. For the avoidance of doubt, this essay does not attempt to argue that the performance mode and character of the drag queen did not exist in the 'real world' at this time, only that there are few to no references to this now near-ubiquitous Black stereotype in cinematic media before 1950. To be clear – cross-dressing and effeminacy had been depicted since the dawn of cinema, white male homosexuality had been inferred by Cecil B. DeMille in 1922 and lesbianism had been hinted at by Marlene Dietrich in 1930 (Benshoff and Griffin 2006). Black blues singer Gertrude 'Ma' Rainey had recorded multiple songs about aggressive Black male homosexuality and lesbianism in the 1920s, and her former protégé and latter rival Bessie Smith's own bisexuality was an open secret during the Harlem renaissance of the early twentieth century (Davis 1998, 39–41, 171; Friederich 2017). Emerging from a world of razzle dazzle theatrics where musicians shared the stage with exotic dancers, snake charmers, fire-eaters and sword swallowers, female impersonator Richard Wayne Penniman had already constructed a performance persona in the shape of the tottering vocalist and piano player 'Princess Lavonne' before adopting the stage name 'Little Richard' in 1953 (Hamilton 1998, 167). Indeed, 'men who sang, danced, and dressed in "imitation of the action and manners of women"' (Long 2004, 72) and environments where commercial sex and gender impersonation were linked had been known to African American communities since the late 1800s, and as urban historians indicate, 'they lived their life and they didn't bother anybody' (Grantmyre 2011, 983–6). Certainly by the time that Little Richard was learning his craft and applying his already considerable vocal talent to the secular stage, there were a number of established female impersonators on the circuit such as 'Patsy Valida' and 'Queen Sonya' with whom Little Richard worked, and from whom he partially took cues and elements of his own character (Hamilton 1998, 172; Ribowsky 2020, 80).

Thirdly, being well aware of being perceived as a sexual threat by white conservatives, Little Richard consciously adopted the trappings of homosexuality and the 'sissy' as a deliberate ploy to defuse and deflect accusations of sexual interest in the young white women attending his shows. This was serious and lethal business; on 28 August 1955, less than a month before the release of 'Tutti Frutti' (Penniman and LaBostrie), 14-year-old Emmett Till had been abducted, tortured and shot dead in Mississippi following testimony that he had behaved suggestively towards a white woman, 21-year-old Carolyn Bryant – and the two men who later admitted the crime were found not guilty of the murder (Tyson 2018). In this environment, as Hamilton (1998, 162) explains, when Little Richard began to attract audience attention from white teens, he 'dispensed with the drag queen's skirts, but he retained her sequins, her makeup, her pompadour, her strutting self-confidence and her way with words'. Speaking later in his career, Little Richard confirmed that

> it wasn't just a gay thing. To be black and work for white girls, I had to look that way. If I didn't wear make-up and look feminine, I couldn't work the white clubs, they wouldn't let me be with the white girls. The more effeminate I looked, they didn't mind me being with the white women. They'd say, 'Oh Richard, there ain't nothin' to him.' I had on the make-up, I had on the eyelashes, I wore it all … and I found out that, when I wore these things, and the more effeminate that I looked, the more I was accepted. I wasn't rejected because weren't nobody afraid of me, I wasn't a threat to be around a white girl. I don't have to wear it at all now, but now I like it. (Little Richard, *The Late Late Show* with Tom Snyder 1997)

To summarise the opening part of this essay, Little Richard constructed a performance persona for the stage during the early 1950s which was ideally suited to the rapidly proliferating visual media of cinema and television. This performance persona drew on existing Black stereotypes that were common currency in contemporary culture, whilst incorporating and foregrounding the gestures and presentation of African American female impersonators. Whilst on the one hand this was a clearly defensive move for both Richard and his newly visible band following the nationwide success of his first hit single in 1955, it also functioned as an appropriately outrageous visual accompaniment to the new music that Little Richard developed and performed as part of the emerging rock and roll genre.

Characters

As individuals within a societal structure, we each perform versions of ourselves dependent on context and audience – mother, sister, daughter, colleague and so on – either as solo actors or as part of an ensemble (Goffman 1956, 56–86). There is added complexity to this role-play in the case of musicians and dramatic actors within Western culture, and a further level of entanglement when we consider the requirements for consistency, content and 'front' that media celebrity and stardom place on individuals. In other words, in each of the performance modes to be discussed here, Richard Wayne Penniman performing as Little Richard is presenting a specific performance of self, either as a performing musician within a cinematic fictional narrative, and so to a certain degree 'acting' despite that he is 'playing himself'. This includes operating as a musician on stage and so presenting the performance persona necessary to interact with an audience in the delivery of the musical material and its accompanying gestures. Additionally, within this, Little Richard presents as the 'I' who inhabits the world of the song and is delivering the sung and played narrative as if it were a first-hand account of experience. Finally, Richard exists as the creative artist who exists and operates in the offstage 'real world' and who constructs and delivers a show in the name of musical and dramatic creativity. This tripartite distinction of selves within performance music (and to a lesser extent drama) has been described as that of the performer, the persona and the protagonist. In other words, (1) the person who puts on the costume, (2) the persona which delivers the performance and (3) and the fictionalised personality that inhabits the world of the song (Moore 2012, 181–2).

Whilst there is a distinction between these three roles, there is also a perceived homology between them reinforced by the illusion of spontaneous composition by a protagonist–composer in performance, which remains one of the most important ingredients in rock reception and a phenomenological overlap between the performance persona and 'authenticity' (Gelbart 2003, 213; Moore 2012, 182). Finally on this point, there is a clear willing 'suspension of disbelief' on the part of an audience in the separate identity and activation of a working performance persona, indicated by the acceptance that 'Little Richard' is the *stage name* of Richard Wayne Penniman (Schechner and Brady 2020, 199).

Modes

Between 1956 and 2017, Little Richard appears on screen in three distinct performance modes:

1. *Where the music is a feature of a dramatic production.* In this mode, Little Richard's performance is presented in the context of a narrative where he is not the central character driving the story but is a featured character or guest artist who signifies 'music'. Examples of this mode include early film appearances such as *The Girl Can't Help It, Don't Knock the Rock* and *Mister Rock and Roll* and later cameo appearances on television such as *Baywatch* (1985), *Columbo* (1991) and *The Simpsons* (2003). In each of these instances, Little Richard either plays himself or a character who closely resembles the Little Richard performance persona within the fiction of the story.
2. *Where the music is a focus of a documentary presentation.* In this mode, the focus of the presentation is to capture, present and in some cases comment on a musical performance event featuring Little Richard as a performer operating in front of a live audience. Examples of this mode include *It's Little Richard* (1964), *The London Rock and Roll Show* (1973) and *Let the Good Times Roll* (1973). In each of these instances, Little Richard is presenting his performance persona, and the presentation features both 'behind-the-scenes' and interview segments.
3. *As part of an interview that may include a musical performance.* In this mode, Little Richard is presented as an interview subject talking about an aspect of his life and career, or to promote a forthcoming event such as a performance, or the release of a book or album. Examples of this mode span Richard's entire performing career and include *American Bandstand* (1964), *The Dick Cavett Show* (1970), *Late Night Line Up* (1972), *The Late Late Show with Tom Snyder* (1997), *Letterman* (1982, 1984), *Donny & Marie* (1976, 1998, 2000), *The Tonight Show Starring Johnny Carson* (1986), *The Arsenio Hall Show* (1990) and *Three Angels Broadcasting Network* (2017). In this mode, Richard presents as a performance artist who is explaining the nature and context of his work and/or in his performance persona delivering a musical performance in support of the interview content before a studio and viewing audience.

Operational definitions

It is possible to examine the ways in which Little Richard deployed his performance persona in cinematic and televisual media through three theoretic lenses. Firstly, a 'performative' lens, secondly the lens of 'stardom' and finally with an understanding of 'expressive coherence'.

Performativity

As Schechner and Brady (2020, 231) explain, 'performative' is a both a noun and an adjective. As a noun and in relation to Little Richard, there is a constituting power in the way that over time Richard performs the act of creating himself as a cultural icon. In other words, when Richard says 'I am the King of Rock and Roll', the active, concrete performative connotation is 'I bound and encompass this musical domain'; 'I am the architect of Rock and Roll' becomes 'I build/construct this musical genre from disparate elements'; 'I am the originator' reads performatively as 'I bring forth this new form as an act of creation'. Simply put, these statements have a fixative function in culture akin to declaring 'I name this ship', 'I promise' or exclaiming 'it's a girl' at the birth of a child.

Performative as an adjective inflects what it modifies with performance-like qualities. For example, we might think of gender performativity – specifically, the notion that gendered identities are constituted through stylised repetitions of bodily acts (Butler 1988) – and consider a similar perspective in the social construction of race (Pfeifle 2014; Smedley 2007). Again, applying this notion to Little Richard, we might think of the repeated performative gestures inherent in the establishment and operation of his performance persona; the choice of a specific musical repertoire; the way that he stands (and latterly sits) at the piano whilst playing for an audience and/or in the studio; his signature falsetto whoops and screams which were much imitated but arguably never equalled; the way he engages with an audience through his gaze; the way he moves on stage, particularly when entering and leaving; mode of dress in performance, including (without being limited to) use of make-up, style of clothing and hairstyles which are consistently straightened in the fashion of the day (conk in the 1950s, bouffant and pompadour in the 1960s and 1970s and Jheri curl in the 1980s, 1990s and early twenty-first century); the ritualised elements of his physical performance – heel on the piano, the removal and tearing up of his clothing before throwing it into the audience; leaving the stage whilst the band is still playing; and so on. Additionally, we might consider the performative behaviours which bound and define his interview persona. Specifically, his use of African American slang in conversation; the intonation and melody of his speech; verbal tics such as his occasional yet persistent, hesitating stutter; hand, eye and bodily gestures whilst speaking that indicate not only his cultural background but also a combination of gendered motions normally associated with females; his consistent and political reference to his lack of recognition as a result of his Blackness; sassiness, and the willingness to speak truth to power from his platform; the working of his major song titles into conversation, particularly 'Good Golly Miss Molly' and the use of catchphrases, most notably 'shut up' and 'Awop-Bop-A-Loo-Mop-Alop-Bam-Boom'. The confirmation of the effectiveness of Little Richard's performative gestures and presentation is that they are adopted by other performers to connote 'Little-Richard-ness' in a particular performance environment. This last point is critical in measuring Little Richard's performative impact firstly in cinema and secondly in television. Specific examples include (without being limited to)

- Eddie Murphy as 'Little Richard Simmons' in *Saturday Night Live* (1981)
- Meshach Taylor as 'Hollywood Montrose' in *Mannequin* (1987)
- Danny John Jules as 'The Cat' in *Red Dwarf* (1988–99, 2009–20)
- RuPaul and similar drag queens (1993–)
- Wesley Snipes as 'Noxeema Jackson' in *To Wong Foo, Thanks for Everything! Julie Newmar* (1995)
- Chris Tucker as 'Ruby Rhod' in *The Fifth Element* (1997)

In this last case, it is worth noting that musician and auteur Prince Rogers Nelson – known simply as 'Prince' – was originally cast in this role. This is significant as Prince (1) has a similar gravity in popular culture to Little Richard in his presence as a stylistic agent provocateur, musical innovator and creative artist and (2) that Little Richard commented several times publicly that he saw Prince's work as a natural progression of his own. The below comment is a typical example:

> When I see Prince today … you know, Prince today is Little Richard in this generation. [To camera] Don't get mad about that Prince! I looked just as good

as you look today. [Wagging finger] I was wearing purple before you was wearing it! (Little Richard, *The Tonight Show starring Johnny Carson*, 4 March 1986)

Also, whilst Prince was primarily a guitarist and multi-instrumentalist, it is possible to trace multiple lines of foundational performative influence from Little Richard in his work as a male African American performance artist, several of which are listed above in 'performativity as an adjective'.

Stardom

For Wojcik (2003, 234) 'stardom' occurs through an actor's recurrence across a number of films in different roles. In the case of Little Richard, this is extended to be a recurrence through different media: (1) as an actor playing 'himself', (2) as an actor playing a character with another name that is modelled on his Little Richard performance persona, (3) as a performer on stage, (4) as a media celebrity, (5) as an animated caricature and finally, as indicated above in the definitions of 'performative', (6) as a set of autonomous performance gestures deployed by third parties which connote 'Little-Richard-ness'. Recognition of the actor in a series of films – and in the case of Little Richard, performance modes – creates 'a double identification in which we see not only the character but also the star. This recognition is crucial both to the star's function in the text and his or her extratextual success' (Wojcik 2003, 234).

Working with applied film theory, Kracauer (1997, 99) notes that 'The typical Hollywood star resembles the non-actor in that he acts out a standing character identical with his own or at least developed from it, frequently with the aid of make-up'. In this way, aside from the obvious reference to cosmetics, it is possible to view the continuity of character mobilised by Richard Penniman as Little Richard as characteristic of a 'star'.

Finally, in this definition of stardom such as it applies to Little Richard, Pattie (2007, 11) highlights the paradoxical notion that contained within the separation between the simultaneous yet separate existence of the performer/stars and their performance persona is not that an audience accepts as real that which is patently unreal; rather it is that an audience accepts that reality, or 'authenticity', as a performance, without necessarily accepting that its status as performance invalidates it as a true expression of the star's authentic self. Put differently, the audience believes in the star's performed self, while being aware that that self is itself a performance.

Expressive coherence

As described by Naremore (1988, 68–71), 'expressive coherence' in performance is a concept which requires that the actor presents their character with sincerity and continuity in changing settings or contexts. Drawing on Goffman's (1956, 51) notion of 'synecdochic responsibility', Naremore explains that in order for an audience to accept a performance as real either within the fiction of the narrative or, as with Little Richard, as a complete musical performance persona, there must be a fit between setting, costume and behaviour and an attention to every detail in order to project competence and confidence. For example, as individuals, to maintain a continuity of character, we ideally sustain a baseline of operational professionalism in the workplace regardless of our emotional circumstances – happy, sad, excited, grieving, bored, apprehensive and so on. For an actor (or musician) their 'front' is maintained regardless of performance or social circumstances. In other words, Richard Penniman always behaves like Little Richard when he is in the public eye, regardless of the mode of performance in play at the time. Further, as part of the Little Richard mythology and in support of expressive coherence, Richard Penniman behaves like Little Richard in private. That is to say that an audience expects stories of private behaviour to live up to their expectations of his persona. Examples of this would be the stories of his sexual appetites and physical stamina consistent with the power and ferocity of his onstage performance. In summary, there is an expectation that there is coherence between the performer's social/performance front – his outward performance and appearance – and his 'true' inner self (Goffman 1990, 56).

The motion pictures, 1956–7

The Girl Can't Help It (1956) – Director, Frank Tashlin

Little Richard's first appearance on screen in a feature film was in Frank Tashlin's *The Girl Can't Help It*, a musical comedy vehicle for 'blonde bombshell' actress Jayne Mansfield. Released in December 1956, the film tells the story of a 'Mr Big' mobster – Fats Murdock, played by Edmond O'Brien – who is determined that his girlfriend Jerri Jordan (played by Mansfield) should be a popular singing star despite her seeming lack of vocal ability. The film is musically notable for including not only appearances by Little Richard, but also musical performances from Julie London, Gene Vincent, Eddie Cochran, Fats Domino and The Platters, leading to its reputation as being as of the 'most potent' of the early celebrations of rock and roll captured on film (Norman 2008, 98) and a clear indication of Hollywood's desire to monetise the emerging youth culture. This notion of exploitation is further exemplified by the depiction of the fictional backstage machinations inherent in engineering popular music stardom as the driving element of the film's plot.

Little Richard's music appears at three key points in the film, each time connoting modernity and progress. In the first instance, the title song is played over the film's opening credits following an opening monologue narrated by principal actor Tom Ewell. This opening sequence is significant for several key juxtapositions through which the film sets up a transition from the technologies and contexts of the 'old world' to the new youth culture. (1) The introductory segment opens in a tight Black-framed 4:3 'Academy aperture' ratio, akin to the boxy image size of a television screen image, before Ewell, costumed in the Black and white evening dress of the establishment, appears to expand the frame to the 1.65:1 'widescreen' presentation associated with modern cinema. This might be taken to represent the expanding world view offered by emerging media capabilities. (2) Following the increase in aspect ratio, the image then transitions from Black and white to 'gorgeous life-like colour by DeLuxe', a change in presentation which might be interpreted in a number of ways, most obviously that the new world includes multiple hues, tints and pigmentation beyond the many shades of monochrome previously considered as the standard. (3) Ewell describes the presentation saying 'our story is about music. Not the music of long ago, but the music expresses the culture, the refinement, and the polite race of the present day'; the monologue is then drowned by the blaring C dominant 7 chord described by the horns in the title song's introduction. The first verse showcasing Richard's impassioned, tenor vocal then plays over Ewell's muted chattering figure and a title montage which presents the key elements of the rock and roll culture; the camera, and so the audience's attention, shifts away from the establishment figure of a formally dressed, middle-aged white man (Ewell was aged 47 years at the time of the film's release) towards the shining technology of a jukebox and various wide shots of five male–female pairings of Lindy-Hopping and jiving dancers. All of the dancers appear to be white, although picked out in contrasting primary colours – a representation of the cultural appropriation of Black styles and a demonstration of the location of hegemonic power. The dance moves and gestures themselves are connotative of frenzied sex, and the implication presented for the first time and repeated later in the film is that rock and roll – and particularly Little Richard's expression of rock and roll – is associated with bodily freedom and a throwing off of established social limitations and boundaries (Weems 2008, 170). In this first presentation of the title song, Little Richard and The Upsetters' performance is heard, but not seen.

The second instance of Little Richard's performance is played over a roughly ten-minute block, which starts sixteen minutes into the film, providing sustained exposure for Little Richard as a musician. In the first part of this timing block, as in the film's opening sequence, Little Richard is once again clearly heard, but not seen. Richard's recording of *The Girl Can't Help It* (Troup 1956) plays as non-diegetic sound accompanying the iconic sequence which depicts Mansfield walking through a reconstructed street scene to meet her on-screen love interest at his apartment. Mansfield's 'hotness' as she strides in time to Little Richard's pounding, relentless twelve-bar rock and roll is accompanied by a number of sexually explicit visual jokes: the moaning horn section evokes the heavy-breathing throes of a sexual encounter; the rising temperature of a delivery man gazing at the passing lead actress is shown to be enough to wholly melt a forty-pound block of ice as Richard's blistering vocal overloads his microphone; Mansfield's exaggerated hip-swinging swagger induces a clear reference to male ejaculation from a milkman staring from the steps of the brownstone block; and as Mansfield climbs the stairs to her destination, another man's stare shatters the lenses of his glasses. All of this is accompanied by the insistent, driving groove of Little Richard and the Upsetters, the new rhythm to which this oldest of all dances is being played out on screen.

This block culminates in one of the film's key expositional sequences: the reveal of Mansfield's character's sexily costumed body. This is soundtracked by Little Richard's final performance in the film. This time, he is seen as well as heard as he delivers two songs which feature as diegetic sound. The scene takes place in an unnamed nightclub,[1] and opens on Little Richard's silver-tipped boots. The camera pans upwards as the Upsetters band – in this guise, four horns, an electric

---

[1] The dialogue and visual editing of the film contradicts and confuses the exact location. Specifically, when Henry Jones's character 'Mousie' describes the events of the evening to Edmond O'Brien as 'Fats Murdock', he says that Ewell's character 'picked her up at her place [at] 9:25, cab to the Hi-Hat, Late Place, Jungle Room, Tree Anon, Sunrise, cab back, left her at her front door 2:40.' This does not synchronise with the previously presented visuals where the Hi-Hat club is at least the third location that the characters visit where the billing is for 'The Chuckles, 3 shows nitely [sic]'. Within the narrative fiction of the film, it may be that Little Richard was not a featured act at the club on the night in question and that the characters visited the same location twice – the second time in a differently laid out performance room – but it is most likely a minor continuity error.

bass, drums, electric guitar and Richard on piano – back Richard who sweats and tosses his unruly hair out of his face as he plays standing up. The band lip- and finger-syncs to a recording of *Ready Teddy* (Marascalco 1956) as the horn players underline the phallic allusion of their instruments' shape by thrusting their hips during the stop-time sections of the song. Richard is resplendent in a silk, gunmetal suit, his performance tightly wound and intense whilst his gaze is focussed off camera, beyond the constructed presentation of the scene. The song ends, clearing space for expositional dialogue. It is worth noting that in this scene the bass drum head (a key marketing space in the presentation of many pop bands) bears the legend 'Mr Tutti Frutti – Little Richard', emphasising an intertextual reference to Little Richard's extra-textual existence.

Following the reveal of Mansfield's figure, Little Richard and the band tear into a lip-synced, propulsive version of *She's Got It* (Marascalco and Penniman 1956) as Mansfield slinks to the powder room. This moment in the film breaks important ground in its implied advocacy of miscegenation; as both Palmer (1995, 139) and Ribowsky (2020, 77) indicate, the tribal moves of Richard and the band sweating and thrusting intercut with Mansfield bumping and grinding across the dance floor connote to some a subliminal stamp of interracial conjugation. This is in addition to the cultural understanding that 'rock and roll' means 'having sex', crashing headlong into one of the societal taboos of the time.

The scene is further notable in its illustrative juxtaposition of fantasy and reality for several reasons. Firstly, Richard and the band are playing in what is presented as an exclusive nightclub complete with a maître d'hôtel, boothed seating and floor show; as film director John Waters comments in reference to this scene, 'Rock and Roll [at this time] was not played in "nice" places' (*John Waters on 'The Girl Can't Help It'* 2004). Secondly, Richard and the band appear to be the only African Americans in the scene, an illustration of the racial segregation that persisted in some areas of the United States during the 1950s; it is interesting to note that the only Black characters in the film are presented as either musicians or the hired domestic help depicted in later scenes. Thirdly, as the scene unfolds, the characters continue to move in time with and relative to the pulse of the music being 'performed' in the club by Richard and the band. As indicated above, Mansfield's iconic 'reveal' of her red sequinned dress, itself an intertextual allusion to the costumes worn by Jane Russell and Marilyn Monroe in *Gentlemen Prefer Blondes* (1953) and a further emphasis of her sex-symbol status, stands out as a signature moment in moving-picture visual history (Pazda, Elliot and Greitemeyer 2011). Finally, where all the other musicians featured in the film perform only part of their songs whilst being frequently interrupted by dialogue from the characters, Little Richard here offers three songs effectively back-to-back and largely in toto.

In this first appearance on film, many of the performative gestures that Little Richard will display as part of his performance persona for the next six decades are present. He is playing the piano standing. His signature falsetto whoop features prominently as part of the vocal line. Most significantly, he is playing himself as a character, further blurring the lines between the performer, his persona and the protagonist who lives within the fiction of the song and the film (Moore 2012, 181–2).

These above elements are repeated in Richard's subsequent motion picture appearances in *Don't Knock the Rock* (Sears 1956) and *Mister Rock and Roll* (Dubin 1957), contributing to the expressive coherence of his on-screen presentation. As before, Little Richard performs on-screen with the Upsetters, and once again, the bass drum features its intertextual/extratextual advertisement.

In both films, Little Richard performs two songs: *Don't Knock the Rock* includes *Tutti Frutti* and *Long Tall Sally* (Johnson, Blackwell and Penniman 1956), whilst *Mister Rock and Roll* features *Lucille* (Collins and Penniman 1956) and *Keep A-Knockin'* (Penniman 1957) on its original prints. The wildly libidinous nature of Little Richard's performance persona is again underscored by his gestures in *Don't Knock the Rock*. As described in his autobiography, Richard appears

> hammering the piano, staring ferociously as the camera moves in for a close-up, throwing his head from side to side, arms flailing like a tree in a tornado, Richard puts on a spectacular performance. Bowing graciously, as though he has just played a Chopin nocturne, he wallops straight into 'Long Tall Sally,' as sax player Grady Gaines solos on top of the grand piano. The wild freedom of it changed the lives of hundreds of thousands of young people. (White 2013, 80–1)

In support of White's suggestion of influence, Richard's visual image in this scene is regarded as significant enough to warrant the production of a marionette in 2020. Missing from White's description is that during the 'Long Tall Sally' piano solo, Richard makes another of his signature performance moves; whilst feverishly working the piano keys, Richard places his right heel on top of the piano and rhythmically grinds his groin from a standing position into the front of the instrument whilst feigning nonchalance at his mime. As graphic a move as this appears to modern viewers, even in contemporary times the signification should have been clear. That this element of Richard's performance made the final cut of the film and past censors at a notoriously conservative point in entertainment history indicates that the line from the blues song was retrospectively true in terms of double-voiced utterance and the secondary meaning of gesture amongst youth: 'The men don't know, but the little girls understand' (Dixon 1960).

In summary, during the twenty-four months between the release of the *Tutti Frutti* single in October 1955 and the opening of the motion picture *Mister Rock and Roll* in October 1957, Little Richard established a consistent cultural performance presence as the founding figure in the youth culture of rock and roll. The use of the definite article to describe Richard's position here is deliberate: whilst his emergence took place at the same time as Buddy Holly and Elvis Presley, Little Richard represents the literal cultural Blackness which both precedes the stardom of the latter figures and provides the context and content against which both of the white performers would be subsequently measured. This artistic primacy was known to Little Richard and was consistently referenced in his interviews throughout the rest of his public life; as he explained to Arsenio Hall in 1990, 'I'm not conceited, I'm convinced.'

Conclusion

This essay has argued that Little Richard (1) extended the range of cultural characters available to Black performers depicted in cinematic media to include the new 'outside' archetype of the drag queen, (2) was a catalytic and political artistic presence in cinematic media at a time when the music of African Americans was increasingly *heard* but not *seen* and (3) consolidated his own performative legacy through an expressive coherence of gesture, text and context sustained over six decades.

Although Richard Wayne Penniman passed away on 9 May 2020 aged eighty-seven, the performance character that he brought into the public consciousness through his early recordings and cinematic appearances – Little Richard – appears to live on. Little Richard's direct performative influence is evident in the work of Jimi Hendrix, James Brown and Prince, each of whom adapted and deployed elements of Richard's performance through multiple media. Little Richard's presence as a cultural character has been absorbed into the mainstream and is exemplified by the characters and actors identified earlier in this essay.

In his wider career, Richard's vacillation between the sacred and the profane is illustrative of the tension between wanting to be unique but needing to belong, which characterises so much of the project of modernity (Penman 2019, 141). It could be further argued that on screen Richard was only ever typecast as himself; but so what? Is it not the mark of a true star that they are only required to be what passes for themselves on screen?

Presented in cinema during 1955 and 1956, Little Richard was able to signify excitement, courage, determination and a headlong propulsive flight into the future which embraced the social and technological possibilities of the age and dismissed the conservative limitations of post-war America. His message of exploration, freakishness and the celebration of bodily pleasure was transmitted not only to Black people as a subset of American society, but to the young as a subset of the world. This was achieved by placing the Black queer outsider aesthetic at the heart of rock and roll.

The final word falls to Little Richard, captured on film reflecting on his professional achievements following an incendiary performance at Wembley Stadium in the UK.

> You've got to remember that it's big money today, it wasn't big money when I was out before. But it's big money, and don't nobody own me – can't nobody claim me, can't nobody shoot me cause ... they haven't given me anything, I couldn't borrow nothing, they didn't help me, I just lived on the mercy of God and I made it through blood and sweat and guts. (Little Richard, *The London Rock and Roll Show* 1972)

References

Benshoff, Harry M., and Sean Griffin (2006), *Queer Images: A History of Gay and Lesbian Film in America*, Oxford: Rowman & Littlefield.

Bogle, Donald (2001), *Toms, Coons, Mulattoes, Mammies, and Bucks: An Interpretive History of Blacks in American Films*, 4th edn, New York: Continuum.

Butler, Judith (1988), 'Performative Acts and Gender Constitution: An Essay in Phenomenology and Feminist Theory', *Theatre Journal*, 40 (4): 519–31. doi:10.2307/3207893

Cohen, Stanley (2002), *Folk Devils and Moral Panics*, 3rd edn, London: Routledge.

Collins, Albert, and Richard Penniman (1956), 'Lucille', [Song] Specialty Records.

Crawley, Ashon (2020), 'He Was an Architect: Little Richard and Blackqueer Grief'. Available online: https://www.npr.org/2020/12/22/948963753/little-richard-black-queer-grief-he-was-an-architect?t=1608985466258 (accessed 5 January 2021).

Davis, Angela Y. (1998), *Blues Legacies and Black Feminism: Gertrude 'Ma' Rainey, Bessie Smith, and Billie Holiday*, New York: Pantheon Books.

Dixon, Willie (1960), *Back Door Man*, Chicago: Chess.

Don't Knock the Rock (1956), [Film] Dir. F. F. Sears, S. Katzman (Producer), USA: Columbia Pictures.

Down and Out in Beverly Hills (1986), [Film] Dir. P. Mazursky, P. Mazursky (Producer), USA: Touchstone Films.

Friederich, Brandon (2017), 'Ma Rainey's Lesbian Lyrics: 5 Times She Expressed Her Queerness in Song'. Available online: https://www.billboard.com/articles/news/pride/7824784/ma-rainey-lesbian-lyrics (accessed 5 January 2021).

Gelbart, Matthew (2003), 'Persona and Voice in the Kinks' Songs of the Late 1960s', *Journal of the Royal Musical Association*, 128 (2): 200–41. Available online: http://www.jstor.org/stable/3557496 (accessed 5 January 2021).

Gilmore, Al-Tony (1975), *Bad Nigger!: The National Impact of Jack Johnson*, London: Kennikat Press.

Glenn, Cerise L., and Landra J. Cunningham (2009), 'The Power of Black Magic: The Magical Negro and White Salvation in Film', *Journal of Black Studies*, 40 (2): 135–52. Available online: http://www.jstor.org/stable/40282626.

Goffman, Erving (1956), *The Presentation of Self in Everyday Life*, London: Allen Lane.

Goffman, Erving (1990), *The Presentation of Self in Everyday Life*, London: Penguin.

Goings, Kenneth W. (1994), *Mammy and Uncle Mose: Black Collectibles and American Stereotyping*, Bloomington: Indiana University Press.

Grantmyre, Laura (2011), '"They lived their life and they didn't bother anybody": African American Female Impersonators and Pittsburgh's Hill District, 1920–1960', *American Quarterly*, 63 (4): 983–1011. Available online: http://www.jstor.org/stable/41412801 (accessed 5 January 2021).

Green, Laura (1998), 'Stereotypes: Negative Racial Stereotypes and Their Effect on Attitudes toward African-Americans'. Available online: https://www.ferris.edu/htmls/news/jimcrow/links/essays/vcu.htm (accessed 5 January 2021).

Grein, Paul (2020), 'Little Richard Never Won a Grammy, but He Brought Down the House at the 1988 Grammy Awards'. Available online: https://www.billboard.com/articles/news/awards/9374831/little-richard-1988-grammys-best-new-artist-rant (accessed 5 January 2021).

Hamilton, Marybeth (1998), 'Sexual Politics and African-American Music; Or, Placing Little Richard in History', *History Workshop Journal* (46), 160–76. Available online: http://www.jstor.org/stable/4289584 (accessed 5 January 2021).

John Waters on 'The Girl Can't Help It' (DVD Extra) (2004), [Film] Dir. N. Algar, UK: Second Sight Films.

Johnson, Enotris, Robert Blackwell and Richard Penniman (1956), 'Long Tall Sally', [Song] Specialty Records.

Kracauer, Siegfried (1997), 'Remarks on the Actor', in S. Kracauer (ed.), *Theory of Film: The Redemption of Physical Reality*, 2nd edn, 93–100, New York: Oxford University Press.

Long, Alecia P. (2004), *The Great Southern Babylon: Sex, Race, and Respectability in New Orleans, 1865–1920*, Baton Rouge: Louisiana State University Press.

Lott, Eric (1992), 'Love and Theft: The Racial Unconscious of Blackface Minstrelsy', *Representations* (39), 23–50. doi:10.2307/2928593.

Marascalco, John, and Richard Penniman (1956), 'She's Got It', [Song] Specialty Records.

Marascalco, John S. (1956), 'Ready Teddy', [Song] Specialty Records.

Mister Rock and Roll (1957), [Film] Dir. C. S. Dubin, USA: Paramount Pictures.

Moore, Allan F. (2012), *Song Means: Analysing and Interpreting Recorded Popular Song*, Burlington, VT: Ashgate.

Naremore, James (1988), *Acting in the Cinema*, London: University of California Press.

Norman, Philip (2008), *John Lennon: The Life*, London: HarperCollins.

Palmer, Robert (1995), *Rock & Roll: An Unruly History*, London: Harmony Books.

Pattie, David (2007), *Rock Music in Performance*, Basingstoke: Palgrave Macmillan.

Pazda, Adam D., Andrew J. Elliot and Tobias Greitemeyer (2011), 'Sexy Red: Perceived Sexual Receptivity Mediates the Red-Attraction Relation in Men Viewing Woman', *Journal of Experimental Social Psychology*, 48 (3): 787–90. doi: https://doi.org/10.1016/j.jesp.2011.12.009.

Penman, Ian (2019), *It Gets Me Home, This Curving Track*, London: Fitzcarraldo Editions.

Penniman, Richard (1957), 'Keep A-Knockin' (But You Can't Come In)', [Song] Specialty Records.

Penniman, Richard and Dorothy LaBostrie (1955), 'Tutti Frutti', [Single] Specialty Records.

Pfeifle, Jason (2014), 'Racial Imperatives: Discipline, Performativity, and Struggles Against Subjection', *Contemporary Political Theory*, 13 (3): e1–e3. doi:10.1057/cpt.2013.30.

Ribowsky, Mark (2020), *The Big Life of Little Richard*, New York: Diversion Books.

Schechner, Richard, and Sara Brady (2020), *Performance Studies: An Introduction*, 4th edn, London: Routledge.

Smedley, Audrey (2007), 'The History of the Idea of Race … and Why It Matters'. Paper presented at the Race, Human Variation and Disease: Consensus and Frontiers, Warrenton, Virginia.

The Arsenio Hall Show (1990), [TV programme] CBS.

The Girl Can't Help It (1956), [Film] Dir. F. Tashlin, USA: 20th Century Fox.

The Late Late Show with Tom Snyder (1997), [TV programme], Dir. T. Snyder, CBS.

The Simpsons (2003), 'Special Edna'. [E7, S14] Dir B. Anderson, USA: Fox, Disney.

The Tonight Show Starring Johnny Carson (1986), [TV programme], Dir. R. Weiner, NBC.

Troup, Bobby (1956), 'The Girl Can't Help It', [Song] Specialty Records.
Tyson, Timothy B. (2018), *The Blood of Emmett Till*, 1st Simon & Schuster trade paperback edn, New York: Simon & Schuster.
Weems, Mickey (2008), *The Fierce Tribe*, Colorado: University Press of Colorado. https://doi.org/https://doi.org/10.2307/j.ctt4cgq6k.17 (accessed 5 January 2021).
White, Charles (2013), *The Life and Times of Little Richard: The Authorised Biography*, London: Omnibus Press.
Wojcik, Pamela Robertson (2003), 'Typecasting', *Criticism*, 45 (2): 223–49. Available online: http://www.jstor.org/stable/23126345 (accessed 5 January 2021).

2

There's always gonna be queens on the rag: Madonna and queer intertextuality

Sarah Perks

If people keep seeing it and seeing it and seeing it, eventually it's not going to be such a strange thing.
– Madonna, *The Advocate Magazine Interview*, 7 May 1991

The category is ...

Madonna is entering her fifth decade of fame and fourth decade of significant attention by academia, predominantly, but not exclusively, in the field of cultural studies, dubbed 'Madonna Studies'. Madonna first released a single in 1982 and an album in 1983, which became dance club hits; her second album a year later, *Like A Virgin*, launched her as a global mainstream pop music star with a distinctive fashion style. Her career and activities were never solely music; she first appeared in a low-budget film *A Certain Sacrifice* in 1979, and her rising star was beginning to show as she shot the film *Desperately Seeking Susan* on the streets of New York in 1984. Her relationship with the screen is as much a part of her work as her music and dance, participating in front of the camera in twenty-one features to date, and she has worked behind it directing and producing films including *W. E.* (2008). As a pop star, she has embraced formal and narrative experimentation in the music video, creating much more than visual recording of her performances, inspiring debate and subject to as much attention as her album and theatrical film releases; indeed, *Justify My Love* (1990) became a smash VHS release when banned by MTV. Voted her best music video by *Rolling Stone* magazine, *Express Yourself* (1989) was the most expensive ever made at the time for five million dollars, an intertextual science fiction crotch-grabbing collaboration with Hollywood director David Fincher, whilst others from her current seventy-five-strong back catalogue mined everything from European cinema history to time lapsing to soft porn to religious iconography.

It is not the author's intention to catalogue this immense body of work here but to point out that the screen presence of Madonna is as vital to her cultural significance as live performance and music recording. Indeed, her screen presence, performance and music are often interdependent: many of her leading roles include her singing talent, notably *Dick Tracy* (1990) and *Evita* (1996), providing the soundtrack directly in *Truth or Dare* (1991) and indirectly in *Desperately Seeking Susan* (1985) and *Who's That Girl?* (1987). Where music is not part of the package, the critical reception was often less favourable, particularly *Shanghai Surprise* (1986) and *Body of Evidence* (1993).

For cultural studies, she arrived at the moment its development was forking along textual analysis and audience reception lines, ahead of, albeit anticipating, the popularity of intersectionality, third-wave feminism and queer theory. However, the vast body of work that has been generated in academic literature on the star has focused on a single aspect of her practice, predominantly her relationship with race, gender or sexuality. Now just shy of thirty years after the publication of the first major academic book of essays – *The Madonna Connection: Representational Politics, Subcultural Identities, and Cultural Theory* edited by Cathy Schwichtenberg – the questions raised feel surprisingly relevant as the book's central questioning of appropriation is very much a popular debate now. At the time, the book and others were ridiculed by more mainstream press reviews – 'a scholarship blindly infatuated with the solipsistic tenets of deconstruction, hogtied by jargon and critical dogma' explained the *New York Times* (Kakutani 1992); it was just the beginning of Madonna Studies, and now her career is directly linked to the wider acceptance of the study of popular culture into academia.

In bed with Madonna

It is also thirty years ago that Madonna made a concert film *Truth or Dare* – released as *In Bed with Madonna* in the UK – that followed her Blond Ambition World Tour (April to August 1990). Days before the tour, Madonna had rushed through the filming of her *Vogue* video, a collaboration with Luis Xtravaganza Camacho and Jose Gutierez Xtravaganza, New York–based dancers she had met in clubs who had set up the Vogue House of Xtravaganza. She hired them to join her tour, alongside five other male dancers: Kevin Stea, Carlton Wilborn, Salim Gauwloos, Oliver Crumes and Gabriel Trupin (who died of AIDS complications in 1995). A further team included her two backing singer–dancers Niki Haris and Donna DeLory, her brother Christopher, hairstylist Sharon Gault, her personal assistant Melissa Crowe and the much shouted at production and technical team. The film quickly veered away from a traditional concert film and into a behind-the-scenes documentary, at times arranged (Madonna was funding it after all – she was also executive producer). But it never appears scripted in the way reality TV became, and the film afforded a huge amount of freedom to its then 25-year-old director, Alek Keshishian. He recalls,

> When I was shooting, I wasn't particularly aware. I was in this bubble where that was just all accepted. When I started editing, those are the moments where you're making certain choices because you have to give up so much of the footage you've shot. I felt instinctively that I wanted to get across how in Madonna's world homosexuality was just a fact of life. These dancers, who she felt so close to, they were going through that age of AIDS. There was still so much stigma against it. I felt personally the power of putting that out, but I had no idea that it might resonate with others quite the way it did. (Coscarelli 2016)

The black and white slightly grainy 16-mm footage was intended as cinema verité style; only the music number performances were in full 35-mm colour. The film was screened out of competition at Cannes and became one of the highest grossing documentaries ever at the time.

The film really does capture an extraordinary performance from Madonna, at a career-high moment when she was supremely confident; it manages to feel authentic in a way that films made by pop stars rarely do, revealing her as bitchy, funny, relatable, maternal and hard-working. She creates her temporary tour family, but then she is also seen with her real family, worrying about her wayward brother Martin and what her father might think about the show (he simply says, 'It's great'). Her closest sibling Christopher stands by her as a beacon of trust; however, in reality, he was soon to be furious with her. In the interview quoted at the start of this chapter for *The Advocate*, a gay culture magazine, she is promoting the film when she outs him (Shewey 2007; original interview archived). Three of the dancers sue her afterwards for their own 'outings' and representation in the film, which she dismisses as an instance of 'they were not ready for her to tell them they were ready'. All the footage is fairly unextraordinary to the general viewer of 2020; however, in the AIDS-pandemic obsessed America of thirty years ago, the cast were not as relaxed about becoming the gay mainstream as Madonna was. The film has been covered extensively by critics, commentators and academics alike and there is much to analyse – her treatment of other celebrities, the sexual assault on Sharon that is laughed at, visiting the grave of her mother, to name a few, but it is the significance around queer intersectionality that creates longevity for cultural studies.

Queer eye for the straight guy

Oliver is the only straight dancer, and he also gets the most screen time in the film, explained away by Madonna as because he was not out partying like the other ones. Whether that's true or not, he does seem singled out by her for attention, and he is wearing Madonna merchandise in every scene (t-shirts and hats in particular). It seems a strange choice to allow him to be the sole perspective on the Gay Pride in NYC, at this moment still a subcultural 'underground' event, not the mainstream family-friendly parade of today. In real-life, Oliver later acknowledges his coming of age here and how he learnt to become a LGBTQ+ ally. On screen, Madonna actually succeeds in marginalising his voice: 'There always gonna be queens on the rag, you just have to expect that of me' she quips to him, although as if to balance, she also admonishes the others for picking on him. A documentary, *Strike a Pose*, was released in 2017 that investigated what happened to the seven male dancers from the tour and their subsequent journeys post–*Truth or Dare*.

It would be hard to deny that Madonna purposefully positions herself as a spokesperson for others, and cultural studies has never been able to fully reconcile this problem of who can speak for whom. Much academic writing on her is limited to this debate in *The Madonna Connection* publication:

> The extent to which Madonna poaches from the repertoires of subcultural groups or celebrates those 'others' in whose names she speaks is the subject of thoughtful and nuanced discussion throughout this anthology in ways that indicate new directions for cultural studies. (Schwichtenberg 1993, 53)

Unfortunately, the claim seems a little grand considering that the structure of the book was neatly divided along lines of gender and race. Already at this point in 1993, the new direction of third-wave feminism had already been signalled by Kim Crenshaw's work on intersectionality and Judith Butler's influential

Gender Trouble exploring gender as societal construct. Perhaps one of the most important observations that the academic grouping of this anthology could have investigated further is hidden in the introduction as an almost throwaway comment:

> Much of Madonna's later work (i.e., *Express Yourself, Vogue, Justify My Love*, the *Blond Ambition Tour* and *Truth or Dare*) deals explicitly with representations of sexuality that have particular resonance for gay and lesbian audiences but are typically misread or ignored by the mainstream. (Schwichtenberg 1993, 58)

The transferring of the sub-cultural into the mainstream was of course nothing new if we consider Elvis, Bowie, Queen and many others before, but it is this *ignorance* precisely that Madonna was setting up as her challenge, however clumsily. Yes, as novelist Andrew O'Hagan points out, she is 'peddling ethnic, feministical and gay ideas to fashion whilst taking none of the risks and absorbing none of the real flak'. This is exactly what she purposefully sets out to do; she even *positions* herself as able to do this ('This was the opportunity of their lives. And I know that they've suffered a great deal in their lives'). How we precisely register the value of this is where things come unstuck, particularly around where flak might actually mean life or death for someone from a sub-cultural minority, or how much of this is actually done in the service of capital and therefore exploitation. And where this value in shifting mainstream perceptions can be measured, or indeed what impact narratives of intersectional care and resistance can achieve in a mainstream context? Unfortunately, and out of the scope of this article, Madonna was to receive much more flak later in her career for daring to peddle possibly the only part of her identity other than cis white female she could legitimately lay claim to: age.

Paris is burning

Truth or Dare was seen by a huge audience, much more than a documentary released the year before about vogueing and ballroom culture by director Jennie Livingston called *Paris is Burning* (1990). The critical reception, particularly by the LGBT community, has been largely positive for this film, though bell hooks asks us to consider how the Black males of the ballroom are also limited in their representation. Her analysis is equally applicable to *Truth or Dare*: 'The film's politics of race, gender and class are played out in ways that are both progressive and reactionary' (hooks 2014, 149). She adds,

> So far I have read no interviews where Livingstone discusses the issue of appropriation. And even though she is openly critical of Madonna, she does not convey how her work differs from Madonna's appropriation of black experience. To some extent it is precisely the recognition by mass culture that aspects of the black life, like 'voguing' fascinate white audiences that creates a market for both Madonna's product and Livingston's. (hooks 2014, 152)

In *Paris Is Burning*, the dancers are seen estranged from any type of community or family outside of the ballroom; Madonna claims them as her family ('all the children I temporarily claimed as my own'), and in doing so, she still positions them in the margins and her as the saviour figure. She is the maternal figure of perfect fantasy – white womanhood – that bell hooks articulates reinforces a white male patriarchy for the Black gay male experience, who willingly embrace it through their (performance of) white female star worship.

Madonna also encapsulates the fixation on stardom of ballroom culture that hooks emphasises through her exploration of Dorien Carey in *Paris Is Burning*. Both Dorien and Madonna assume it is everyone's aspiration to be a star, and here, hooks argues via Richard Dyer, that stars are filling the void of creating the fictional notions of individual freedom under capitalism. However, when Madonna quizzes her two backing singer–dancers Niki and Donna on whether they want to be famous, they seem much less keen on the idea than her. Beyond the Black gay male fantasies of white women, hooks describes effectively how Dorien articulates the positive experiences of the ballroom, equally applicable to Madonna's representation:

> Carey speaks profoundly about the redemptive power of the imagination in black life, that drag balls were traditionally a place where the aesthetics of the images in relation to black gay life could be explored with complexity and grace. (hooks 2014, 155)

hooks develops her argument into a Madonna-specific chapter in *Black Looks*, with some positive reflection: 'And indeed what some of us like about her is the way she deconstructs the myth of the "natural" white girl beauty by exposing the extent to which it can be and is usually artificially constructed and maintained' (hooks 2014, 159). Yet it is Madonna's 'emphasis on black male experience' that has her and her Black female friends mark her down as the quintessential white girl outsider colonialising Black culture (hooks 2014, 159). Not to disagree with this hypothesis, but to surface the problematic issue of hooks and her friends are also, in fact, largely speaking on behalf of the gay Black male experience.

Revisiting the film thirty years on, journalist Emma Madden says, 'remains one of the most morally contentious documents of the spoiled, rich white-girl fantasy' (Madden 2020). There is less generally written about Madonna and class: when she calls the dancers 'poor' she does so in full knowledge of her own working class made good 'rags to riches' story. Indeed, hooks ends her chapter reminding us of this: 'Perhaps when Madonna explores the memories of her white working-class childhood in a troubled family in a way that enables her to understand intimately the politics of exploitation, domination and submission, she will have a deeper connection with oppositional black culture ... acts of resistance that transform rather than simply seduce' (hooks 2014, 164). However, Madonna wasn't actually working class; she downgraded her engineer father to mechanic to create a perfect Detroit Cinderella story, and whilst this doesn't particularly undermine hook's persuasive points about race, it does render her advice pointless. More interestingly perhaps, there is yet to appear any writing anywhere on Kevin, the only Asian-American character in her dance troupe and on camera, also the troupe leader, who doesn't get to utter a word, though we do see him smile and dance.

What are you looking at?

Here is where Kimberlé Crenshaw's theories of intersectionality arrive at the same time for cultural studies (1989–91) and have influenced much of the direction since. Crenshaw initially used cases of employment legal cases to explain her precis on the damage of single disadvantage models: 'The refusal to allow a multiply-disadvantaged class to represent others who may be singularly-disadvantaged defeats efforts to restructure the distribution of opportunity and limits remedial relief to minor adjustments with an established hierarchy' (Crenshaw 1989, 145). Whilst there would certainly still be questions around Madonna's leading role in the activity, she is actively pursuing Crenshaw's call to action: 'The goal of this activity should be to facilitate the inclusion of marginalised groups for whom it can be said: "When they enter, we all enter."' (Crenshaw 1989, 167).

Crenshaw further pushes how we might conceive Madonna's ambitions with the notion of identity politics, particularly with regard to the representation of AIDS: Madonna is 'recognizing as social and systemic what was formerly perceived as isolated and individual' (Crenshaw 1991, 1). She also notes the issue of misreading – what here might also be understood as the ignorance of the mainstream: 'While the descriptive project of postmodernism of questioning the ways in which meaning is socially constructed is generally sound, this critique sometimes misreads the meaning of social construction and distorts its political relevance' (Crenshaw 1991, 12). It seems the space of queer intersectionality might be at particular risk here in *Truth or Dare* due to misreading through its reduction of some voices and allowance for Madonna and Oliver to have the majority of the screen time. The notion of coalition by Crenshaw, however, might offer a resolution here:

> If, as this analysis asserts, history and context determine the utility of identity politics, how, then, do we understand identity politics today, especially in light of our recognition of multiple dimensions of identity? More specifically, what does it mean to argue that gendered identities have been obscured in antiracist discourses, just as race identities have been obscured in feminist discourses? Does that mean we cannot talk about identity? Or instead, that any discourse about identity has to acknowledge how our identities are constructed through the intersection of multiple dimensions? A beginning response to these questions requires that we first recognize that the organized identity groups in which we find ourselves are in fact coalitions, or at least potential coalitions waiting to be formed. (Crenshaw 1991, 14)

In 2019, episode one of season two of the American FX Television series *Pose* creates an intertextual feedback loop as it discusses the dichotomy at the heart of Madonna's use of voguing for her new hit single. This is a historical drama, so it is written in contemporary times about a historical moment in 1990. They can't agree on whether it is a great thing that Madonna, one of the most famous women on the planet, is bringing attention to the vogue ballroom or to what degree she is exploiting their scene, to appreciate or to appropriate if you like. The debate reopened, it is articulated through Pray Tell (Billy Porter) claiming it made them look like a fad, whilst Blanca (Mj Rodriguez) is full of phase and excitement ('This song is our ticket to acceptance'). Whilst cultural studies might have moved on at this point, *Vogue* magazine sums it up in a final irony of the feedback loop-loop. On the debate between the two characters, the journalist in Vogue writes,

> Both perspectives are valid, but the irony now is that 'Vogue' is remembered as neither of those things – instead, it's looked at with hindsight as a seismic shift for queer culture in the broadest sense, as it hit the mainstream for the very first

time. Yes, there are valid questions around Madonna profiting off a movement that was spearheaded by a marginalized community she was not a part of, but, in her own way, she gave back. Even the year before 'Vogue' was released, the liner notes for her album Like a Prayer came not with a series of thank yous to those who had helped her with the record, but an urgent message describing the 'Facts About AIDS' to encourage safe sex, the most visible step yet in her efforts to promote AIDS/HIV awareness. And while she might occasionally miss the mark, who knows the number of young, queer people of color who saw Madonna's video playing on MTV and recognized within it a community that promised a lifeline. The possibility of upping sticks and moving to New York City, where, within the four walls of the ballroom, they could find a small slice of freedom. (Hess 2020)

In *Truth or Dare*, there is an extremely cringeworthy moment (at least to 2020 standards) where Madonna describes her tour family as emotional cripples and as her children, infantilising their demeanour and experiences ('I love having children to watch over'). Her behaviour echoes that of the role of a house mother in ballroom culture, though this is likely coincidence. In 'truth', several of the dancers were HIV positive and struggling to deal with their situation. For some, vogueing has never been able to leave its identification with AIDS behind, and for others, it has transcended this view or is comfortable to continue to use the association to raise awareness.

In his book *Crip Theory*, Robert McRuer explores the direct relationship between heteronormativity and able-bodied normativity as part of his ongoing critique of neoliberal capitalist structures. Whilst he does not directly analyse Madonna, he does briefly engage her as an ally in the rejection of performative heterosexuality and describes her as a 'queer theorist'. Madonna is quite literally pushing everyone out of the closet with *Truth or Dare*, and whilst some of it might be in the pursuit of capital – or if we follow the McRuer's logic through pushing towards (however unknowingly) to building the type of capital that embraces diversity, normalising to increase its capital – there is also an argument for her work's combination of visual transgression and activist messaging that pushed against the normative boundaries that served to restrict representations of LGBT minorities of colour and the AIDS narrative of victim and 'dis-ability'. Her transgression here is not to coerce her tour family into normalising images (e.g. gay marriage) but to push further than has been seen in mainstream film previously, for example by combining her own transgression, the blowjob on a bottle of Evian, with two men French kissing at the height of the AIDS epidemic. McRuer outlines,

> At the same time that AIDS theory and queer theory, and AIDS theory as queer theory, have developed, the disability rights movement and the academic field that has come to be known as disability studies have mobilized similar in- sights. Disability activists and theorists have argued, for instance, that disability should be understood as a minority identity, not simply as a 'condition' of lack or loss to be pitied or 'overcome'. This minority identity has been forged through the common experience of able-bodied oppression – although nothing 'naturally' links people with mobility impairments to people with cognitive disabilities to those who are deaf or blind, a common disability identity has been claimed across such experiences and in opposition to able-bodied hegemony. At the same time that this minority identity has been shaped, however, theorists/activists have also argued that the division into two neat categories (able-bodied and disabled) is ideological, more about maintaining a particular system of power than about accurately describing reality; they have insisted that, in fact, all of us inhabit different kinds of bodies and have a range of bodily experiences. (McRuer 2002, 223)

The cinematic technique the documentary employs in terms of 'truth' is that of black and white reality footage and colour concert performances, which has traditionally been used to emphasise a division between fact (black and white reality/Kansas) and fiction (colour pop performances/Oz). But it is a false division that this device intentionally emphasises here, the film is playful with ideas of truth and reality, purposefully blurring lines between fact and fiction, for example, when she stages them all sat on the bed talking, or that the colour pop concert performances are in some way more *real*. Madonna's screen presence throughout this film and in her videos of this period does nothing *but* attack ideological constructs and neoconservative values, overtly (explicit material) and covertly (non-traditional family values). The few queer representations in mainstream culture of 1990/1991 are of able-bodied, often white, LGBTQ+ individuals; here Madonna presents a queer intersectionality of multiple bodies of colour that suggests AIDS is not marginalised to either the individual or as a lack of ability. Therefore, it makes sense that McRuer would consider her a queer theorist, as she is closer than most to his examples of collaborative intention (or coalition) behind crip theory:

> As I hope Crip Theory has consistently suggested, we need a postidentity politics of sorts, but a postidentity politics that allows us to work together, one that acknowledges the complex and contradictory histories of our various movements, drawing on and learning from those histories rather than transcending them. (McRuer 2006, 202)

Madonna is transgressing but she is not transcending. Likewise, her use of vogue and other queer references places her firmly in the pastiche category of intertextuality – she draws attention to the imitation through performative techniques, rather than just a recording of the reality. This confirms Richard Dyer's (2006) projection of pastiche: 'A knowing form of the process of imitation, which itself always holds us inexorably within cultural perception of the real and also, thereby, enables us to make sense of the real.'

'I can't live in New York because all my friends are dead'

Truth or Dare doesn't delve into Madonna's backstory in New York, just that she has her own apartment there. The Madonna myth/story is that she moved to New York City's East Village in 1978 with thirty-five dollars and a huge ambition to be a dancer. Her authenticity for gay fans is heavily connected to this narrative, particularly how she explains she was encouraged to make this move by her hugely influential (and gay) ballet teacher Christopher Flynn back in Detroit. Madonna was therefore in New York through a period largely considered a cultural heyday, including Studio 54 and the last days of disco, CBGBs and punk/no wave, and the arty, new wave Danceteria. It was while working in this club that she became close to fellow worker artist Keith Haring, and this puts her at the heart of the centre of the artistic scene. She goes out with Jean-Michel Basquiat, flat shares with designer Martin Burgoyne and finally cements herself as the queen of the East Village on screen in *Desperately Seeking Susan* (1985). In *Truth or Dare*, it is only made known that she has an apartment there in New York when she falls ill and therefore is not cavorting around with the others in a hotel bedroom. On screen, she dedicates a prayer to close friend Keith Haring at her last concert, which is also an AIDS benefit; Martin died of AIDS in 1986 and Keith and Christopher both died of AIDS in the 1990s.

Her formative New York years and her immersion in the 'underground' scene of New York explain both her early relationship with queer culture and also the source of her many intertextual references – particularly those from art history and arthouse cinema. Alongside the choreography by the House of Xtravaganza in her Vogue video, there are paintings by Tamara de Lempicka, one of Madonna's favourite artists and an infamous 1920s bohemian, a seducer of men and women who always claimed to live beyond the rules of society. In *Deeper and Deeper*, Madonna is clearly paying tribute to Andy Warhol's underground films, such as through casting Udo Kier from *Flesh* (1968) in the video, and to Luchino Visconti's *The Damned* (*La caduta degli dei* 1969), where the sexually ambiguous Helmut Berger impersonates Marlene Dietrich. This video also includes a cameo by Chi Chi LaRue, a drag queen well known as a director of gay pornographic films. When her then-boyfriend Tony Ward appears in her video for *Justify My Love* (1991), she is aware of his status as a gay icon and in nude modelling; he later goes on to play the main role in new queer cinema classic *Hustler White* (1996, Bruce LaBruce). Madonna's intertextuality and appropriation is also clearly influenced by the Pictures Generation of 1980s New York – for example, she is the sole sponsor of Cindy Sherman's 1997 exhibition *Untitled Film Stills* at MOMA, an artist with whose work Madonna has clear parallels in terms of assuming multiple looks and identities for the camera.

Bobby Woods, the director of *Deeper and Deeper* shared Madonna's handwritten concept notes to demonstrate her involvement and commented,

> Madonna wanted to do an Andy Warhol/Edie Sedgwick styled video. She believed, and I think this is accurate, that there was a similar feel to the times of America in the Roaring '20's and the Disco '70's. A wildness. The video was made very quickly. Deeper and Deeper is a great song, one of her best dance records for sure, thanks to Shep Pettibone. The dance sequences in the video are 100% spontaneous. We loaded a dance floor with people, put her record on, and the dancing began. I have danced with Madonna many times. So I can understand why those people wanted to dance with her as well. It's a thrill. She also brought along Udo Kier and Holly Woodlawn who were part of the original Warhol crowd. Her pal Sofia Coppola (who I adore) came along, too, as well as Debi Mazar and Ingrid Casares ... For me, working with her was a lot of fun. First off, she's extremely smart. Secondly, it's all her doing. (Woods 1992)

Whether from her own creativity as the master producer of her works, through her artistic friends and influences or via the professional influence of director, crew and cast, Madonna's screen presence involves an ongoing use of references that mark her out as both queer and avant-garde. In *Truth or Dare*, she states she is a fan of the films of Pedro Almodóvar (and he throws a big party for her) and her Bad Girl video (again with David Fincher) references Wim Wenders's *Wings of Desire* (*Der Himmel über Berlin* (1987). Both Almodóvar and Wenders were already fairly well-known filmmakers; their success was not considered mainstream but arthouse, at the time their work was considered both contemporary and edgy. This is not to show how very postmodern Madonna was, but instead how the breadth of her references mapped on to developments in cultural studies and sort of charted its move from considerations of what we might term avant-garde work into considerations of popular culture. Madonna later returns to cast herself in the Damiel (Bruno Ganz) role in Wenders's *Der Himmel über Berlin*, standing as a winged angel in her short film *Her-Story* (2017), created for international women's day and as a rallying cry against authoritarianism.

Conclusion

Camilla Paglia wrote a much-quoted statement piece in 1990 in the *The New York Times*, overflowing with praise and perhaps a little too optimistic: 'Through her enormous impact on young women around the world, Madonna is the future of feminism' (Paglia 1990). Whilst it doesn't feel like this grand statement bore out – and in fact Paglia and Madonna have been prone to public spats of late – it does feel like there is a lasting argument for cultural studies to consider the relevance of its relationship with Madonna (see Oppenheim 2016). Stuart Hall himself might well have been thinking about Madonna's role as an activist in AIDS awareness in 1992 when he says,

> The question of AIDS is an extremely important terrain of struggle and contestation. In addition to the people we know who are dying, or have died, or will, there are the many people dying who are never spoken of. How could we say that the question of AIDS is not also a question of who gets represented and who does not? AIDS is the site at which the advance of sexual politics is being rolled back. It's a site at which not only people will die, but desire and pleasure will also die if certain metaphors do not survive, or survive in the wrong way. Unless we operate in this tension, we don't know what cultural studies can do, can't, can never do; but also, what it has to do, what it alone has a privileged capacity to do. It has to analyze certain things about the constitutive and political nature of representation itself, about its complexities, about the effects of language, about textuality as a site of life and death. Those are the things cultural studies can address. (Hall 1992, 285)

Whether anyone likes it or not, Madonna does do activism – particularly around AIDS – as a part of her work, and she embodies an immorality of inaction so frequently called upon by cultural studies academics. The examples above show how Madonna formed her own kind of queer intersectionality through her approach to representation on screen. In yet another feedback loop, the film

Truth or Dare was screened at MOMA twenty-five years after its release, therefore becoming the work of (or at least about) an 'artist' in their own right, something Madonna frequently claimed but was rarely taken seriously for. Ryan Gilbey named *Truth or Dare* the world's greatest music documentary ever in September 2019 in *The Guardian*; it is hard to imagine a mention for the preachy *Lady Gaga: Five Foot Two* in thirty years' time. In 2020, Pedro Almodóvar wrote in his Covid diaries of how Madonna constructed the whole party scene in *Truth or Dare* and how she was extremely rude to everyone except Antonio Banderas and, ultimately, did not get their permission for appearing in the film. That Madonna does not get permission for anything is exactly why she is so valuable to cultural studies.

References

Coscarelli, Joe (2016), 'From the Interview: After 25 Years, How Well Has Madonna's @Truth or Dare@ Aged?' *The New York Times*. Available online: https://www.nytimes.com/2016/08/26/arts/music/madonna-truth-or-dare-alek-keshishian.html (accessed 16 November 2020).

Crenshaw, Kimberlé Williams (1989), 'Demarginalizing the Intersection of Race and Sex: A Black Feminist Critique of Antidiscrimination Doctrine, Feminist Theory and Antiracist Politics', *University of Chicago Legal Forum*, 1989 (1): article 8.

Crenshaw, Kimberlé Williams (1991), 'Mapping the Margins: Intersectionality, Identity Politics, and Violence against Women of Color', *Stanford Law Review*, 43 (6): 1241–99.

Dyer, Richard (2006), *Pastiche*, New York: Routledge.

Fouz-Hernández, Santiago, and Freya Jarman-Ivens, eds (2004), *Madonna's Drowned Worlds New Approaches to Her Cultural Transformations, 1983–2003*, New York: Routledge.

Hall, Stuart (1992), 'Cultural Studies and Its Theoretical Legacies', in Lawrence Grossberg, Cary Nelson and Paula Treichler (eds), *Cultural Studies*, London: Routledge.

Hess, Liam (2020), 'Strike a Pose! Why Madonna's @Vogue@ Is Still Relevant 30 Years Later', *Vogue*. Available online: https://www.vogue.com/article/madonna-vogue-video-30th-anniversary (accessed 16 November 2020).

hooks, bell (2014), *Black Looks: Race and Representation*, 2nd edn, London: Routledge.

Kakutani, Michiko (1992), 'Books of the Times; Madonna Writes', *The New York Times*. Available online: https://www.nytimes.com/1992/10/21/books/books-of-the-times-madonna-writes-academics-explore-her-erotic-semiotics.html (accessed 17 November 2020).

Madden, Emma (2020), 'Madonna Showed Us Her Elite Head Games in *Truth or Dare*', *Pitchfork*. Available online: https://pitchfork.com/thepitch/madonna-showed-us-her-elite-head-games-in-truth-or-dare/ (accessed 17 November 2020).

McRuer, Robert (2002), 'Critical Investments: AIDS, Christopher Reeve, and Queer/Disability Studies', *Journal of Medical Humanities*, 23 (3/4): 221–37.

McRuer, Robert (2006), *Crip Theory: Cultural Signs of Queerness and Disability*, New York: New York University Press.

Oppenheim, Maya (2016), 'Feminist Critic Camille Paglia Accuses Madonna of @Maudlin Self Pity@ over Billboard Speech', *Independent*. Available online: https://www.independent.co.uk/news/people/camille-paglia-madonna-billboard-speech-maudlin-self-pity-a7477786.html (accessed 17 November 2020).

Paglia, Camille (1990), 'Madonna – Finally, a Real Feminist', *The New York Times*. Available online: https://www.nytimes.com/1990/12/14/opinion/madonna-finally-a-real-feminist.html (accessed 17 November 2020).

Schwichtenberg, Cathy, ed. ([1993] 2019), *The Madonna Connection: Representational Politics, Subcultural Identities, and Cultural Theory*, New York: Routledge.

Shewey, Don (2007), 'Madonna's X-rated *Advocate* Cover Story', *Advocate*. Available online: https://www.advocate.com/news/2007/07/23/madonna-x-rated-interview (accessed 16 November 2020).

Woods, Bobby (1992), 'Today in Madonna History: November 24, 1992'. Available online: https://todayinmadonnahistory.com/tag/bobby-woods/ (accessed 17 November 2020).

3

Prince's fashion during the *Batman* era: Symbols, silhouettes and the return of purple

Karen Turman

'[*Batman*] is going to be my movie!' Alex Hahn quoted the late musical genius and style icon, Prince Rogers Nelson, as declaring this enthusiastic statement to studio engineer Femi Jiya (2003, 157). Regardless of the irony behind this statement, in that he already had three films to his name – *Purple Rain* (1984), *Under the Cherry Moon* (1986) and *Sign O' the Times* (1987), and was in the process of a fourth *Graffiti Bridge* (1990) – this declaration indicates the point at which Prince was uncharacteristically embracing a project outside of his realm. Prince famously never collaborated on a project of someone else's design, so why would he accept director Tim Burton's offer to contribute to the *Batman* soundtrack? In fact, Prince not only accepted the collaboration, but he also embraced it to the point of conflating the film as the next Prince project and subsequently attempted to absorb the Batman symbol into his own brand. No stranger to the silver screen, he deftly inserted himself into the *Batman* discourse by creating a new character, Gemini/Partyman, and starring in two lengthy cinematic music videos complete with entire plotlines, supporting characters, and high production value involving elaborate set design, dozens of extras, and extensive make-up and costuming. While it is no secret that Prince was indeed a cinephile who essentially skyrocketed to global pop music icon fame on the big screen in *Purple Rain*, his practically autonomous involvement and independent insertion into the *Batman* narrative warrants further scrutiny. How did his performance on both stage and screen during this often-overlooked era of his career affect his style evolution and ultimate branding as a cultural icon?

Prince remains to this day as synonymous with the colour purple as with his self-designed Love Symbol glyph that once replaced his name (1993–2000). Much attention has been paid to Prince's albums and aesthetics throughout the 1980s, with each year yielding a fresh new version of Prince both sonically and visually, from the scandalous bikini briefs emblematic of *Dirty Mind* (1980), to the polka-dot fantasy prints of the *Lovesexy* tour and album (1988b). Nonetheless, biographers and critics often pass over Prince's work during 1989, the last year of Prince's zeitgeist throughout the previous decade that had brought him to the height of his celebrity and fame as an international superstar. Because the only main studio album he released during this year, the soundtrack to Burton's *Batman* (Prince 1989a), was deemed merely a beneficial financial move for Prince, both the music and the surrounding context of the Nude Tour (June to September 1990) have been generally ignored, despite 'Batdance' (1989b) earning him his first number one hit since 'Kiss' (1986b). Initially asked to rewrite two previously recorded songs for the soundtrack, he instead swiftly created an entire album using clips from the testing footage of the film and even created his own character, Gemini/Partyman, to insert into an adjacent narrative, therefore giving himself agency within the project and adding to the *Batman* discourse. This essay aims to pinpoint significant elements of Prince's aesthetic style that surface during this unique and pivotal year during his incredibly prolific career spanning four decades. Through close analysis of Prince's auspicious return to the colour purple as the Joker-inspired superhero villain 'Gemini', the innovative tailoring of his 'Partyman' suit and the reconciliation with his obsession of the Batman symbol, I will explore the ways in which his involvement with Burton's *Batman* film in 1989 proves critical in the evolution of Prince's aesthetic and personal branding that would inaugurate and solidify his style into the 1990s and the latter half of his career.

The most notable aspect to Prince's style in 1989 is the audacious return of purple, his signature colour. Prince, of course, had been uniquely branding himself with the colour purple since the 1970s, as early collaborator and sound engineer Chris Moon recently outlined in 2018. While Prince retired the iconic purple studded trench coat after 1984, the colour itself was also placed metaphorically backstage in his wardrobe, with only a few cameos during the second half of the 1980s until the Partyman suit materialised for the *Batman* soundtrack. While he's not entirely abstaining from wearing purple between 1984 and 1988, the colour is noticeably absent from prominent public moments such as album covers, music videos, and concert costumes. Some examples from 1986 include purple iterations of designs that were famously worn in other hues. For example, the now iconic black crop top and low-waisted trousers with contrasting white buttons worn in both *Under the Cherry Moon* (1986) and the 'Kiss' music video (1986b) also made an appearance in lilac, including matching booties complemented by the billowing white fur coat that would later appear in the 'U Got the Look' (1987b) and 'If I Was Your Girlfriend' (1987a) music videos from the *Sign O' the Times* film (1987). Prince was also spotted around this time in a head-to-toe lavender ensemble with matching boots and trench as well as a plum version of his yellow zoot suit look from the 'Anotherloverholeinyourhead' (1986a) live performance during the Parade tour. In 1988, Prince brings purple briefly back to the stage during the *Lovesexy* tour with a short jumper over white leggings and high-heeled purple boots that extend above the knee and feature a heart ankle chain. While there are several of these extant sightings of Prince in his signature colour, the purple suit worn during the 'Partyman' music video (1989d) for the *Batman* soundtrack is to my knowledge the first full Prince-purple colour suit featured on a large-scale platform since Jim Sherrin's costume designs from the *Purple Rain* tour.

In the *Batman* franchise, purple is the classic colour of its number one villain, the Joker. Since the 1940s, the Joker has been depicted with green hair and a purple suit: from comic book illustrations of the Joker to Cesar Romero's live action interpretation in the *Batman* television series from 1966. In Tim Burton's 1989 film, costume designer Bob Ringwood leaned on fashion aesthetics from the 1940s to create Jack Nicholson's Joker who sports purple in the form of a tuxedo jacket with tails and peaked lapels, fedora hat, gloves and high-waisted plaid trousers. His double-breasted teal waistcoat with shawl lapels and matching silk scarf as bow tie complement the contrasting orange blouse, giving him a classic clown-like appearance. This outfit is clearly a blueprint for Prince's version of the Joker character, as both Partyman and the split-personality Gemini.

As aforementioned, the *Batman* soundtrack constitutes the only time Prince would participate in a collaborative project of someone else's design up until this point, with the exception of his teenage years. Perhaps this is why, after Nicholson suggested to Burton that Prince's songs '1999' and 'Baby I'm a Star' (Prince 1984a) supply the sonic backdrop to key scenes of the film due to Prince's branding with the colour purple and, by association, the Joker's costume, Prince not only accepted the proposal but took it to unforeseen extremes (Ro 2011, 187). Rather than merely providing alternative versions to those original songs, he instead created an entire new album using clips from the film after viewing the testing footage (Ro 2011, 189). In addition to the soundtrack, he invented two of his own characters to insert into an adjacent narrative of his creation, and therefore claimed his own agency within the project by creating space for himself in the *Batman* franchise.

First, the character Gemini appears centre stage in the 'Batdance' video, taunting a long-haired Prince inside his studio while the progressive electro-beats percolate and troupes of dancing Batmen, Jokers and Vicky Vales descend upon him. The iconic look was designed by long-time Prince designers Susan Stella and Helen Hiatt, who contributed to his wardrobe during the *Purple Rain* (1984) and *Sign O' the Times* (1987) eras, then oversaw the department from 1988 to 1990. This half-Joker, half-Batman look clearly references Ringwood's costume design of Nicholson's Joker. The Joker side features the purple cropped tailcoat with peaked lapels, buttercup orange blouse with green tie and pocket square to match the wild curly hairstyle, a purple glove and orange Cuban booties with tiny purple Batman symbols on the zipper pulls. The Batman side of the costume includes a dramatic black cape echoing not only Michael Keaton's costume in Burton's film, but many classic superhero looks in general. In addition, Prince's funk influences, Sly Stone and James Brown, also famously fashioned capes into their stage costumes. Finally, the Gemini costume includes a mirror-cut Batman symbol breastplate, divided in half, and referencing the classic Batman costume, while the whole symbol also appears on his right wrist as another mirror cut-out bracelet, as previously seen in a heart shape during the *Sign O' the Times* and *Lovesexy* tours, designed by Michelle Kasimor Streitz.

The split-sided Gemini suit also reflects the pre–comic book character of the Joker that surfaced on playing cards during the nineteenth century. This figure is often depicted in half-red, half-black attire and make-up, just as the Gemini character is black and purple, complete with white face paint, red lipstick and green hair on only the Joker half of his face. Prince takes this split-design look further a year later in *Graffiti Bridge*, contemporary to the Nude Tour during which he showcased his songs from the *Batman* soundtrack. The costume worn during the 'Elephants and Flowers' performance (Prince 1990a) resembles a black and white harlequin version of the Gemini costume, credited to designer Helen Hiatt. The mock turtleneck chequered poncho resembles a cape, with extra pleated fabric cascading from the right shoulder. During the performance Prince even wears white face paint, which is one of the few times we see him wearing face paint outside of the *Batman* music videos and later in 1994 when he writes 'SLAVE' on his face as a political statement during his contract dispute with Warner Bros. Studios.¹ This look draws from the Harlequin figure that originated in the sixteenth-century Italian improvised theatre tradition of the Commedia Dell'Arte. The stock character represented a mischievous impish trickster, the trouble-making valet-servant to the aristocratic characters. Akin to the court jester in European cultures, this character's prankster function in theatrical narratives fits with the Partyman character's role in the eponymous music video from the *Batman* soundtrack.

With the Partyman suit, created by Helen Horatio and Sarah Daubny, Prince aggressively embraces his purple image in mainstream culture for the first time since *Purple Rain*, but this time as an alter ego. His trickster attitude in the video brings an authenticity to this look as part of his dual identity. Directed by Albert Magnoli, director of *Purple Rain*, the music video centres on a masquerade cocktail party with wealthy guests listening to a jazz combo, recognisable as drummer Michael Bland, saxophonist Candy Dulfer, guitarist Levi Seacer, Jr. and bassist Miko Weaver. Reminiscent of the glamorous parties in Gotham City throughout the *Batman* films, the polite revelry is rudely interrupted when Prince materialises as Partyman and signals to the musicians, his undercover henchmen, to liven up the mood. The track commences, a frenzy of dancing erupts and antics ensue. Partyman rapidly serves all of the masked attendees a special drink ladled from an oversized aquarium serving as mermaid habitat, and by the end of the song, the entire room has been poisoned as the police arrive and Prince and his purple-clad henchmen vanish from the scene of the crime. The playfulness of Partyman recalls his Christopher Tracy prankster character in *Under the Cherry Moon* whom co-star Jerome Benton identified during an interview with Prince scholar DeAngela Duff (2017) as the Prince character whose personality most closely resembles that of Prince himself.

The Partyman costume is faithful to Nicholson's green-haired Joker ensemble, but exchanges the buttoned-up look with the green scarf-tie for an opened orange blouse that reveals a more relaxed and seductive look. The orange blouse sets off the thin sparkling orange pinstripes and small cloth-covered buttons

---

¹ The face paint and split-sided black and white costuming made a strong appearance yet again in 'The Same December' music video off the *Chaos and Disorder* album in 1996. The NPG band members have black and white face paint similar to the Gemini Partyman look from 1989, while Prince wears an entirely black and white ensemble, split down the middle, complete with black top hat and feather boa. He still has 'SLAVE' written on his face, with the addition of the Love Symbol that was his legal name at this point. The name change was in reaction to a contract dispute with Warner Bros., which is parodied in the subplot of the music video.

that march down the asymmetrical front closure, sleeves and lower back of the suit jacket in addition to the outer trouser legs. The orange Japanese characters down the sleeve translate to 'Gemini' in both Hiragana and Kanji scripts. This asymmetrical double-breasted jacket forms a flattering triangle from his wide shoulders, cascading straight down the body and cinching at the waist. Dress historian Casci Ritchie (2019) states that

> Prince really starts to properly find his silhouette during this period. For that period the tailor was really important. It's a hyper silhouette, neither male nor female, completely unusual for typical men's tailoring … The Partyman suit is basically the [blueprint] of Stacia Lang's designs [who worked at Paisley Park in 1990 and was head of wardrobe from 1991 to 1993]. From 1989, all Prince's tailoring came from that point.

As Ritchie mentions, the Partyman suit represents a pivotal moment in the design of Prince's suits. In addition to the now-famous tailored Prince silhouette solidified during Lang's reign as wardrobe director, other distinctive sartorial touches reappear throughout Prince's fashion: from the numerous, tiny, closely applied and cloth-covered contrasting button rows down the trouser legs, up the back of the jacket and along the sleeves that we will see in many of Lang's iconic *Diamonds and Pearls* (1991)/*Love Symbol* (1992) album era suits, to the addition of more purple suits prominently featured in his wardrobe during this time and throughout the rest of his career.

The Partyman suit, as well as Ringwood's Joker outfit and Hiatt and Stella's Gemini costume, echoes the zoot suit aesthetic of the 1930s and 1940s big band swing era. The zoot suit was an innovative and audacious redesign of the three-piece men's suit, popularised by young African American men on dance floors in Harlem, New York in the 1930s and Mexican Americans in Los Angeles during the 1940s. Luis Alvarez comprehensively analyses the sociocultural implications of the zoot suit as sartorial signifier for non-white youth counterculture communities within varying historical and geographical contexts in *The Power of the Zoot: Youth Culture and Resistance during World War II* (2008). An outrageously visible signifier of countercultural identity and rejection of oppressive hegemonic culture towards ethnic and racial minorities, the zoot suit aligns well with the semiotic radicalism outlined in Dick Hebdige's seminal book, *Subculture: The Meaning of Style*. Hebdige points to the inherent social implications of a collective style within countercultural communities, or in this case, 'The challenge to hegemony which subcultures represent is not issued directly by them. Rather it is expressed obliquely, in style. The objections are lodged, the contradictions displayed at the profoundly superficial level of appearances: that is, at the level of signs' (1979, 17). Often conflated with criminality, the socially rebellious look was defined by exaggeratedly wide shoulders, high-waisted wide-legged trousers cinched at both the waist and the pegged ankles and various accessories such as large hats with pheasant feathers extending from the brim, wallet or watch chains cascading from the waistline to below the knee, loudly colour-coordinated pocket squares, blouses, ties, waistcoats, suspenders, and two-toned wing-tip shoes. Oftentimes, zoot suits were fabricated from pinstriped fabric, much like the Partyman suit's thin and sparkly orange pinstripes that complement the purple background.

The zoot suit represents one example of Dandyism within the Black community and the Mexican-American community. I understand the dandy as a person embodying elegant yet socially rebellious style through their art, lifestyle and sartorial expression. Popularised by the British in the nineteenth century, and subsequently theorised by the French, Dandyism had been practiced for centuries by African Americans, as outlined in Monica Miller's work on Black Dandyism. Prince's absorption of the classic men's suit with his own personal twists is a classic example of Dandyism, to the practice of which he was no stranger: As French poet Charles Baudelaire (1961) states in his essay, 'Mon Coeur mis a nu,' 'The Dandy must aspire to be sublime without interruption; he must live and sleep before a mirror' (author's translation). The quintessential dandy aspired to the total sublimation of his existence through a constantly deliberate and self-conscious alignment of style, artistic production and social rebellion. Prince's Dandyism is born of a long tradition of Black entertainers who emphasised their corporeal agency through clothing, asserting a certain level of personal and social independence through the intersection of gender, race and class identifiers. Behind Prince's sartorial flamboyance lies the need for Black entertainers to possess artistic and personal freedom. His choice of clothing, however risqué and outlandish, revealed an outward declaration of his personal, artistic and spiritual freedom to engage with the world in his own way, on his own terms. Miller summarises the importance of sartorial signs and symbols in Black Dandyism:

> For black people, clothing has long been one of the most important ways of communicating self-possession, self-respect, and a knowingness about the semiotic power of clothing and adornment. Black dandyism, as a mode of

creative appropriation, has been not just a strategy of social critique but, as we have seen, a mode of survival. (2013, 153)

Miller's emphasis on semiotics in fashion and its particular significance with Black entertainers, in addition to the sociocultural implications of the semiotics in countercultural style as pronounced by Hebdige, lead us to the next section of this examination of Prince's celebrity branding during the *Batman* era: symbols. Through the analysis of the Partyman suit and Gemini costume, we have established the return of purple to Prince's primary image, the solidifying of an iconic silhouette through the tailored Partyman suit design and the connection to Black history through the cultural contextualisation of the zoot suit inspiration and practice of Black Dandyism in these looks. With this context, we can pivot towards the emerging presence of symbols on his clothing and accessories at this turning point in his style trajectory.

First, the aforementioned Japanese characters in orange that march boldly down the sleeves of the Partyman suit represent a trend in Prince's costuming around this time and may have been inspired by his intense schedule in Japan during the Nude Tour, described by journalist Neal Karlen (1990) as 'a greatest-hits production with lean arrangements and none of the Liberace-on-acid costumes and special effects of the *Lovesexy* tour.' Other sartorial sightings of similar Japanese script include various Nude Tour outfits where, for example, the Kanji character for 'Love' in white repeats down Prince's black one-strapped jumpsuit from shoulder to ankle and again around the inside of the popped collar on his black sheer button-down blouse. In yet another purple suit worn during the tour, the Japanese characters are Katakana and read 'Nude' in white, down both sleeves of the loose-fitting, double-breasted plum jacket. I believe it's safe to assume that Prince didn't speak Japanese, but rather enjoyed the look of the characters as symbols and was becoming increasingly interested in integrating them into his clothing at this point.

Symbols are present throughout Prince's work, notably on album covers and set designs; however, with the exception of the crucifix worn around his neck, he did not consistently wear noticeable symbols until the 'Mountains' video (1986c) at the end of *Under the Cherry Moon* (1986). The flat heart-shaped mirror brooch on the breast pocket of his black cropped blazer becomes incorporated into the set design and looks from the subsequent *Sign O' the Times* tour, of which the album itself is inundated with signs and symbols. Local Minneapolis artist Michelle Kasimor Streitz was contracted to create the heart mirrors which were used as bracelets, as decoration on jackets and trouser legs and as earrings for tour merchandise. For example, Prince wears the mirror heart in the form of a bracelet with the previously mentioned white fur coat and black strapped jumpsuit for the *If I Was Your Girlfriend* music video and *Sign O' the Times* promotional photos. The mirror heart decoration appears yet again one year later during the 'Alphabet St.' music video (1988a) on the back of Prince's teal leather jacket with rhinestone designs on the upper back panel. The heart is clearly a simple and explicit symbol for Prince's wardrobe, in particular during the context of the *Lovesexy* era. Other hearts are featured on his jewellery during this time, in particular on the metal chain around his black over-the-knee 3" heeled boot as well as among the flat metal charms dangling on a necklace chain or attached to a structured Kelly green halter-top printed with randomised black letters and numbers.

In addition to the ever-present heart symbol in Prince's style image between 1987 and 1988, other recognisable symbols surface, including the cross, peace sign, dove, guitar and an early stylised form of the male–female symbol that he would then adopt and transform into what we now recognise as the Love Symbol. I believe this to be the first time we see him wearing this symbol, despite its appearance as early as the album cover of *1999* (1982) that Prince himself drew, hidden upside down in the first '9' of 1999, or the stained-glass windows of the 'bathroom' set and the graffiti outside of the industrial wasteland tunnel that Prince motors through in the 'When Doves Cry' video (1984b), as well as on the motorcycle featured in *Purple Rain*, circa 1984. But during the Nude Tour in 1990, he begins aggressively to integrate this symbol into his clothing and accessories. Most notably, up until this point he almost exclusively wears the crucifix on a long chain around his neck. The first time we see him replacing the crucifix with this early form of the Love Symbol, or Lovesexy symbol as it was referred to by the design team at the time, appears during the 'Scandalous' music video from late 1989 (1989e). This symbol also starts to feature prominently in his clothing, appearing on various shirt collars and on the one-sleeved, fringed black leather jacket that he also wears in *Graffiti Bridge*.

Although this Lovesexy symbol is still associated with Prince as a precursor to the Love Symbol design, its origins lie in the LGBTQ+ community as early as the 1960s. In his seminal book on the gay history of Minnesota, *Land of 10,000 Loves*, Stewart Van Cleve (2012) highlights the first Minneapolis Pride March in 1972 as a pivotal moment in which Mars and Venus signs featured prominently in widely distributed hand-drawn promotional fliers. Scholar of transgender history Joy Ellison's (2019) research examines Prince's image and lyrics as a transgender icon and contextualises the appearance of the Mars–Venus symbol in Minneapolis with Prince's rise in popularity:

> Starting at the same time, you see quite a bit of the Mars into Venus symbol [all over trans culture and] that is exactly where Prince starts with this in 1982. It's just everywhere. You can find it in a Star Street Transvestite Action Revolutionaries pamphlet in 1970. Often the trans symbol is out to the side somewhere, so it looks like the Glam Slam club entrance.

Prince opened the Glam Slam night club in downtown Minneapolis in 1989, inspired by his song on the *Lovesexy* album. The doorway into the club was framed by a yellow neon circle that broke into an arrow pointing upwards and to the left, with subtle hash marks along the arrow to hint at the Venus aspect of the symbol. According to Ellison (2019), this combined Mars–Venus symbol 'became the basis for the contemporary trans symbol'.

Whether or not Prince was aware of the association of the Lovesexy symbol with gay pride or, more specifically, transgender identity, his fixation on displaying this iconography in his fashion choices in particular emerges around the time of his involvement with the *Batman* album and film. Prince created the *Batman* album between the *Lovesexy* and Nude Tours, during which time he transitioned from wearing many symbols with universal meanings to preferring one specific symbol that eventually evolved into the Love Symbol. Originally designed by Sotera Tschetter, Mitch Monson and Liz Luce, the unpronounceable Love Symbol glyph would ultimately become Prince's legal name in 1993, constituting a radical political act as analysed by Zaheer Ali (2017). But prior to the adoption of the Love Symbol to brand his image, in 1989, Prince appeared to be co-opting the Batman symbol. He used the symbol in black and yellow as a backdrop for various sets, including his Nude Tour concert and his 'Electric Chair' performance on *Saturday Night Live* (1989c), as well as the purple zipper pulls on his orange booties for the Gemini costume, both examples of which were for promotion of the film as well as the album. But Prince also started having his design team create looks with the Batman symbol, such as the silver zipper pulls on his black pin-striped booties, a pair that were not part of his costume for the 'Batdance' music video. What was so attractive about this symbol for Prince? The symbol represents masculinity, power, strength, ingenuity, mystery, moral code and goodness within darkness. Batman had two sides: an anonymous, sexy crime fighter and a lonely wealthy man with a difficult family history and no real superpowers. Prince not only seemed to identify with this symbol, but to become fascinated with its pervasiveness in mass culture. Aesthetically, the symbol is graphically clean and simple and immediately recognisable. Warner Bros. expertly executed the marketing of their film with the symbol on merchandise and posters, bringing the Batsignal to life in the real world, so to speak. It's no wonder that Prince ostensibly tried to absorb this ubiquitous symbol while in the process of redefining his own brand as he embarked upon a new decade.

Liz Bucheit, owner of Crown Trout Jewelers in Lanesboro, MN, worked as an independent contractor to create much of the metal jewellery for Prince between 1989 and 1994. Among her first projects were metal wrap-around toe and heel pieces shaped in the Batman symbol that would appear on his boots. She recalls the design department at Paisley Park faxing her a template with minor changes, requesting that she change the Batman symbol just slightly. The shoes were most likely never used, and, rather abruptly, she was given word to stop creating the Batman symbol for Prince allegedly due to possible legal issues. She was then asked to start creating metal accessories in the Lovesexy symbol shape, which would eventually permeate Prince's aesthetics. Bucheit (2018) distinctly remembers creating many metal Lovesexy symbols of varying sizes and proportions, from the zipper pulls on the booties and jackets to the large symbols on the back and sleeve of Prince's one-armed fringed black leather jacket. The boots with the evolved Lovesexy symbol shape can also be spotted in the aforementioned 'Elephants and Flowers' ensemble from *Graffiti Bridge*. In light of the possible legal issues with the *Batman* franchise, the 'Elephants and Flowers' Harlequin look now appears to be a suitable substitute for the Gemini costume, free of *Batman* references, which Prince would develop even further into a cropped jacket with Love Symbol accents during the *Gold Experience* album era in 1995 (Prince 1995). Bucheit's story of the context behind the design evolution of the Lovesexy symbol also sheds light on inconsistencies with the cover of the Nude Tour book featuring three images of Prince wearing a red patent-leather military-style motorcycle jacket with matching trousers and carrying a blue version of the famous Cloud guitar against a yellow backdrop. The shiny red suit, adorned with gold Lovesexy symbols, peace signs and hearts dangling from chains on the shoulder, also appears later in the music video for 'Thieves in the Temple' (1990b) from the *Graffiti Bridge* soundtrack. In one version of the 'for promotional use only' Nude Tour image, the Prince figure on the right wears the Batman symbol mirror bracelet that he sports in the Gemini

'Batdance' costume. In later versions, the bracelet had been eliminated from the image, most likely as a result of pressure from his lawyers.

Perhaps this experience inspired Prince to begin trademarking his own intellectual property and aggressively defending these rights when anyone tried to use it without authorisation. But more importantly, this indicates the critical moment when Prince realised he wanted to craft his own image into a symbol as recognisable as the Batman logo. He wanted his own Batsignal, so he created it himself.

While we can never really know Prince's intentions, and most of this information is based on observation and theory, this often-ignored era is worth analysing as a landmark moment in Prince's style and identity. Is it a coincidence that he agreed to collaborate on Burton's *Batman* film because the *Batman* theme was famously the first song he ever played on the piano as a child (Ro 2011, 187)? Or did this project resonate with him and allow him to look back fondly on his childhood? Prince was thirty-one years old at this time, having enjoyed rock star fame for over a decade. Perhaps this was a moment of reflection as he entered a new phase of life: he experimented throughout his twenties and was thus ready to reflect on and synthesise his self-identity. The Nude Tour was a greatest hits tour: despite repeating consistently over the years that he never dwelled on his past, he was looking back on his music and stripping himself down to the basics, as the title of his tour implied. This era marked the beginning of Prince working with a new band that would transform his sound, the New Power Generation, in addition to the moment he first met his future wife, Mayte Garcia, his muse who would greatly influence his goals and aesthetics, however temporarily. This era also showcased Prince's embracing of his signature colour again, with full, bright purple suits. In addition, he refined his style aesthetic with the custom-tailored suit silhouettes. And finally, he began taking the branding of his image more seriously by creating the blueprint for his own personal Batsignal.

This pivotal moment in branding Prince's celebrity identity falls in line with fashion as a semiological practice. French literary theorist, semiotician and fashion critic Roland Barthes's work analyses fashion itself as a series of signs and symbols that express social meaning. In his essay 'History and Sociology of Clothing, Some Methodological Observations' (1957), Barthes applies Ferdinand Saussure's linguistic theory of semiology to clothing, relating to dress as signifier and signified of the sign, or symbol, itself: 'It goes without saying that dress – which cannot be reduced to its protective or ornamental function – is a privileged semiological field: one could say that it is the signifying function of dress which makes it a total social object' (2006, 11). While Prince's Love Symbol branding would eventually prove to be as successful as the colour purple for signifying his celebrity image to the public, akin to the powerfully explicit meaning behind the Batsignal, the clothing he chose to wear on an everyday basis functioned in much the same way to send a signal out to the world of the branding of his newly redesigned image. The Love Symbol would become his new signature, an explicit sign designed to signify his identity that served simultaneously as iconography for interpretation on the clothing itself. Having soared to stardom in the early days of the now ubiquitous music video, recognising the cinematic value of translating musical performance to the small and subsequently big screen, Prince understood the importance of appearance, style and branding as powerfully associated with the music. Prince was celebrated for his commitment to his music, and by extension, his identity as artist–musician–film star that translated to every facet of his life: with the Love Symbol, the colour purple and an unmistakable silhouette, Prince's iconic new look reflected his total devotion to his celebrity identity at all times, ready for a new tumultuous decade of his already brilliant career.

References

Ali, Zaheer (2017), 'Slave 2 the System: Prince's Labor Activism & the Black Radical Tradition', [Presentation] *Purple Reign: An Interdisciplinary Conference on the Life and Legacy of Prince*, Salford, UK. Available online: https://www.youtube.com/watch?v=uZ12lLE5quc. Accessed 30 December 2020.

Alvarez, Luis (2008), *The Power of the Zoot: Youth Culture and Resistance During World War II*, Berkeley: University of California Press.

Barthes, Roland (2006), 'History and Sociology of Clothing, Some Methodological Observations', in *Language and Fashion*, ed. Andy Stafford and Michael Carter, trans. Andy Stafford, 3–20, Oxford: Berg.

Batman (1966), [TV programme] ABC, 26 January 1966.

Batman (1989), [Film] Dir. Tim Burton, USA: Warner Bros. Pictures.

Baudelaire, Charles (1961), 'Journaux intimes', *Œuvres complètes*, 1247–316, Paris: Bibliothèque de la Pléiade, Gallimard.

Bucheit, Liz (2018), 'Interview' with the author. May 2018.

Duff, DeAngela (2017), [Podcast interview] "Jerome Benton Interview," 12 October 2017. *Grown Folks Music*, Available online: https://www.polishedsolid.com/jerome-benton-interview/. Accessed 30 December 2020.

Ellison, Joy (2019), 'Interview' with the author. April 2019.
Graffiti Bridge (1990), [Film]. Dir. Prince, USA: Warner Bros. Pictures
Hahn, Alex (2003), *Possessed: The Rise and Fall of Prince*, Billboard Books.
Hebdige, Dick (1979), *Subculture: The Meaning of Style*, London: Routledge.
Karlen, Neal (1990), 'Prince Talks', *Rollingstone*, 18 October 1990. Available online: https://www.rollingstone.com/music/music-news/prince-talks-189956/. Accessed 30 December 2020.
Miller, Monica L. (2013), 'Fresh-Dressed Like a Million Bucks: Black Dandyism and Hip-Hop', in Kate Irvin and Laurie Anne Brewer (eds), *Artist/Rebel/Dandy: Men of Fashion*, New Haven: Yale University Press.
Moon, Chris (2018), 'Why Purple', [Facebook post] 18 September 2018. Available online: https://www.facebook.com/photo.php?fbid=670081013378761&set=a.110902705963264&type=3&theater. Accessed 30 December 2020.
Nelson, Prince (1980), *Dirty Mind*, Released October 1980, Warner Bros, Vinyl.
Nelson, Prince (1982), *1999*, Released October 1982. Warner Bros, Vinyl.
Nelson, Prince (1984a), 'Baby I'm a Star', [Song] Released June 1984, Track 8 on *Purple Rain*, Warner Bros, Vinyl.
Nelson, Prince (1984b), 'When Doves Cry', [Music video] Released May 1984, Track 1 side 2 on *Purple Rain*, Warner Bros, Vinyl. Available online: https://www.youtube.com/watch?v=UG3VcCAlUgE. Accessed 30 December 2020.
Nelson, Prince (1986a), 'Anotherloverholeinyourhead', [Music video] Released March 1986, Track 11 on *Parade*, Warner Bros, Vinyl. Available online: https://www.youtube.com/watch?v=Zc99JK9gHDk. Accessed 6 September 2022.
Nelson, Prince (1986b), 'Kiss', [Music video] Released February 1986, Track 10 on *Parade*, Warner Bros, Vinyl, Available online: https://www.youtube.com/watch?v=H9tEvfIsDyo. Accessed 30 December 2020.
Nelson, Prince (1986c), 'Mountains', [Music video] Released May 1986, Track 8 on *Parade*, Warner Bros, Vinyl. Available online: https://www.youtube.com/watch?v=_WmPeLOLDnA. Accessed 30 December 2020.
Nelson, Prince (1987a), 'If I Was Your Girlfriend', [Music video] Released May, 1987, Track 2 side 3 on *Sign O' the Times*, Warner Bros, Vinyl. Available online: https://www.youtube.com/watch?v=DJkCErlAd5c. Accessed 30 December 2020.
Nelson, Prince (1987b), 'U Got the Look', [Music video] Released June 1987, Track 1 side 3 on *Sign O' the Times*, Warner Bros, Vinyl. Available online: https://www.youtube.com/watch?v=_jCuroTbqBI. Accessed 30 December 2020.
Nelson, Prince (1988a), 'Alphabet St.' [Music video] Released April 1988, Second song on *Lovesexy*, Warner Bros, Vinyl. Available online: https://www.youtube.com/watch?v=vP1kZLGG5gw. Accessed 30 December 2020.
Nelson, Prince (1988b), *Lovesexy*, [Album] Released May 1988, Warner Bros, Vinyl.
Nelson, Prince (1989a), *Batman*, [Album] Released June 1989, Warner Bros, Vinyl.

Nelson, Prince (1989b), 'Batdance', [Music video] Released June 1989, Track 9 on *Batman*, Warner Bros, Vinyl. Available online: https://www.youtube.com/watch?v=ulOLYnOthIw. Accessed 30 December 2020.

Nelson, Prince (1989c), 'Electric Chair', [Performance] *Saturday Night Live*, NBC, 24 September 1989. Available online: https://www.youtube.com/watch?v=VlBQxQkE-wE. Accessed 30 December 2020.

Nelson, Prince (1989d), 'Partyman', [Music video] Released August 1989, Track 4 on *Batman*, Warner Bros, Vinyl. Available online: https://www.youtube.com/watch?v=AjY8HvpNu6o. Accessed 30 December 2020.

Nelson, Prince (1989e), 'Scandalous', [Music video] Released November 1989, Track 8 on *Batman*, Warner Bros, Vinyl. Available online: https://www.youtube.com/watch?v=lGHcJ_-Hhps. Accessed 30 December 2020.

Nelson, Prince (1990a), 'Elephants and Flowers', [Song] Released August 1990, Track 5 on *Graffiti Bridge*, Warner Bros, Vinyl.

Nelson, Prince (1990b), 'Thieves in the Temple', [Music Video] Released August 1990, Track 12 on *Graffiti Bridge*, Warner Bros, Vinyl. Available online: https://www.youtube.com/watch?v=FyfF20APPr. Accessed 6 September 2022.

Nelson, Prince (1991), *Diamonds and Pearls*, Released October 1991, Warner Bros, Vinyl.

Nelson, Prince (1992), *Love Symbol*, Released October 1992, Warner Bros and Paisley Park Records, Compact Disc.

Nelson, Prince (1995), *The Gold Experience*, Released September 1995, Warner Bros and NPG, Compact Disc.

Purple Rain (1984), [Film] Dir. Albert Magnoli, USA: Warner Bros. Pictures.

Ritchie, Casci (2019), 'Interview' with the author, April 2019.

Ro, Ronin (2011), *Prince: Inside the Music and the Masks*, New York: St. Martin's Griffin.

Sign O' the Times (1987), [Film] Dir. Prince, USA: Cineplex Odeon Films.

Turman, Karen (2019), 'Gemini, Partyman, and the Nude Tour: Symbols and Silhouettes During the Batman Era', [Presentation] *Prince Batdance Symposium*, Atlanta, GA: Spelman University. Available online: https://www.youtube.com/watch?v=8tDI-AYhpMM&t=10s.

Turman, Karen (2020), 'Prettyman in the Mirror: Dandyism in Prince's Minneapolis', in Kirsty Faiclough and Mike Alleyne (eds), *Prince and Popular Music: Critical Perspectives on an Interdisciplinary Life*, London: Bloomsbury Press.

Under the Cherry Moon (1986), [Film] Dir. Prince, USA: Warner Bros.

Van Cleve, Stewart (2012), *Land of 10,000 Loves: A History of Queer Minnesota*, Minneapolis: University of Minnesota Press.

4

'Meet the long-lost Phillip Jeffries': The elusive cinema of David Bowie

James King

David Bowie's career as a performer has been defined by a series of continuing, playful, highly self-conscious reinventions. These dramatic shifts were reflected not just in his ever-changing musical styles – from the acoustic leanings of his early folk-infused albums, to the glam-rock grandiosity and 'plastic soul' of the 1970s, the New Romantic pop stylings of the 1980s and his turn to industrial electronica in the 1990s – but also in the elaborate succession of stage personas Bowie fashioned for himself. Two of the most notable of these creations, the crazed Martian rock star 'Ziggy Stardust' and the amoral Aryan zombie 'Thin White Duke', were so immersive that Bowie had to kill off the former on stage – in a staggering performance in 1973 at the Hammersmith Apollo, captured by documentarian D. A. Pennebaker in his seminal concert film *Ziggy Stardust and the Spiders from Mars* (1979) – and distance himself from problematic pro-Fascist comments made by the latter in a string of deranged, drug-addled interviews in which he praised both Margaret Thatcher and Hitler. It must be noted that Bowie's crippling cocaine addiction, which lasted throughout much of the 1970s, played a heavy role in this insanity, causing a certain dissolution of boundaries between his 'real-life' self and these fictitious, fractious onstage personas. Mercifully, he recovered from this addiction, regained his senses and continued to evolve as a performer throughout the subsequent decades: touring, releasing records, acting both onstage and on-screen and even starting up an internet service provider – the short-lived 'BowieNet' – before his death on 10 January 2016, at the age of sixty-nine.

The origins of David Bowie's theatrical personas can be traced back to his tenure studying the dramatic arts under renowned theatre practitioner Lindsay Kemp at Sadler's Wells in the 1960s, an eclectic education that ranged from avant-garde theatre and mime to *commedia dell'arte*. It is also worth noting that one of Bowie's earlier career breaks came when he went on tour with Marc Bolan's rock duo Tyrannosaurus Rex throughout February and March 1969, billed not as a musician but as a mime act. So when it comes to considering Bowie's career as a film actor, and the considerable body of screen performances he amassed over a half-century, arguably we can do so giving it equal critical weight and consideration as we do his musical output – for Bowie, acting was not a mere side project or tangential diversion from his music career, but an integral part of his artistic practice from the very outset. This essay will take a short survey of the cinematic contributions of David Bowie – noting his collaborations with a remarkably wide range of film-makers, including Nic Roeg, Nagisa Ôshima, Julian Schnabel, Martin Scorsese, Julien Temple, Alan Clarke, Tony Scott, Jim Henson and Christopher Nolan, to name but a few – before going into a more detailed textual analysis of his brief but memorable appearance as Special Agent Phillip Jeffries in David Lynch's notorious *Twin Peaks: Fire Walk with Me* (1992), a performance which in many ways embodies the enigmatic quality of the screen persona Bowie ultimately left us with: elusive, unknowable, defying simple explanation and always seemingly just out of reach.

Following a walk-on role in the BBC drama series *Theatre 625*, in a 1968 episode titled 'The Pistol Shot', and an appearance in Michael Armstrong's black-and-white short film *The Image* (1969), David Bowie's cinematic career began in earnest in 1976 with a starring role in Nic Roeg's iconic sci-fi feature *The Man Who Fell To Earth*. After the enormous success of Roeg's previous film, the supernatural thriller *Don't Look Now* (1973), Paramount Pictures had agreed to finance an adaptation of Walter Tevis's 1963 satirical novel about an alien who crash-lands in New Mexico – coming to earth in search of water to transport back to his home planet, which has been ravaged by drought – before he falls prey to alcoholism, capitalism, television-addiction and sexual decadence. The book offers a strange and sombre critique of post–Second World War American culture and materialism, and given he had risen to fame with such celestial-facing tracks as 'Space Oddity' and 'Moonage Daydream', and had only recently retired his Martian persona Ziggy Stardust, in many ways, Bowie was the perfect casting choice for the role of the titular enigmatic extraterrestrial: Thomas Jerome Newton.

Director Nic Roeg had previous experience working with Rolling Stones frontman Mick Jagger in his debut feature *Performance* (1970), so it seems the British film-maker was undaunted by the prospect of wrangling a lead performance out of a rock star with very little professional acting experience, and all the narcotic dependency that their lifestyle may entail. By his own admission, in a remarkably candid interview with Virginia Campbell of *Movieline* in 1992, Bowie claims to have still been in the midst of a heavy cocaine addiction throughout the entire production:

> I just threw my real self into that movie as I was at that time. It was the first thing I'd ever done. I was virtually ignorant of the established procedure, so I was going a lot on instinct, and my instinct was pretty dissipated. I just learned the lines for that day and did them the way I was feeling. It wasn't that far off. I actually was feeling as alienated as that character was. It was a pretty natural performance ... a good *exhibition* of somebody literally falling apart in front of you. I was totally insecure with about 10 grams a day in me. I was stoned out of my mind from beginning to end. (Campbell 1992)

However, despite his supposed narcotic sedation – a claim refuted by his co-star Candy Clark, it is worth noting – few can contest that Bowie *looked* the part of a man who had just fallen to earth. Stick-thin, with pale, almost translucent white skin and a shock of burnt-red hair, Bowie's appearance in the film is undeniably otherworldly. An injury sustained in 1962 during a playground quarrel over a girl with childhood friend George Underwood had left Bowie with anisocoria – a permanently dilated left pupil – which here further served to create a disarming, alien appearance.

There is a key sequence two-thirds of the way through Roeg's film where the 'true identify' of Thomas Jerome Newton is revealed. With the aid of bespectacled lawyer Oliver Farnsworth (Buck Henry), Newton has amassed a small fortune patenting his advanced alien technology and unleashing it onto the US marketplace. However, a heady mix of alcohol, women and television have started to distract him from his mission of returning to his home planet. After a fight with his mistress Mary-Lou (Candy Clark), who he has been trying to break things off with, Newton heads into the bathroom wearing a gaudy oversized dressing gown, sipping on a large glass of gin, his alcoholism really starting to take hold by this point. Newton regards himself in the large well-lit mirror of this garish 1970s hotel bathroom, sets down his drink and strips naked. He stares down at his genitals (cropped only just out of frame), grabs hold of them with both hands and then tweaks each of his nipples. It's a remarkable moment of physical exposure from Bowie as an actor, letting the full extent of his spindly, pallid, almost emaciated physique be laid bare before the rolling camera. Then he turns to the wall-mounted magnified shaving mirror and stares deep into his bloodshot eyes. The camera zooms in on the small rectangular mirror as Newton pulls down the skin around his cheekbones and inspects the underside of his eyeballs. He grabs a couple of pairs of tweezers from the cabinet, uses one set to lift up his eyelid and the other to dig deep into the eye itself. The camera tracks left around the back of Newton's head, his bright red hair mercifully obscuring our view, as he plucks something right out of the eye-socket. At this point, we cut back to the bedroom, where Mary-Lou is perched on the edge of the bed, painting her fingernails pink. She blows them dry, calls out for 'Tommy' and lurches up to her feet, clutching her glass of gin, ice cubes clinking. The camera pans to follow Mary-Lou as she moves across the shag carpet, over to the bathroom door. She knocks. Calls out for Tommy again. Asks if he's all right in there. Knocks some more. Then she rattles the door handle – it's locked. Increasingly concerned, she demands to be let in. Eventually Newton unhooks the latch and the door slowly creaks open. Mary-Lou lets out a blood-curdling scream, and we cut to reveal the 'true' alien form of Thomas Newton: bald-headed, body completely hairless, with giant yellow cat's eyes where his blue irises and dilated pupils once were. Mary-Lou is so shocked by this revelation that she drops her glass of gin and urinates herself – and yet somehow the figure of Thomas Jerome Newton seems much less strange when made up in these alien prosthetics. He simply looks like a man in a suit, an artificial costume, lacking that uncanny, otherworldly, *indescribably odd* quality that Bowie just naturally possesses – the androgynous creature we saw fully exposed in the mirror a few moments before.

After his acclaimed turn in *The Man Who Fell to Earth*, Bowie starred in David Hemmings's 1978 black comedy *Just a Gigolo*. Set in post–First World War Berlin, Bowie plays a disaffected Prussian officer who returns home after the end of the Great War and, unable to find employment elsewhere, goes to work in a brothel. Despite featuring such cinematic luminaries as Sydne Rome, Kim Novak and Marlene Dietrich in her final on-screen performance, the film was a critical and commercial disaster, leading Bowie to famously deride it as his '32 Elvis Presley movies rolled into one' (MacKinnon 1980). Bowie blamed Hemmings's penchant for partying and not applying himself fully for the film's failings, as he reveals in his interview with Virginia Campbell:

> I'm such a control freak that I would like to buy Gigolo back – this is a pipe dream of mine – and redo the entire thing. It actually read very well. If only Hemmings had applied himself. But David was too fond, like myself at the time, of having a good time. (Campbell 1992)

It was after this tumultuous production that Bowie finally managed to break free of his addiction to cocaine, relocated to West Berlin and entered a bold new phase of musical innovation, producing a trio of highly regarded LPs that came to be known as his 'Berlin Trilogy': *Low* (1977), *Heroes* (1977) and *Lodger* (1979). It seems fitting, then, that his next on-screen appearance would be in Ulrich Edel's German-language drama *Christiane F.* (1981). Based on the 1978 non-fiction book *We Children from Zoo Station*, the film tracks the harrowing descent of thirteen-year-old West-Berliner Christiane Vera Felscherinow from her bored adolescence into a sordid life of heroin addiction and prostitution.

While Bowie's main contribution to the film was allowing a liberal use of his music throughout, he does make a notable appearance in the narrative itself, in a crucial sequence right before Christiane tries heroin for the first time. The young girl – in a stunning debut performance from Natja Brunckhorst – has managed to secure a couple of tickets to a David Bowie concert through a connection of her mother's and, once there, edges her way right towards the front of the crowd. Already experimenting with drugs with school friends at the local club, slowly sliding into habitual abuse, the teenager gobbles down a handful of tranquilisers and gapes up at the stage as the incandescent Bowie appears from the wings. With some particularly creative editing, utilising concert footage from a performance that actually took place in New York, the newly drug-free Bowie struts up to the microphone – dressed in a bright all-American sports jacket, his hair cropped short, looking clean-cut and with some actual colour in his cheeks. He gazes down into the crowds and shares a brief look – a moment of cosmic recognition – with this lost young girl as she teeters on the verge of full-blown addiction, before launching into his first song. It's a strange and enigmatic moment, serving no obvious narrative purpose, and yet it remains one of the film's most powerful and indelible images, testament to the shimmering screen presence Bowie commands, even in the briefest of appearances.

The following year Bowie starred in Alan Clarke's TV adaptation of the Bertolt Brecht one-act play *Baal* (1982). He had recently garnered considerable respect as a stage actor during a lengthy Broadway run of Bernard Pomerance's *The Elephant Man*, where he played the lead role of John Merrick for a stint of 157 shows between 1980 and 1981 – earning particular praise for his highly expressive physical performance, wearing no stage make-up whatsoever, drawing heavily upon his experimental theatre training at Sadler's Wells. Bowie brings much of this theatricality to Clarke's BBC production of *Baal*, playing the eponymous role of the dissolute poet, troubadour and murderer. The play opens with a stark direct-to-camera monologue from Bowie – heavily made up as the womanising vagrant with tobacco-stained teeth and a scraggily red beard, wearing a grubby sweat-stained undershirt and always carrying a poorly tuned banjo. In true Brechtian form, the production is littered with distancing devices – fourth-wall-breaking direct address, split-screen sequences, spoiler-revealing intertitles – and is punctuated throughout with songs and fragments of musical commentary. Most notably it is here, for the first time on-screen, that we seamlessly see Bowie integrate his musical talents into an acting role. The songs are raw and coarse, accompanied only by the strumming of Baal's banjo, and yet Bowie adapts the lyrics to suit his own distinctive voice, commits to them fully, lending the songs a power and gravitas that is quite startling, as if they were sordid lost b-tracks from one of his earliest acoustic recordings.

In 1983, Bowie featured in two relatively high-profile productions: Tony Scott's Manhattan-set vampire thriller *The Hunger* and Nagisa Ôshima's poignant Japanese prisoner-of-war drama *Merry Christmas, Mr. Lawrence*. While Scott's film is a visually stylish endeavour – with a glossy noir-infused aesthetic akin to his brother's recent sci-fi thriller *Blade Runner* (Ridley Scott 1981) – in which Bowie plays the 200-year-old vampire companion of Catherine Deneuve, the production was reportedly riddled with studio interference and resulted in a rather incoherent and insubstantial affair. As Bowie himself claims,

> Tony Scott had one particular vision of this movie. The script Tony, Susan [Sarandon] and I talked about was different from the sensibility of the actual film. He had no power at all and had to bow to demands. I have every respect that he kept his cool throughout the whole proceedings and actually got the film finished. Let's say that it was a case of 'More blood!!!' Tony was trying to pull back from such situations and treat things in a more psychological manner. And this is Tony Scott we're talking about. (Campbell 1992)

The most memorable sequence of the film involves Bowie's character – simply called 'John', a name reflective of much of the film's level of originality – who is suffering from an incurable condition in which he has started aging at an incredibly accelerated pace, his vampiric immortality finally failing him. We watch as John sits in the waiting room of genetic specialist Dr Sarah Roberts (played by Susan Sarandon), visibly aging before our eyes. Over the course of an afternoon, with the aid of slick editing and considerable make-up – liver spots appearing, hair greying and falling out, wrinkles forming – Bowie's character turns from a virulent 30-year-old into a decrepit old man, unrecognisable even to his close neighbours. In an act of desperate frustration, he returns home and kills an innocent teenage girl who comes over to his palatial Upper West Side apartment to play violin. But even the blood drawn from this final act of violence cannot break his curse, and eventually Catherine Deneuve puts his skeletal form to rest in a wooden coffin, seals it and leaves him to wither away for all eternity, caught between life and death. It's a sombre and restrained performance from Bowie, filled with melancholy allusions to dependency and addiction, a trauma no doubt still fresh in his mind.

By contrast Nagisa Ôshima's *Merry Christmas, Mr. Lawrence* features what is widely considered to be Bowie's most credible and accomplished cinema performance. A classy Japanese–British co-production, put together by the now-iconic producer Jeremy Thomas, and co-written by Paul Mayersberg – who had previously adapted the screenplay for *The Man Who Fell to Earth* – Ôshima's film is based on Sir Laurens van der Post's experiences in a Japanese prisoner-of-war camp during the Second World War, as depicted in his books *The Seed and the Sower* (1963) and *The Night of the New Moon* (1970). Bowie plays the rebellious South African Major Jack 'Strafer' Celliers, whose arrival at the internment camp both lifts the spirits of the captured British soldiers and threatens the fragile peace brokered with the prison guards by the diplomatic Lieutenant Colonel John Lawrence (Tom Conti), who is fluent in both Japanese language and culture. We first see Bowie's character in a long shot from behind, in a military court tribunal, after overhearing that Celliers is a 'very difficult man' – a paratrooper who waged guerrilla warfare on Japanese soldiers in Indonesia, before surrendering to them in order to spare the lives of the local villagers who had sheltered him. Despite his face being completely obscured (we can only see the back of his head, a scruff of strawberry blonde hair), from the way the scrawny figure stands – a clenched fist held behind the back; an angular, relaxed gait – it is undeniably Bowie. The man's physical presence is too distinctive to not be instantly recognisable. Throughout the film, Bowie's character glides about like a strangely serene agent of chaos – casually defying the prison guards' orders, stealing food, picking flowers, breaking other prisoners out of solitary confinement – both enraging and enthralling camp leaders Sergeant Hara (Takeshi Kitano) and Captain Yonoi (Ryuichi Sakamoto). We also see, through a series of dream-like flashbacks, a tragic incident from Celliers's bucolic childhood back in South Africa, in which Bowie convincingly plays the teenage version of his character without the assistance of make-up or digital 'de-aging' techniques that have become commonplace in modern film-making.

When it comes to describing Bowie's ability to switch between characters of vastly different ages and backgrounds, *chameleonic* would be an understatement.

Perhaps the most remarkable moment of the film comes nineteen minutes in, as Jack Celliers sits on a cot-bed in his jail cell, awaiting what is assumed to be his execution via firing squad. Two Japanese soldiers march in and demand he get up to his feet. Celliers looks at the guards, exhales slowly, seemingly resigned to his fate. But then he does something very strange – he starts swirling his fingertips around the inside of his packer hat. Then he brings them up to his face and starts rubbing them over his cheek. Slowly we realise he is miming the act of applying shaving cream, performing the last rituals of a condemned man. The guards look on in stunned confusion as he continues to act out drawing a razor blade over his stubble. He enters into pleasant conversation with an imaginary barber, asking after their children, as he shaves the rest of his neck, his jaw and his upper lip. Then Celliers starts scooping invisible food out of the bottom of his hat, chews it down and sobs momentarily before regaining his composure. He looks up to the baffled guards and says, 'Tea? Yes, I'd like that' and takes an imaginary cup from them, pours some down his throat, before bringing two fingers to his lips and dragging languorously on an unseen cigarette. He licks his lips, exhales invisible smoke and savours the moment. Finally, he looks down, and we cut to a close-up shot of the filthy jail cell floor, where we see the shadows of his fingers as they tap ash from the tip of his imaginary cigarette and let it fall to the ground – his boot appears in frame and the scuffed toecap stubs out the fantasy tobacco butt, twisting in the dirt, really grinding it into the ground, before Celliers finally rises to his feet. It's an extraordinary sequence of mime, and one that again recalls his early theatrical tutelage under Lindsay Kemp.

Throughout the rest of the 1980s, Bowie confined himself mostly to smaller supporting roles, albeit in an impressively diverse range of projects: playing by turn a hitman in John Landis's 1985 comedy caper *Into the Night*; Pontius Pilate in Martin Scorsese's controversial biblical epic *The Last Temptation of Christ* (1988); a slick advertising executive in Julien Temple's ill-fated period musical *Absolute Beginners* (1986) and an uncredited cameo in the Monty Python-created pirate comedy *Yellowbeard* (1983). If there was one thing Bowie refused to be, it was typecast. Just like his musical evolutions, Bowie's choice of film parts was reliably unpredictable, and so it seems fitting that in 1986 he agreed to take on a lead role in the Jim Henson children's fantasy *Labyrinth* – not only starring opposite Jennifer Connelly as Jareth, the villainous Goblin King, but also writing and performing a number of original songs for the production: 'Underground',

'Magic Dance', 'Chilly Down', 'As the World Falls Down' and 'Within You'. Ever the fearless performer, Bowie seemed undaunted by the prospect of acting in a film populated almost entirely by puppets.

Bowie first appears on-screen twelve minutes into the film, after Jennifer Connelly's character Sarah, a self-absorbed teenager frustrated with having to spend the evening babysitting her stepbrother Toby, has become so distraught by his incessant crying that she wishes the infant be taken away by goblins. Predictably, as soon as she leaves his room, lightning strikes, thunder claps and her baby brother's cries are silenced. Sarah creeps back into his bedroom, flicks the light switch – but the electricity has cryptically cut out. Rain lashes against the window and wind rustles the curtains as Sarah approaches her brother's crib, only to find it empty. An owl flies up against the window pane and goblin puppets start scuttling around the edges of the bedroom, visible to the audience but always staying just out of Sarah's line of sight. There's more thunder and lightning as the window shutters suddenly burst open and the barn owl flies inside the bedroom. It circles Sarah, wings flapping, as she screams and tries to bat it away. Then we see its shadow transform and grow into that of a man. Glitter flies through the air as the figure of Bowie as Jared the Goblin King is finally revealed: a high-collared black cape flapping in the wind, curtains billowing behind him, face clad in Ziggy Stardust-esque glam-rock make-up – all black mascara, white foundation and blue eyeshadow – and donning a giant feathery blonde wig. Hands planted akimbo on his hips and wearing a mischievous smile, Jared starts talking in an exaggerated version of Bowie's lilting Brixton drawl, folds his arms and explains to Sarah that he's kidnapped her brother. Then Jared claims he's brought Sarah a gift: reveals a crystal ball in his leather-gloved hand, which he proceeds to expertly roll over the front and back of his palm. In an act of human puppetry – the crystal ball tricks actually performed by choreographer Michael Moschen, an accomplished juggler, who crouched behind Bowie just out of shot – Jared begins to roll the crystal ball back and forth between the length of both arms with a magician's grace, as he implores Sarah to forget all about her baby brother. When she refuses, he transforms the crystal ball into a snake, dangles it between his hands, then throws it in Sarah's face. She wails as the reptile wraps itself around her neck, before abruptly turning into a silk scarf and fluttering down to her feet – where it transforms yet again into a goblin puppet and scuttles out of frame, laughing. Jared then lays out the quest Sarah must undertake, venturing through the titular labyrinth, if she is ever to regain Toby. They are then magically transported just outside the labyrinth walls and

Jared fades into thin air. Bowie is clearly having a lot of fun playing the camp role of the Goblin King – in his first attempt at family-friendly fare – and he carries this joyous energy throughout the rest of Jim Henson's film as he sings and dances about with goblin puppets, clambers up Penrose stairs, rolls more crystal balls around, all the time wearing wildly inappropriate turquoise tights and a codpiece.

The 1990s proved, arguably, a less fruitful decade for Bowie when it came to his screen performances. With a few exceptions – such as David Lynch's *Twin Peaks: Fire Walk with Me* (1992), which we will return to shortly – the period was littered with films that were forgettable, at best. He starred opposite Roseanna Arquette as a British bartender in search of a green card in Rich Shepard's poorly received New York comedy caper *The Linguini Incident* (1991), and an aging gangster struggling to keep the peace in Andrew Goth's independent Manchester-set crime thriller *Everybody Loves Sunshine* (1999). He also featured as feared gunslinger Jack Sikora in Giovanni Veronesi's Spaghetti Western *Il Mio West* (1998). One of his more memorable performances from the period was in Julian Schnabel's art biopic *Basquiat* (1996), in which Bowie – who had been a contemporary and friend of the doomed Manhattan painter – played the role of iconic pop artist Andy Warhol, adorned in the requisite blonde bowl wig and heavy facial prosthetics. Speaking in Warhol's signature whispery sotto voce, it's a remarkably tender performance, and one that for the most part avoids caricature. Often featured in scenes alongside Dennis Hopper, who plays the influential art dealer Bruno Bischofberger, Hopper and Bowie make a surprisingly effective comedic duo and offer some soft satire of the New York art scene of the era amidst the film's more morbid depictions of the prodigious artist's descent into drug addiction.

The twenty-first century saw a further slowing down of Bowie's cinematic output, with his last leading role being that of the terminally ill supernatural neighbour in Nicholas Kendall's Canadian family drama *Mr. Rice's Secret* (2000). Then there was a string of self-conscious cameos, often simply appearing on-screen as himself, in films such as Ben Stiller's fashion-assassin satire *Zoolander* (2001), Eric Idle's mockumentary *The Rutles 2: Can't Buy Me Lunch* (2002) and Todd Graff's teen musical comedy *Bandslam* (2009). However, he did produce one final standout performance in 2006, playing the enigmatic Serbian inventor Nikola Tesla in Christopher Nolan's period thriller *The Prestige*, the tale of two rival illusionists obsessively trying to outdo each other in a game of deadly brinkmanship on the stage-magician circuit in nineteenth-century London.

Bowie enters the narrative with typical theatrical flamboyance: strutting across a wooden stage, a tesla coil hanging overhead spraying sparks of static electricity, sharply dressed in a three-piece suit and silk necktie, hair slicked down in a neat centre-parting, sporting a pencil-thin moustache. He marches through a cloud of electricity, crosses the stage and shakes the hand of Hugh Jackman's character Robert Angier, then clasps onto it firmly – tells him to hold out his other hand. Angier does so and Tesla's assistant (Andy Serkis) places an oversized lightbulb in it, which promptly lights up, as if by magic, powered solely by the static charge passing between the two men. It's a playful moment, drawing heavily on Bowie's persona as the perpetual trickster showman. In the following scene, Tesla and Angier have lunch together, overlooking the Colorado mountains. Tesla cautions the young magician over the perils of obsessive innovation: 'Society only tolerates one change at a time. The first time I tried to change the world, I was hailed a visionary. The second time, I was politely asked to retire.' Again, one cannot help but note a hint of self-reflexivity here – Bowie being an artist who has drawn ire as well as praise from critics and fans alike for his continual reinventions and stylistic evolutions.

Although he only appears for a few minutes in an early sequence of David Lynch's *Twin Peaks: Fire Walk with Me* (1992) – a feature-length prequel to the ground-breaking television series – as the long-lost Cajun FBI agent Phillip Jeffries, in many ways, it is a quintessential David Bowie screen performance. Following the hugely acclaimed and ratings record-breaking first season of *Twin Peaks* (1989–91) – David Lynch and Mark Frost's postmodern television coup that centred on the investigation of the mysterious murder of high school prom queen Laura Palmer in the small, isolated Pacific North-Western town of Twin Peaks – the second season went off the rails narratively and creatively. This can be blamed in part on studio pressure from ABC to prematurely reveal the identity of Laura Palmer's killer, but it was also due to Lynch's creative attentions being diverted by his filming another feature film – the Nicolas Cage and Laura Dern road-movie romance *Wild at Heart* (1990) – and a sharp decline in viewership over the second season led to the show's abrupt cancellation. In an effort to wrap up the multitude of loose threads left hanging in the final episode, a series of stand-alone films set within the 'Twin Peaks universe' were planned, the first being *Fire Walk with Me*. However, the film's reception at the Cannes Film Festival in 1992 was so hostile, with audiences booing and hissing in frustration – due in part to the film's radical departure in tone from the mostly light-hearted soap-opera stylings of the television series, but also in its defiant refusal to address any of the unanswered questions posed by the series finale – and its commercial performance so poor that plans for further film instalments were scrapped. Fans would have to wait another twenty-five years for the answers to some of those hanging questions, when Showtime produced a triumphant revival series *Twin Peaks: The Return* (2017), helmed again by Lynch and Frost, and featuring most of the surviving original cast. Lynch had intended for Bowie to have a direct involvement in the show's revival, but illness and ultimately death prevented him from reprising the role of Special Agent Phillip Jeffries; however, the character does make a notable appearance in the new series utilising unused footage shot during the production of *Fire Walk with Me*.

In the years since its disastrous premiere, *Twin Peaks: Fire Walk with Me* has undergone a drastic – and much justified – critical reappraisal, with academics such as Todd McGowan now calling it 'Lynch's most important and original film' (2007, 131) and *Village Voice* critic Calum Marsh (2013) hailing it his 'masterpiece'. While such euphoric praise may be as equally hyperbolic as that of the Cannes audience's rabid reaction decades prior, the film certainly contains some of Lynch's finest work as a director, not least in the sequence involving Bowie's character FBI Special Agent Phillip Jeffries, who mysteriously reappears after vanishing on a secret assignment in Argentina two years ago. This scene takes place in the Philadelphia offices of the FBI, opening with an exterior shot tilting up to reveal the city's famous cracked Liberty Bell. There is an air of mounting suspense as drum cymbals are brushed slowly and composer Angelo Badalamenti's signature suspended synthesiser chords ring out over the soundtrack as we cut to the drab interior of the FBI offices. Special Agent Dale Cooper (Kyle MacLachlan) strides through the open doorway of this wood-panelled room, marches across the thin blue carpet and approaches his supervisor Deputy Director Gordon Cole's desk. Cooper gets down on his knees and leans in to the half-deaf Cole (played by Lynch himself), and softly states, 'Gordon. It's 10:10am on February 16th.' Cole looks to his wristwatch to confirm the time and date as Cooper continues, 'I was worried because of the dream I told you about.' Cole nods quizzically, spiral cords leading to a pair of plastic hearing aids dangling from his ears. We then cut to a wide-angle shot of a long corridor, with a succession of fire doors propped open, as in a hospital ward. A CCTV camera hangs from the ceiling tiles in the top centre of the frame, pointing down this ominous corridor. Dale Cooper marches in from frame right, stops in his tracks in the middle of the corridor, turns around and looks up directly into the lens of the CCTV camera, an intense stare fixed on his face. The next shot is a close-up of a television monitor, where we see the black-and-white closed-circuit camera feed of Cooper stood staring in the centre of the corridor, his trim suited figure flickering on-screen. Another cut pulls us back to a wide shot to reveal a security guard at his desk – littered with an upturned Maglite torch, a clipboard and a set of videotape playback controls – as he watches three TV monitor screens, Cooper stood in the middle one. Cooper then marches out of the CCTV monitor shot frame left and suddenly appears from frame right in the wide shot, stands behind the security guard and inspects the three TV monitors: two showing empty corridors, and the third one on the far right depicting the entrance to the FBI office building, a parking lot visible through the glass doors.

Agent Cooper repeats this process of going out into the corridor, staring up into the CCTV camera and then returning to the security guard's office and reviewing the security footage. His behaviour is baffling, but the intensity he brings to the task creates an overwhelming sense of tension – of anticipation. *Something is coming.* And sure enough, there is a cut to a medium shot of a blue metal elevator door sliding open. The bell rings out. Fluorescent light spills out of the elevator car and onto an American flag stood in the corridor, next to a wall-mounted FBI seal and a metal plaque with the number 7 engraved into it. On the soundtrack, menacing low synth chords reverberate. We cut back to the wide-angle corridor shot as Cooper marches out and stands in position staring up into the CCTV camera once more. Then we return to the elevator shot, doors hanging open. Suddenly David Bowie as Special Agent Phillip Jeffries marches out wearing a white zoot suit and a bright floral Hawaiian shirt, sporting a towering bleach-blonde quiff. The camera has to tilt up ever so slightly to keep the quiff in shot as Jeffries exits frame right. Back in the corridor Cooper still stands staring up at the CCTV, as Jeffries silently paces up behind him. Seemingly unaware of Jeffries's presence, Cooper whips back into the security guard's office – where he finds his image mysteriously frozen on the CCTV feed. He watches as Agent Jeffries walks right past him on the screen. A close-up shot reveals Cooper's worried face as he calls out for Gordon. He runs out into the corridor, calls for Gordon again and sprints towards his office.

Back in Gordon Cole's office, as Cooper's cries echo down the corridor, Phillip Jeffries stumbles in through the open doorway, baggy trousers flapping about, bright red leather shoes glistening under the fluorescent lighting. We cut to a wide-angle shot of Cole and the previously unseen Special Agent Albert Rosenfeld (Miguel Ferrer) rising from their desks in shocked unison as Jeffries staggers into frame. A stunned Cole asks him, 'Phillip, is that you?' Cooper rushes into the office behind Jeffries – who looks totally lost and dazed beneath his deep tan, with a bloodied split lower lip. Cole declares, 'Cooper, meet the long-lost Phillip Jeffries. You may have heard of him from the academy.' Jeffries shifts his weight between heels, starts wringing his hands, eyes darting between Cooper and Albert. Then he wags his forefinger about and speaks in a thick Cajun accent:

> Well, now, I'm not gonna talk about Judy. In fact, we're not gonna talk about Judy at all. We're gonna keep her out of it.

Cooper twists around, shocked, calls out to Gordon – who holds up his hand to silence him: 'I know, Coop.' Jeffries points an accusatory finger at Cooper, a deranged grin spreading across his face: 'Who do you think this is there?' Suddenly, the glow of TV static starts to ripple over the entire frame, ever so slightly superimposed over the scene. Albert grabs Jeffries's elbow, looks him over, asks, 'Suffered some bumps on the old noggin, Phil?' At this point, another shot is superimposed over the office scene: that of a short African American man with a flat top haircut, wearing a white papier-mâché mask with a long, thin, pointed Pinocchio-style nose; dancing about in an all red suit, shirt and tie; snarling and baring teeth. Gordon Cole adjusts his hearing aid, 'What the hell did he say there, Albert? That's Special Agent Dale Cooper.' Jeffries approaches Gordon's desk, as the masked man continues to dance about, superimposed over their images. Gordon: 'For God's sakes, Jeffries, where the hell have you been?' As the image of Cole's office slowly fades away, we are shown the medium shot of the dancing man more clearly, clutching a wooden twig like a strange voodoo instrument, smoke whirling around behind him in the dark. Off-screen now Cole's voice rings out: 'You've been gone damn near two years.' More TV static is superimposed as white noise fills the soundtrack, drowning out Cole's voice.

At this point in the sequence, any vestige of classical continuity editing breaks down completely. We are transported to a totally different location: a wide-lensed high-angle shot reveals a filthy wood-panelled room above a convenience store, three giant windows partially covered up in brown paper, the glass smeared in dust and grime, blocking out all sunlight. The shot is one of Lynch's most iconic compositions – inspired by the painter Francis Bacon's technique of dividing up the canvas into distinct areas of rival energies. At the top of the frame, an old lady, her grandson and a bearded homeless man sit on a rotting sofa, propped against the room's back wall and windows, flanked on either side by two more vagrants perched on spindly chairs, one seated next to an unplugged jukebox and an old-fashioned drinks cabinet. At the bottom centre of the frame we recognise the MAN FROM ANOTHER PLACE (Michael J. Anderson), the iconic dancing dwarf from the *Twin Peaks* television series – dressed in his trademark red suit, shirt and tie – sat at a Formica table opposite BOB (Frank Silva), the silver-haired, denim jacket–clad evil spirit and killer of Laura Palmer, who is laughing maniacally. Four bowls of creamed corn sit on the table top between them. To the far left of the frame, in an inexplicable spotlight, the masked man dances next to an overturned plastic milk crate and a steel bucket. Off-screen we hear Phillip Jeffries's Cajun drawl: 'I sure as hell wanna tell you everything. But I haven't got a whole lot to go on.'

To attempt to describe the following series of shots would be a lengthy and fairly arduous endeavour, but needless to say, things descend into further Lynchian surrealism as the inhabitants of the room engage in some sort of Kenneth Anger-esque black magic ceremony: lights flicker dramatically; thunder cracks; plumes of smoke emerge; characters dance about, slap their knees, talking in reverse; the child's face turns into that of a monkey; Michael J. Anderson rubs the Formica table top and fiddles about with his creamed corn; the bearded homeless man watches the proceedings dispassionately; TV static keeps rising superimposed over everything, white noise crackling. Throughout the sequence, we hear barely audible fragments of dialogue from Special Agent Phillip Jeffries off-screen:

> Oh, believe me, I followed … It was a dream. *We live inside a dream* … The ring. Ring. It was above a convenience store … Listen up, and listen carefully. I've been to one of their meetings … Hell, God, baby, damn, no. *I found something* … And then there they were. (emphases in original)

Eventually the snow of TV static engulfs the convenience store scene completely and we return to Gordon Cole's office, where we see a close-up of Phillip Jeffries screaming, wailing in agony. In a succession of mute jump cuts, interspliced with yet more TV static, we see Jeffries sat in a chair opposite Cole's desk, desperately relating a story to Gordon, Cooper and Albert, arms wildly gesticulating – the information withheld from the audience. Then we are presented with a low-angle shot of a telephone wire against a grey overcast sky, and Gordon yells out off-screen: 'He's gone. He's gone.' This is followed by a close-up shot of Jeffries's chair, now conspicuously empty. The conventions of classical continuity editing slowly return as we are presented with a wide shot of Albert holding a telephone receiver to his ear, stood next to Cooper in the corner of the room. Albert relays information: 'I've got the front desk now. He was never here.' Gordon Cole adjusts his hearing aid in medium close-up as Cooper asks him: 'Gordon, what's going on?' The action then moves back to the security guard's office, where we see an over-the-shoulder shot of Gordon Cole watching the three CCTV monitors, replaying video footage of Jeffries striding past Cooper. The video feed freezes, and a wide shot reveals Cooper holding the CCTV playback control, stood next to Gordon, both men's eyes glued to the screen, still in shock. Cooper comments, 'He was here.' They nod. Gordon asks, 'But where did he go?' And finally we cut back to the over-the-shoulder shot of the three CCTV monitors. Bowie's image flickering on-screen in freeze-frame, barely recognisable, but definitely *there*.

As the rest of the film unfolds, the narrative soon returning to the town of Twin Peaks to follow Laura Palmer (Sheryl Lee) through the fateful last few days of her life, there is never any direct explanation given regarding the role, function or fate of Special Agent Phillip Jeffries. Even in the revival series twenty-five years later, where he appears first through unused footage from the feature film – glimpses of his violent misadventures in Argentina – and then later through CGI as a disembodied spirit trapped in what can only be described as an oversized teakettle, Jeffries remains an enigmatic, elusive and unknowable figure. An agent of chaos whose appearance literally causes the fabric of reality to unravel. And yet one of the lines he utters during this delirious and formally disruptive sequence in *Fire Walk with Me* contains what is perhaps the most crucial key to unlocking the mysteries of the film and the television series: 'We live inside a dream.' As in many of his film roles – Thomas Jerome Newton in *The Man Who Fell to Earth*, Nikola Tesla in *The Prestige* – Bowie's performance as Phillip Jeffries carries the aura of a man who has travelled beyond the realms of normal human perception, returning from strange dimensions bearing mystical secrets, and yet somehow he seems deeply wounded by the experience and has paid a heavy psychic toll for his intrepid explorations.

Throughout his parallel careers as both musician and actor, the only true constant with David Bowie was his insatiable appetite for innovation and evolution. He never stayed put in one place, artistically or geographically, never stood still or repeated himself for the sake of stability or crowd-pleasing. He took risks, both in his music and in his film choices – sometimes they paid off, and sometimes they led to disaster. Bowie tried on many masks and outfits, not just on stage but also in terms of his sexuality, his lifestyle and his spiritual beliefs. He experimented tirelessly, trying out different things, discarding what didn't work – and sometimes what did. There was a restlessness to his creative output that made him many things, but boring was never one of them. Unlike many film stars who carefully cultivate a consistent persona, carrying it across multiple performances, Bowie's path was much more chameleonic – playing aliens and war veterans, hitmen and bartenders, gigolos and vampires, FBI agents and goblin kings and experimenting always with different costumes and accents. Perhaps the one true unifying facet of his film career was the otherworldly quality he brought to each role through his unconventional physical appearance: the dilated pupil, the burnt red hair, his spindly insect-like physique. In the end, after featuring in over thirty films, spanning more than half a century, he forever retained the aura of a man who had just fallen to earth.

References

Campbell, Virginia (1992), 'Bowie at the Bijou', *Movieline*, 3 (7). Available online: https://lebeauleblog.com/2017/04/17/david-bowie-bowie-at-the-bijou/.

MacKinnon, Angus (1980), 'The Future Isn't What It Used to Be', *NME*, 13 September 1980. Available online: http://www.bowiegoldenyears.com/press/80-09-13-nme.html

Marsh, Calum (2013), 'Twin Peaks: Fire Walk with Me is David Lynch's Masterpiece', *Village Voice*, 17 May 2013. Available online: https://www.villagevoice.com/2013/05/17/twin-peaks-fire-walk-with-me-is-david-lynchs-masterpiece/.

McGowan, Todd (2007), *The Impossible David Lynch*, New York: Columbia University Press.

Filmography

Absolute Beginners (1986), [Film] Dir. Julien Temple, UK: Goldcrest Films International.
Baal (1982), [Film] Dir. Alan Clarke, UK: BBC.
Bandslam (2009), [Film] Dir. Todd Graff, USA: Summit Entertainment.
Basquiat (1996), [Film] Dir. Julian Schnabel, USA: Eleventh Street Production.
Blade Runner (1981), [Film] Dir. Ridley Scott, USA: The Ladd Company.
Christiane F. (1981), [Film] Dir. Ulrich Edel, Germany: Solaris Film.
Don't Look Now (1973), [Film] Dir. Nic Roeg, UK/Italy: Casey Productions.
Everybody Loves Sunshine (1999), [Film] Dir. Andrew Goth, UK.
Just a Gigolo (1978), [Film] Dir. David Hemmings, Germany: Bayerischer Rundfunk.
Labyrinth (1986), [Film] Dir. Jim Henson, USA: Henson Associates.

Merry Christmas, Mr. Lawrence (1983), [Film] Dir. Nagisa Ôshima, UK/Japan: Nation Film Trustee Company.
Mr. Rice's Secret (2000), [Film] Dir. Nicholas Kendall, Canada: New City Productions.
Performance (1970), [Film] Dir. Nic Roeg, UK: Goodtimes Enterprises.
The Hunger (1983), [Film] Dir. Tony Scott, USA: Metro-Goldwyn-Mayer.
The Image (1969), [Film] Dir. Michael Armstrong, UK: Border Film Productions.
The Last Temptation of Christ (1988), [Film] Dir. Martin Scorsese, USA: Universal Pictures.
The Linguini Incident (1991), [Film] Dir. Richard Shepard, USA: Isolar.
The Man Who Fell to Earth (1976), [Film] Dir. Nic Roeg, UK/USA: British Lion Film Corporation.
The Prestige (2006), [Film] Dir. Christopher Nolan, USA: Touchstone Pictures.
The Rutles 2: Can't Buy Me Lunch (2002), [Film] Dir. Eric Idle, USA: Above Average Productions.
Twin Peaks: Fire Walk with Me (1992), [Film] Dir. David Lynch, USA: New Line Cinema.
Wild at Heart (1990), [Film] Dir. David Lynch, USA: Propaganda Films.
Yellowbeard (1983), [Film] Dir. Mel Damski, USA/UK: Seagoat Films.
Ziggy Stardust and the Spiders from Mars (1979), [Film] Dir. D. A. Pennebaker, USA: Mainman.
Zoolander (2001), [Film] Dir. Ben Stiller, USA: Paramount Pictures.

5

Where the popular meets the esoteric: *Videodrome* (1983) and *Holy Motors* (2012)

Ellen Smith

Many pop stars have made the transition to cinematic acting roles, often as a means of furthering their cultural significance and adding a new layer to their persona. For musicians such as Cher, Jennifer Lopez, Whitney Houston and Lady Gaga, this transition has been rewarded with commercial success and recognition at mainstream awards ceremonies, allowing them to be cemented further into our shared popular culture as multidisciplinary artists. Fans of the pop star also play a key role to their success as actors, and are often gratified by a careful formula of positioning the star in a new context whilst retaining some recognisable elements of their persona as a musician. In some cases, the filmic character is almost indistinguishable from the star, such as Madonna's Susan in *Desperately Seeking Susan* (1985), which derives a purer sense of pleasure and satisfaction for fans of the pop icon. Meanwhile Madonna, through the assured success of essentially playing herself, was able to boost the status and sales of her subsequent single '*Into the Groove*', which features in the film. For other pop stars, however, the transition to screen has been less driven by commercial pursuits and safely building on their familiar image. Some have appeared in more offbeat, low-budget works by arthouse film-makers, where their established persona and its fans are perhaps less indulged.

Thompson (1995, 38) says that this alternative approach is the pop star 'paying their dues', and that 'the seeming modesty of a judicious blend of cameo and low budget roles can actually represent the ultimate in long-term status enhancement.' Thompson names Tom Waits as the ultimate 'dues-payer', whose 'bulging portfolio of drunkards and low-rent psychopaths' (1995, 38) on-screen have become a key cultural reference point, providing inspiration for other musicians and characters. Therefore, this approach does not come without a pay-off, as the pop star is given an opportunity to build recognition amongst an alternative/cult audience, who make up an important part of the collective cultural consciousness. However, these kinds of roles are arguably less about tactical dues-paying and more indicative of the pop star's true creative interests and choices, even if they are smaller and less spectacular. The casting of a pop star in any film generates new layers of meaning, but in more alternative, low-budget spaces, where a director's artistic stamp and idiosyncrasies are given greater freedom and emphasis, the musician's presence in a film does not feel primarily like a selling point or vehicle to demonstrate their multiple talents but rather a more autonomous decision to be involved in a film-maker's pure vision. Two works that exemplify this are David Cronenberg's *Videodrome* (1983), starring Blondie's Debbie Harry, and Leos Carax's *Holy Motors* (2012), which features an appearance from Kylie Minogue. In these texts, conventional storytelling is eschewed in favour of strange logic and a unique cinematic language, whilst the nature of media and performance itself come under interrogation by both Cronenberg and Carax. Harry and Minogue's personas at first seem unrecognisable and even underused, at odds with the impenetrable worlds they are placed in. However, their presence is of course not without purpose, and they arguably play a key role in the films' critique, anchoring the works in a sense of self-awareness and intertextuality between the filmic world and real-world culture. These films can tell us what happens when the popular meets the esoteric; what is lost, what is kept, how it comes about and what the effect is.

Often, a pop star's acting role is constructed with the star and their persona already in mind. Both Harry and Minogue, however, were both considered for their parts after the project had already been realised, and neither primarily through recognition of their work as musicians. Cronenberg, though unavoidably aware of her Blondie fame, wanted to work with Harry after admiring her first significant excursion into acting with *Union City* (1980), a low-budget neo-noir produced shortly after Harry's commercial breakthrough with Blondie's third studio album *Parallel Lines* in 1978 (Lucas 1983, 35). He approached Harry with a script for *Videodrome* not yet decided on an ending, but Harry, already a fan of the film-maker's earlier work and 'fascinated with his worldview', agreed to the role 'on good faith that it would all work out' (Harry in Naftule 2019).

Kylie Minogue's involvement in *Holy Motors* was even further removed from her music career, and came about through her and Carax's mutual friend

French film-maker Claire Denis. Denis, no stranger to infusing her work with references to popular music (she also cast *OutKast*'s André 3000 in a supporting role in her 2019 film *High Life*), befriended Minogue in a French hair salon and recommended her to Carax. Carax maintains he knew nothing of the pop star's career other than her collaboration with Nick Cave on the single '*Where the Wild Roses Grow*', though this claim perhaps seems in line with Carax's own persona and mystique. Even having begun her career as an actress in Australian soap operas, Minogue largely abandoned screen roles after her feature film debut in *The Delinquents* (1989), which, like Harry with *Union City*, came about during her commercial breakthrough as a musician. After that came the critically panned *Street Fighter* (1994) where she starred alongside Jean-Claude Van Damme, followed by a blink-and-you'll-miss-it appearance in *Moulin Rouge!* (2001) almost twenty years later. When interviewed about *Holy Motors*, she said,

> I was starting to think this is not for me, that maybe acting's in the past. But I guess I put the energy out there – what I needed was the Nick Cave of the film world to go 'You, I know what to do with you. I'm going to bring something from you that I know you can do.' And, ironically, the only thing that Leos [Carax] knew about me was my duet with Nick Cave. (in Smith 2012)

Her pairing with Carax is undoubtedly unconventional, Minogue a global pop megastar and household name (except in the Carax household) and Carax an enigmatic French arthouse film director known for his singular, cryptic style. In comparison to someone like Debbie Harry, Minogue's rise to pop stardom was far more manufactured and tied to record sales and charts climbing, though her enduring longevity in the mainstream has perhaps meant she has been able to deviate from this slightly, hence a late-career left-field project like *Holy Motors*.

In the film, Minogue plays Eva, a vague character who is implied to have the same 'job' as the film's lead Mr Oscar (played by Denis Lavant) – that is, be driven around in a white limousine and perform in various unusual acting 'appointments' to no audience or camera, sometimes for the service of others and sometimes for no obvious reason at all. Before Eva and Oscar must attend to their next appointments, Eva/Minogue performs the original song 'Who Were We' (written for the film by Carax and musician Neil Hannon) in an abandoned building with Oscar watching, and the two display a sense of sadness and frustration regarding a past romantic relationship between them that led to a child. Eva's next appointment then begins, and Oscar watches on as she, now dressed as an air hostess, and another 'actor' jump from the top of the building to their deaths (Oscar also 'died' in an earlier appointment before it is revealed to be staged). The presence of the global pop icon in this highly ambiguous scene, within the latter half of a film defined by its near-incomprehensible ambiguity, is certainly jarring at first glance. It is made even more jarring perhaps with the credentials of Minogue's scene partner Denis Lavant, a unique, selective actor who has appeared in nearly all of Carax's works and, like Carax, operates far from the mainstream cultural consciousness. In retrospect, Debbie Harry's *Videodrome* male co-star James Woods is also a revealing casting choice, as Cronenberg seemed to predict his persona's trajectory as it moved further and further in line with that of the paranoid Max Renn (or someone who has endured Renn's ordeal and lived to tell the tale), in his promotion of right-wing conspiracy theories and disinformation on social media.

Harry and Cronenberg perhaps have a little more in common than Minogue and Carax, which allows Harry's transition into his vision to feel slightly more seamless. They both found their artistic voices alongside each other in the late 1960s and 1970s, connecting with a milieu in which new subversive ideas and energies were gaining traction. Harry, a former go-go dancer and Playboy bunny, developed her own unique world view as an independent artist emerging in the radical New York punk and new wave music scenes, and was involved with several bands and sounds before settling with Blondie – namely, The Wind in the Willows, The Stilettos and The Angel and the Snake (an early prototype of Blondie). The release of Blondie's *Parallel Lines* saw Harry and the band deviate from the brooding punk sound of earlier projects and announce themselves as a pop group, with hit singles from the album such as 'Heart of Glass' and 'Hanging on the Telephone' forming the more ubiquitous idea of Harry's sound and image. Even with this sudden ubiquity (she made an appearance on The Muppet Show), Harry's punk origins and independence were seemingly never compromised, as Blondie's hook and pop-orientated work became just one element in the band's eclectic style, which also incorporated elements of rock, reggae and early rap. Over in Canada, Cronenberg entered the arthouse film scene with shorter works: *Stereo* (1969) and *Crimes of the Future* (1970), followed by his first more widely distributed works *Shivers* (1975) and *Rabid* in (1977), establishing his associations with the body horror genre and a transgressive style of film-making.

With *Videodrome*, the director's eighth work, came a marked engagement with the zeitgeist of the era, one of technological hyper-development, consumerism and the ongoing debate surrounding the effects of consuming sensational media, brought to the fore with the arrival of the videotape. In the film, Max

Renn (played by Woods), the president of small TV station CIVIC-TV, which specialises in 'everything from softcore pornography to hardcore violence', stumbles on a pirate broadcast from an unidentified location called Videodrome, depicting extreme torture and murder of its subjects. In an attempt to unearth the signal's origins, Max becomes hallucinative and finds himself entangled in a mind control conspiracy engineered by a shadowy corporate entity. Harry plays Max's aptly named lover Nicki Brand, a sadomasochistic radio personality who also becomes fixated with the broadcast. After her real self disappears to 'audition' for Videodrome, she appears only as a simulacrum that communicates with Max during his hallucinations. The film expresses a deep mistrust with how reality is presented and the limits of our perception of it, whilst suggesting that technology and the media are potentially capable of replacing that reality with a new hyper-reality. The filtering of these contemporary ideas through Cronenberg's cautionary tale intrigued Harry, and her co-star Woods would later remark that she was herself an artist connected to this cultural zeitgeist in a promotional interview for the film (Morgan 2017). Evidence of this can be found in some of Blondie's lyrics, which seem very much in tune with the media saturation, consumer culture and post–sexual revolution excess of the era, though often with a slightly more accessible, playful approach compared to Cronenberg's nightmarish visions. The ideas surrounding self-preservation within the Blondie songs 'Fade Away and Radiate' and 'Die Young Stay Pretty' are not too far away from *Videodrome*'s philosophy and Nicki's character arc, the former about movie stars surviving death via their screen image and the latter a mantra for living fast and uninhibited. After sex-obsessed Nicki cannot be satiated by the offerings of the material world and ostensibly meets her demise, she is able to live on as a vivid, highly sexualised representation of herself with the television screen as her host body. Hampton (2016) says that Harry's performance 'casts a spell of stillness that establishes a taut equilibrium of self-preservation and self-destruction'. These two conflicting ideas, of self-preservation and self-destruction, summarise many of *Videodrome*'s central ideas and are encapsulated by the final scene of the film where, after Nicki tells Max Renn that he too can 'leave the old flesh' by killing his body and be preserved in a hyper-real body, Max utters the iconic closing call to arms 'long live the new flesh' before committing suicide.

In this way, Nicki is perhaps not too far removed from something Harry herself could conceive. In fact, Harry's persona does indeed become enmeshed with her character's in a number of ways. In a review of Blondie's debut album, Tucker

(1981) states that Harry is a 'possessor of a bombshell zombie's voice that can sound dreamily seductive and woodenly Mansonite within the same song' and that she performs with 'utter aplomb and involvement throughout, even when she's portraying a character consummately obnoxious and spaced out, there is a wink of awareness that is comforting and amusing yet never condescending'. A few of these characteristics that make up Harry's pastiche, chiefly her 'spaced out', 'zombie' nature, are transferred to Nicki, whose disposition in the film is detached and desensitised to almost everything around her, a result of her oversaturation – so detached and saturated that she can only be pleasured by masochistic acts of self-harm such as putting out a cigarette on her bare chest. This nonchalant, post–sexual revolution condition once again calls to mind the pop star's own music, such as her blasé, tongue-in-cheek reflection on a failed relationship in Blondie's 'Heart of Glass', or the retelling of taboo sexual fantasies involving a police officer in 'X-Offender'. With her Blondie character, Harry would often take archetypes of female beauty and subvert/caricature them, most memorably her bleached-blonde bombshell hair with visible dark roots that draw attention to the artifice of the style. This irony was sometimes misread as an invitation for objectification, much to the frustration of Harry who was very much involved in the postmodern layering of her persona. Meanwhile in *Videodrome*, Nicki craves this objectification behind closed doors whilst her radio/TV persona and aesthetic choices suggest otherwise. After she becomes a screen simulacrum, she is represented by highly sexualised images and sounds, seen notably in the scene where Max pushes his face into his anthropomorphic television on Nicki's command. The screen displays Nicki's teeth pressed against her open lips whilst moans of pleasure can be heard, almost resembling one of Harry's own parodies of female beauty and exaggerated eroticism.

There is a sense, however, that both Minogue and Harry were prepared to de-emphasise their personas in various ways and place a level of trust in the direction of Cronenberg and Carax, based on pre-established respect and 'good faith' as well as the desire to work with film-makers offering something a little more alternative to their practices. Minogue's transformation is far starker than Harry's, whose image evidently shares similarities with Nicki. But perhaps for more casual Blondie listeners, who might only be familiar with the bouncy, playful facet of Harry's persona, Nicki would be something more jarring and unrecognisable. Harry expressed this idea in an interview about *Videodrome*, revealing that Nicki's ambivalent and unpalatable nature was not always the planned choice for the character. But, nevertheless, Harry complied: 'What we were looking for was something that would take me out of the image people had of me, you know Blondie and being a singer, and sort of being this cute pop-sy little character. We did however want something at first like comedy, something that would be light and charming and people would really love me. So Nicki is not exactly that' (in *The Making of David Cronenberg's Videodrome* 1982).

For Minogue, being unrecognisable was a preference, a chance to prove herself in a new context: 'My fear was that the inverted commas around my name and what I've worked so hard at to create is a creation that almost eclipses me. I didn't want to be in this film and suddenly there's a right screech, and then, "What the hell is Kylie Minogue doing here?" I'm not Kylie Minogue in that' (in Smith 2012). As Minogue alludes to here, there is a risk in representing a pop star as something close to themselves, particularly in conceptually convoluted films like *Videodrome* and *Holy Motors*, where the viewer could easily be withdrawn from the headspace of the work if the pop star's performance draws attention to itself for the wrong reasons. In casting a pop star, both directors are required to tread a razor line between creating a playfully self-aware reality and conveying sophisticated ideas. It can be said that both *Videodrome* and *Holy Motors* achieve this, as they explore contemporary and complex issues; yet to state that they are totally 'serious' works would be a misrepresentation of their tone. Both films display an offbeat sense of humour in their gravitation towards exaggeration and absurdity, which the pop star's presence only serves to enhance.

Despite this exaggeration, however, Harry and Minogue's personas are arguably somewhat stripped down and understated. For Nicki, this comes from her detached disposition and for Eva, despite Minogue's best efforts, from the limited emotional depth she is granted in her short scene, which purposely does little to clearly outline her background or importance. Her singing voice is also softened and raw, sounding less polished and raw than the usual layers of pop production would allow. When reflecting on her role in *Videodrome*, Harry stated that 'Nicki doesn't carry the story; she doesn't have enough screen time to make a difference' (in Hampton 2016), implying she perhaps felt slightly lost in the film. However, this comment likely came about once Harry learnt that many of her scenes had actually been removed from the final cut. Originally, Nicki was positioned as one of the film's 'villains', a confirmed accomplice of Bianca O'Blivion (played by Sonja Smits) who seeks to 'reprogramme' Max for her own cause. In the final version, Nicki does still play a part in Max's mind control but her role is more passive; it is unclear which side she is on, whether 'auditioning' for Videodrome has fulfilled or undone her. In one deleted scene that would have been the film's finale, Cronenberg nearly complicated things further with a sex scene in the Videodrome world between Woods, Harry and Smits, an orgasmic endorsement of the post-death 'new flesh' featuring melting faces and mutated sex organs. Cronenberg removed the scene after he felt the special effects were unconvincing and bordering on comic, citing the failure of the alien sex scenes in Nicolas Roeg's *The Man Who Fell to Earth* (1976) (Browning 2007, 70) as what dissuaded him – coincidentally another film that features a pop star in David Bowie. In the distributed version of *Videodrome*, Harry/Nicki is crucial but decentralised, perhaps an act of aforementioned razor-line treading by Cronenberg, who streamlines his vision into a lean eighty-nine minutes without overusing the pop star or moments of extreme body horror.

The most striking and immediately noticeable loss in Harry and Minogue's screen de-emphasis, however, is their hairstyles. For Harry, her bleached-blonde hair is essential to her image and gave her band its name as catcallers would frequently shout 'blondie' at the singer. The Blondie song 'Platinum Blonde' is dedicated to the implications of blonde hair, whilst Cateforis (2011, 97) claims it is a key component of the singer's pastiche of pop culture tropes in its 'tribute to the 1950s bleached-blonde bombshell'. On her blondness, Debbie Harry (in MacInnis 1990) has stated, 'In a sexual sense, I'm talking about movie stars now ... I mean there's a chemical reaction where this blonde sort of innocence and purity, combined with this extreme, sensual, magnetic, adult, mature, womanly sexuality, is very, very explosive on the screen. I think that's what makes it so attractive to people. It's very subconscious.' This explanation almost bears resemblance to the dialogue from the TV interview scene in *Videodrome* where Max Renn and Nicki Brand are invited on 'The Rena King Show' to discuss mediated sex and violence, in what Nicki calls a climate of 'overstimulated times'. Cronenberg moves the site of subconscious suggestion away from Harry's hair, which is now brunette, and places it on her vivid red dress, which she is seen wearing again once she becomes the sexualised simulacrum of Max's hallucinations. During the interview, Woods's character remarks, 'That dress ... It's very stimulating. It's red. You know what Freud would have said about that dress?' Whilst Harry's blonde hair evoked old-school cultural reference points in its 'allusions to Marilyn Monroe, Jayne Mansfield, Kim Novak and other flaxen dames of distinction' (MacInnis 1990), Cronenberg severs her from these loaded associations and disrupts the audience's familiarity with the pop star's persona. For Nicki, the low-key brunette hair helps her to assimilate (blonde would be too revealing), concealing her hidden tendencies as she expresses concern about the dangers of those same tendencies. Yet Max picks up on her hypocrisy and wilful participation in overstimulation (wearing a red dress), sparking his sexual interest in her.

In *Holy Motors*, Eva/Minogue's hair is a short pixie cut, a style the pop star has never been strongly associated with, again maybe a technique in severing her from her real-life persona to avoid the 'right screech' watershed moment Minogue feared. In a film littered with references to cinema history, particularly French cinema, Eva's hair also deliberately brings to mind Jean Seberg's famous pixie crop in Jean-Luc Godard's *Breathless* (1960), whilst the 'character' for her next appointment is also called Jean. Mr Oscar's limousine driver Céline, the only character who displays unambiguous familiarity with the shape-shifter, is played by Édith Scob. In one scene, Scob wears a pale blue mask with only the eye holes removed, an allusion to her most celebrated role in Georges Franju's *Eyes Without a Face* (1960), and it seems many casting choices serve as intertextual references. Minogue's casting is unique in that she is an intertextual reference to a different art form in real-world popular culture, whilst also appearing as an avatar of Seberg and performs a song in what seems like an evocation of the musical film genre. By layering these references and partnering Minogue with Lavant, Carax seems to suggest that the popular and the esoteric markers of culture, whether in music or cinema, past or present, are linked, interchangeable and must be preserved. Carax is also lamenting a bygone era of cinema throughout the film by making these allusions, whilst heralding in the digital age (there is an extended sequence where Mr Oscar uses motion capture technology for one of his appointments), though not without scepticism. As Cronenberg prophesies a world where the human body and mind can become interconnected with technology as a means of hyper-real preservation, Carax's Mr Oscar must negotiate his own purpose in a technologically hyper-developed world. He wants to preserve his craft, what he calls 'the beauty of the act', but has reservations towards the accelerating modernisation around him: 'I miss the cameras. They used to be heavier than us, then they became smaller than our heads, now you can't see them at all. So sometimes I do find it hard to believe in it all.'

At the start of her career, Kylie Minogue's pop persona was defined by the wholesome 'girl next door' characters of her TV soap acting. Later, it developed into something slightly more sexually mature and flirtatious, appealing to her increased LGBTQ+ following. *Holy Motors*'s Eva possesses none of these attributes, and carries herself with a weariness and melancholy. It is unclear, however, whether the scene between Mr Oscar and Eva is a real interlude in their acting appointments and the two really did have a relationship, or whether this is just another staged appointment for both of them. The scene occurs once the film has finally settled into a rhythm; Mr Oscar finishes one appointment, is driven to the next whilst changing his costume and make-up, performs and so on. The only insight into what could be Mr Oscar's real self happens during the transition period in the limousine, until Carax teases greater clarification via Eva's scene. After alienating its audience, the film presents a chance to see what is under the mask, to learn who people like Mr Oscar and Eva really are, until the scene is lost once again to ambiguity. Perhaps if we were able to follow Eva to her next appointments as we do with Lavant's Oscar, she would eventually arrive at something close to Kylie Minogue, performing as a pop star. Carax seems to imply there is a level of shape-shifting that everyone in society must perform, particularly our entertainers, providing a real-world example in Minogue by presenting her as something completely unfamiliar. Mr Oscar's more outlandish acting appointments are punctuated with universal vignettes grounded in the everyday, such as his 'role' as a father collecting his young daughter from a party, the abrupt transition reminding the viewer how easily a public and private persona can become enmeshed. Minogue herself alludes to these ideas in her own interpretation of the film, 'I was definitely intrigued about "Who Were We," which different faces do we present to society. I know I'm a chameleon – even in music, I'm changing my guise a lot and all of that' (in Smith 2012). Mr Oscar is given an information file for his appointments from an agency, and for a pop star like Kylie Minogue, being told exactly how to act and what to look like in this way is not an unfamiliar concept. In both *Holy Motors* and *Videodrome*, there is a suggestion that we never truly know the performers and tastemakers of society who we invite into our lives, especially as that society moves further towards modernisation and digitalisation. By casting real performers/pop stars, the suggestion becomes applicable to real-world culture too. After all, in the real world, Debbie Harry's true character has been buried under a pastiche of pop culture tropes and caricatures of female beauty, whilst the idea of Kylie Minogue 'in inverted commas' (as the star puts it) has been, for the large part of her career, constructed by those around her.

Where Carax is reluctant to reveal what truly lies beneath the mask, Cronenberg answers by suggesting there lurks an insatiable desire for forbidden stimulation, which can and will be exploited by the greedy corporate architects of a consumer-capitalist society. Those who outwardly seem most concerned about this condition are the ones who participate in it most recklessly, like Harry's Nicki Brand. Brand's public persona is at odds with her private desires, as she spends her days blithely advising the callers to her 'Emotional Rescue' radio show, secretly detached from their mundane familial and relationship issues, waiting until something truly dangerous and unorthodox comes along, as it eventually does with the Videodrome broadcast. It is as though Nicki has grown out of the real world and its traditional mechanisms, particularly in regards to sex, and seeks the next step (even if it means destruction) in her hyper-real self, the new flesh. Whilst Max Renn's interests in Videodrome largely stem from the search for cutting edge programming for his TV station, Nicki's fixation reveals a dark, ugly underbelly to an overstimulated society and its media figures, a daring role to embody for real-life celebrity Harry. Similar to *Holy Motors*, Videodrome asks us to reassess our perception of those media figures, of our performers and entertainers, by drawing attention to their inherent artifice. Nicki's shift from agony aunt to sexual deviant is not the film's only character revelation. Professor Brian O'Blivion (played by Jack Creley), the enigmatic 'media prophet' who originally helped to create the Videodrome broadcast, is revealed to have died before the events of the film, despite appearing as the third guest on 'The Rena King Show' via television screen. Like Nicki, he presents a deceptive version of himself to the public eye, one constructed via thousands of videotapes he recorded before his death – a prototype of the Videodrome technology and its potential for hyper-real self-preservation.

Videodrome and *Holy Motors*, two unique and essential meetings of pop star and celluloid, present a strong case for the popular's ability to enhance an esoteric viewing experience. For postmodern icon Debbie Harry, her role in *Union City* and its pathway into *Videodrome* was the start of a series of selective appearances in more offbeat, transgressive and/or horror-adjacent works, where she would continue to, as Thompson (1995) puts it, 'pay her dues' in supporting/cameo parts. Her next sizeable character after *Videodrome*'s Nicki Brand would be Velma Von Tussle in John Waters's *Hairspray* (1988), a work from another key purveyor of cinematic transgression. Emerging in the punk scene, it was already in Harry's nature to lean towards the provocative, and it seems she did not have to stray too far from her pop persona or artistic preoccupations to do so with *Videodrome* or later roles. For pop sweetheart Kylie Minogue, *Holy Motors* was more of an outlier in her career and a chance to prove herself with an alternative audience once again, following on from previous criticism and accusations of miscasting in projects such as *Street Fighter*. It could be questioned whether Harry and Minogue's roles in *Videodrome* and *Holy Motors*, which are small and unconcerned with being major selling points, could have been played by a non-pop star to the same effect. However, their inclusion has proven to generate a wealth of additional meaning in their intertextuality and pre-established associations, whilst challenging the viewer to apply the films' ideas surrounding media, performance and technology to a real-world context. The fact that they are small roles and aren't major selling points is key, as the pop star is crucial but not indulged, allowing a purer vision. The more revealing question could be whether their roles (if the films were made at different times) could be swapped, if Debbie Harry could play Eva and Kylie Minogue, Nicki Brand. The former does not seem like an unlikely possibility, whilst the latter pairing would prove more difficult for Minogue who, despite ostensibly having more autonomy over her persona later in her career, struggled to break away from the manufactured image induced by her soap opera origins for so long. In other words, the leap from low-stakes TV romance with Jason Donovan to masochistic sex scenes with James Woods might have proven too extreme for the executives at her record company and fans alike. Therefore, there may be a limit in how the popular interacts with the esoteric, much to *Holy Motors*'s dissent. The differences between these two pop stars also comes from our increasingly complicated relationship with celebrities in the digital age, a climate Cronenberg and Carax both warn us to approach with caution.

References

Browning, Mark (2007), *David Cronenberg: Author or Film-maker?*, Bristol, UK: Intellect Books.
Cateforis, Theo (2011), 'Camp! Kitsch! Trash! New Wave and the Politics of Irony', in T. Cateforis (ed.), *Are We Not New Wave?*, 95–122, US: University of Michigan Press.
Hampton, Howard (2016), 'Experience Necessary: Deborah Harry in Videodrome', 26 December, *The Criterion Collection*. Available online: https://www.criterion.com/current/posts/4357-experience-necessary-deborah-harry-in-videodrome. Accessed 21 September 2022.
Lucas, Tim (1983), 'Videodrome', *Cinefantastique*, 14 (2): 32–49.
MacInnis, Craig (1990), 'Deborah Harry and the Blondie Mystique', *Toronto Star*.
Morgan, Kim (2017, June 28), 'Kim Morgan on David Cronenberg's *Videodrome*'. Available online: https://thenewbev.com/blog/2017/06/kim-morgan-david-cronenbergs-videodrome/. Accessed 21 September 2022.

Naftule, Ashley (2019, October 2), 'Her Side of the Story: Debbie Harry Talks about Her Life in Blondie in Her New Book', *Phoenix New Times*.

Smith, Nigel (2012, October 17), 'Australian Megastar Kylie Minogue on "Holy Motors" and Why She Feels Like She's Just Beginning', *IndieWire*. Available online: https://www.indiewire.com/2012/10/australian-megastar-kylie-minogue-on-holy-motors-and-why-she-feels-like-shes-just-beginning-44118/. Accessed 21 September 2022.

The Making of David Cronenberg's Videodrome (1982), [Film]. Dir. M. Garris, US: Nice Guy Productions.

Thompson, Ben (1995), 'Pop and Film: The Charisma Crossover', in J. Romney and A. Wootton (eds), *Celluloid Jukebox: Popular Music and the Movies since the 50s*, 32–43, UK: BFI.

Tucker, Ken (1981, April 8), Blondie by Blondie Album Review. *Rolling Stone*. Available online: https://www.rollingstone.com/music/music-album-reviews/blondie-247907/. Accessed 21 September 2022.

6

Translating personas: French singers on film
Andy Willis

French cinema has had a long relationship with stars from other cultural forms. For example, a number of significant French film stars of the post–Second World War era had established careers in the music industry alongside or before moving into film acting. Through a number of case studies, this chapter will consider the relationship between the star persona created by a number of performers within the music industry at different historical moments, and how that was transferred into film roles. As Lisa Taylor has noted, 'Music stars make the most effective transference to mainstream cinema when the character played draws upon the star persona already established by the culture and media industries.' (2004, 159) Writing in the wider context of a discussion of Prince's film acting, she discusses Madonna and her star turn in *Desperately Seeking Susan* (1985) as an example of this. One might also cite David Bowie's appearance in *The Man Who Fell to Earth* (1976) as typical of this trend. Whilst this is certainly true of a range of French pop stars' appearances on film, this assumption can be challenged when one considers singers who managed to sustain a film career beyond the moment of their most noteworthy music stardom.

Yves Montand: a star translated

The first case study considers the popular post-war singer turned actor Yves Montand. It is often overlooked in Anglo-Saxon writing about French cinema that Montand had begun his show business career as a singer. As Pamela M. Moores puts it, 'Montand is also known in France as a popular music-hall singer who maintained his considerable success over many years. This was his original claim to fame' (1991, 132) Furthermore, one of the cornerstones of his star persona was established in these early years – that is, his association with the French working class. As Guy Austin observed, 'His early career as a singer in the music-hall tradition saw him pejoratively defined by his class when nicknamed *le prolo chantant* (the singing pleb)' (2003, 20). The first part of Montand's acting career reflected these origins and the duality of his developing star persona.

His early films included *Étoile sans lumière* (Star Without Light 1946), set in the film industry as silent production turned to sound, which starred another high-profile singer transferring their star image into film, Édith Piaf. Piaf had been a major influence on Montand's career, so it is not surprising to see him supporting her transfer to the cinema. The year 1946 also saw Montand appear in *Les Portes de la nuit* (Gates of the Night). A more serious affair, directed by Marcel Carné and written by Jacques Prévert, the film reflected on the immediate post-war era and the impact the conflict had on its characters and wider French society. Perhaps not surprisingly, given his emergence from the music industry, Montand would also play a singer in films such as *Souvenirs perdus* (Lost Souvenirs 1950), and as himself, reflecting his popularity at the time, in a number of light musical comedies such as *Paris est toujours Paris* (Paris is Always Paris 1951), *Paris chante toujours* (Paris Still Sings 1951) and *Saluti e baci* (1953).

As he became more established as a star, Montand would develop and expand the non-musical aspects of his persona. In this manifestation, the image drew on the performer's background and association with the French (and Italian migrant) working class and his commitment to social justice and class politics. He had been born Ivo Livi and had grown up in an Italian migrant family in Marseilles; and whilst many of his films tended, as Guy Austin notes, to 'situate Montand far from his roots' (2003, 20), as he became more established, his choice of collaborators is significant. By the mid-1950s his left-wing politics were becoming well known in France, and in 1956, he had embarked upon a controversial singing tour of the USSR. From this period onwards, a number of the roles that Montand accepted saw him collaborate with directors who shared a left-wing world view. This saw him accepting acting work with directors such as Giuseppe De Santis (*Unominie e lupi*/The Wolves 1956), Gillo Pontecorvo (*The Wide Blue Road* 1957), Alain Renais (*La Guerre est Finie*/The War is Over 1965) and Costa-Gavras (*Z* 1969 and *The Confession* 1970), as well as providing the narration for Chris Marker's 1963 documentary *Le Joli Mai* (The Lovely Month of May). Therefore, in France, and to a certain extent within Italy and Europe more generally, Montand's star persona was increasingly of someone who is honest, reliable and committed and was closely associated with his, and his wife Simone Signoret's, left-wing politics. Austin sees *Z* as a key work in developing this newer screen persona for the singer. He argues that

> *Z* posits Montand's character as a multifaceted star, a man of glamour, physical prowess and sex appeal as well as political intellect. These were already attributes of Montand as a singer and public figure, but had not yet been incarnated by him on screen with any success. *Z* changed that and crystallised the image of Montand at the end of the sixties as a political *and* glamorous film star. (2003, 22)

In contrast to this, in the Hollywood productions which he sporadically appeared in from 1960 and continued to do so throughout that decade, Montand was a performer who R. Barton Palmer described as one of the, 'sexy European actors and actresses to capture the interest of American filmgoers in the 1950s' (2010, 17). In what was his most intense engagement with Hollywood, with films such as *Let's Make Love* (1960), *Goodbye Again* (1961) and *My Geisha* (1962), Montand was consistently cast rather simplistically as a suave Gallic lover. Indeed, these were characters who seemed more concerned with romantic conquest than social change. In America, Montand found, as many other French actors, such as Charles Boyer and Louis Jordan had before him, by transferring to Hollywood, European actors had to adhere to broad national stereotypes, which often meant leaving their already existing, and often more nuanced, French 'image' behind whilst adopting a much more simplistic one.

Typical of this transition for Montand within this period is *Let's Make Love*. The actor was cast in this film following a highly successful run of his one-man singing and dancing show in New York and a short tour of the United States. Reviewing the show, Richard Watts Jr. writing in *The New Yorker* stated that 'all our singers, including Mr. Sinatra, could sit at his feet and take a lesson from him', whilst other commentators affirmed his blue-collar persona noting that 'he looks as if he drives a taxi by day' (Montand, Hamon and Rotman 1992, 296–7). Little of this musical persona would translate into this first Hollywood film. In *Let's Make Love*, Montand starred alongside Marylin Monroe, playing Jean-Marc Clément, a billionaire who, when accidently cast to play himself in a Broadway satire, has to learn how to sing and dance in order to get closer to Monroe's Amanda. In something that might have been considered an in-joke within France, Montand hires Milton Burle, Bing Crosby and Gene Kelly to assist him in learning the art of entertaining as he can't deliver a funny line, sing or dance. Indeed, perhaps surprisingly given his clear ability, throughout the film Frankie Vaughn, playing Tony, gets much more opportunity to showcase his singing talents than Montand. The latter and his co-authors reflected upon this fact, noting that he,

> a singer-dancer-mime hailed by critics across the United States for his sure and supple touch and timing, had been side-lined into the role of a stiff and lumpish young man whose only spectacular number was a sketch that lampooned his clumsiness. So he had just fifty skimpy seconds of real-life Montand, in the scene where his character dreams he can outdance Astaire. In other words he was a foil. American producers whose female stars feared strong competition loved to pair them with a Continental, a Latin lover who exuded a torrid mythic aura without threatening the status of the fragile star. (Montand, Hamon and Rotman 1992, 312)

Whilst Montand does get to perform the songs 'Incurably Romantic' and 'Let's Make Love' in the film, the Hollywood gossip columns also found much to write about during the film's production. It was this aspect of the extra-textual production of *Let's Make Love* that cemented a certain persona, the gallic lover, for Montand in the United States. As stated in his co-written memoir, 'This is the point where legend takes over' (Montand, Hamon and Rotman 1992, 312), it was during the making of the film that rumours of an affair between Montand and Monroe began to circulate. This 'fact' was seemingly supported by a cover of *Life* magazine on 15 August 1960, which contained a close-up of the pair, actually a publicity photo from the last scene of the film, apparently in a romantic tryst. The affair would continue to be a part of Montand's 'legend' from that moment onwards, and he would still be asked about it in as late as a 1988 interview on *Late Night with David Letterman*.

Whilst Montand had developed a much more complex and mature star persona by the 1970s through a variety of different roles in a variety of European films, his other Hollywood work, such as *Goodbye Again*, *My Geisha* and *On a Clear Day You Can See Forever* (1970), continued to trade on his romantic image. By the 1970s, Montand had been a star in France for over thirty years and in that time had managed to develop and change the way in which audiences perceived him. Indeed, the singer-actor was taken so seriously in France regarding his political comments that in the mid-1980s, he was variously raised as a serious potential candidate for the Presidency of France (Austin 2003, 25). This fact, perhaps more than anything else, shows the chasm between his nuanced star persona in France, one that straddled music and film and extended across decades, and the shallow and limited one developed in Hollywood.

The emergence of French youth cultures: the *Yé-Yé* girls as 'unconstructed' stars

Marking a distinct change in the media industries from the period Montand developed as both a singer and film star, and the youth cultures that emerged in France during the late 1950s, as elsewhere globally, showed a distinct influence from the United States. Unlike other musical trends of earlier periods, these mark a notable impact within France of styles and trends that originated outside French cultural traditions. Those who were part of the emergence of youth culture in France are often given the label *Copains*, the translation of the term as friends, buddies or pals emphasising a strong sense of perceived collectivity. Whilst Briggs (2015) articulates the emergence of the *Copains* as marking beginnings of a French youth culture, the term is also often used to refer to it in a more commercialised form. In doing so, there is a clear sense of French youth culture beginning to have distinct (if linked) groupings.

One of the most noteworthy of these was the appearance in the late 1950s of a number of local rock 'n' roll acts in France. At first, the musical style was associated, negatively, with youth gangs. These were labelled as the *blouson noirs* (black jackets) and were made up of groups of youngsters dressed in jackets seemingly inspired, like other youth groups around the world, by the rebellious attitude personified by Marlon Brando's character in the 1953 film *The Wild One*. As David Looseley notes, the origins of this trend can be connected to the release of 'Rock Around the Clock', which became a hit in France in 1956, echoing its success in North America and other parts of Europe. This, along with the impact of Elvis Presley, led to a number of French performers offering local versions of the American style. These ranged from the 'half-imitation, half-parody' of Henry Cording and his Original Rock and Roll Boys, who released '*Va te faire cuire un oeuf, man!*', to the more serious attempts at rock and roll style offered by the likes of Danyel Gérard and Richard Anthony (Looseley 2003, 23). Looseley goes on to argue that the real impact of rock 'n' roll was felt in the early 1960s. He states that this was the period when it became a cornerstone of an emerging, and what by this time was becoming something that could be argued was a distinctive French youth culture.

The second case study focuses on a number of young female singers, often referred to as the '*Yé-Yé* girls', who were closely associated with the *Copains*. This case study will explore how this group of performers came to be seen to typify

French-ness in the 1960s. This would result in performers, such as Françoise Hardy, also appearing in a number of small parts in films such as *Nutty, Naughty Chateau* (1963) and *What's New Pussycat?* (1965), which were often carefully constructed to represent a particular version of French-ness, youthfulness and modernity. The intertextual relationship between French music and cinema stars at this particular historical moment is further reflected by the fact that actresses such as Brigitte Bardot and Anna Karina also released records that drew on their cinematic star personas.

Copains seemed to be becoming a more distinct, arguably commercialised and less aggressive, form of youth culture marked out by a clear commodification of its components, most notably music performers. This trend is perhaps most typified by the appearance of, initially, the Europe 1 radio show *Salut les Copains*, followed in 1962 by a youth orientated glossy magazine of the same name which promoted the idea of a *Copains* culture. In this more commercialised form, the *Copains* became associated with a particularly French musical cycle labelled Yé-Yé. This process, the creation of a commodified *copains* culture, articulates a shift from something that could be read as cutting-edge, new and challenging, typified by the idea of the *blouson noirs*, to a softer incarnation, driven by the needs of the media industries developed to exploit youth culture that could be read as part of the establishment.

What is notable about the *Yé-Yé* moment is the fact that a number of the emerging performers associated with it initially rejected the idea of being a 'star'. This, as Briggs notes, put them somewhat at odds with the rock 'n' roll performers who seemed to desire the role of idol. He argues that within the culture industries focused on *Yé-Yé*, there was a clear attempt to develop personas for performers such as Françoise Hardy, Sylvie Vartan and Sheila that emphasised their status as a simple *copain*. This distinction between star and *copain* is also notable for its gender divide. Whilst the likes of Johnny Hallyday increasingly assumed the role of a star, the young women of the *Yé-Yé* moment emphasised the fact that they were like their fans, utilising the idea of their being examples of the elevation of 'the girl next door' to stardom. It worked, as Briggs states, and 'many enjoyed "commercial success equal to, if not greater than, their male counterparts"' (2015, 33).

As one might expect of such a cultural moment, a number of *Yé-Yé* stars attempted to transfer their popularity onto film, and television, screens with a number making appearances on screen in the early to mid-1960s. In such instances, the singers tended to appear in roles that closely reflected their existing pop culture personas. Françoise Hardy, for example, was one of the female singers that Looseley describes as having been 'projected as skittish, fun-loving and wholesome' (2003, 27), in an attempt to counter the more antisocial behaviour of the rock 'n' rollers associated with *blouson noirs*. The wholesomeness of Hardy's image is reflected in the head and shoulder images used on her early record covers. These often caught the performer in simple outfits such as cardigans, suede jackets or black dresses, and in 'ordinary' situations such as holding an umbrella in the wind or standing in the street against a distressed poster. As noted, Hardy would accept a number of small roles in films such as *Château en Suède* (*Nutty, Naughty Chateau* 1963) and *What's New Pussycat* (1965) that utilised her popularity in France and beyond.

The popularity of female *Yé-Yé* singers and the manner in which they seemed to connect with young audiences also inspired a number of film stars to attempt to trade on their cinematic popularity and release records. In this category, film stars such as Anna Karina and Brigitte Bardot joined the *Yé-Yé* scene, releasing records to cash in on their high profile. Karina had established herself as an actress in France in the early 1960s working with a number of directors associated with the *Nouvelle Vague*, most notably Jean-Luc Godard, and her first releases were associated with her films. For example, in 1965, her name was on the release of songs from *Pierrot Le Fou* (1965) and *Le Voleur De Tibidabo* (The Thief of Tibidabo 1964). Karina would have more conventional hit records later in the decade with songs written for her by Serge Gainsbourg, from the television production *Anna* (1967), such as '*Sous Le Soleil Exactement*'. Here, once again, the persona of the 'singer' is inexorably connected to that of the film star.

Unlike the *copains* persona of the extraordinary-ordinary young woman, Bardot was already an established international film star with a 'sex-kitten' persona linked to the representation of her sexuality in films such as *And God Created Woman* (*Et Dieu ... créa la femme* 1956). Whilst Bardot had released a record to coincide with the success of that film, '*Et Dieu ... créa la Femme*' 1956, as well as another film-related release '*Sidonie*' (from *Vie Privée* 1962), she would begin releasing records more consistently in 1963. This year saw the likes of singles '*El Cuchipe*' and '*Invitango*', which were taken from the album *Brigitte*, followed by another album *B. B.* in 1964. Whilst the covers of both these albums contained shots of Bardot that emphasised her sexuality and played on her existing star persona that had been established in her films, the images that accompanied the track listing on *B. B.* show the star dressed in jeans and a black turtle neck sweater, every bit the *copain*. The design and marketing team were obviously seeking to utilise Bardot's extraordinariness but also at the same time presenting her as being like other female singers of the period. By 1968, when Bardot released another album, *Bonnie and Clyde*, the *copain* moment had given way to other manifestations of youth culture such as hippies and the more psychedelic music associated with them.

In the first category, the persona of the young female music performer being both an everyday *copain* and a star can be found in the 1966 French film *Masculin-Feminin*. In this film, high-profile *Yé-Yé* singer Chantel Goya appears as a young woman seeking to make a record for RCA, the company that had in fact released Goya's first record, *C'est bien Bernard*, in 1964. Godard is said to have cast her after seeing her perform the song on French television and utilised anecdotes from her own experience in the film. For example, Goya had spoken of her accidental meeting on the street with a Japanese man, who she thought was a tourist, who asked her directions to the RCA offices. She assisted him and gave him a copy of her new record. The man turned out to be a radio station owner in Japan and upon his return he encouraged the playing of her record, resulting in a hit in the country. In the film, it is suggested that Goya's character has become popular in Japan through good fortune rather than talent (Deluxe 2013, 80–1).

The appearance of Goya, as Madeleine, in the film seems to directly draw on her developing image as a singer who had just released her first records. When she first appears in the café where Paul (Jean-Pierre Leaud) is seated reading, she seems every bit the young *copain*. She wears an overcoat, woollen sweater, black skirt, black loafers and a bob style hair, the sort of combination so familiar from the many images of young singers on record sleeves, not least from Goya herself on the cover of '*Si Tu Gagnes Au Flipper*' from 1965, and the pages of *Salut les Copains*. The way in which the character of Madeline seems so closely modelled on Goya has been noted by Hassan Melehy, when he observes that 'questions of identity and authenticity permeate *Masculin féminin*. The soundtrack plays six of Chantal Goya's songs, usually in an ambiguously diegetic fashion that raises the question of whether they are also sung by Goya's character Madeleine' (2018, 155).

Godard seems particularly interested in interrogating the constructed nature of stardom. Throughout the film there are moments that suggest a constructedness regarding Madeline's star image. Using Goya as the film's central character allows Godard to suggest wider reflections on the manufactured nature of the 'everyday' and 'unconstructed' *copain* – that is, that the stardom of the *copain* is as constructed as the performance of one offered by Goya as Madeline. Again, as Melehy suggests, 'This division between Madeleine and her media persona continues outside the studio building: a journalist catches her and asks superficial questions to which she gives untruthful answers, including an account of her taste for Bach in phrases she borrows from Paul' (2018, 155). This theme is continued within the costume decisions made by the film-makers. In another scene, Madeline wears a peacoat with the letter C emblazoned on the pocket and a striped scarf that has a large G visible – the blurring of the character of Madeline and the pop star playing her further displayed for the audience aware of Goya's other popular cultural existence.

Johnny Hallyday: the chameleon

The final case study of the chapter will focus on French pop star Johnny Hallyday, who unlike Montand and similar to a number of the *Yé-Yé* girls, only occasionally appeared in films but did so across his long career. Halladay emerged just before the phenomenon of the *Yé-Yé* singers, and his career continued long after their early to mid-1960s heyday.

It was from the rebellious youth cultural moment of the late 1950s that Jean-Phillipe Smet emerged as Johnny Hallyday, initially performing at Le Golf Drouot dance hall on the Rue de Montmartre in Paris before releasing his first record, *'T'aimer follement'* (Loving You Madly), in March 1960 (Looseley 2003, 24). From the outset, Hallyday can be seen as a performer adopting a star image or persona. In this regard, Looseley notes that it was suggested in the French popular press at the time of his emergence as a star that he was in fact American, going so far as to suggest that the singer was actually from the city of Tulsa. This myth was encouraged by the fact that Hallyday himself was happy to

> be billed initially as a US citizen living in France, a ruse dreamt up by Lee Halliday, the American husband of Johnny's cousin Desta, who together had brought him up. And as with many of the manufactured stars of the late 1950s, his managers (Georges Leroux, then Johnny Stark) and his record labels (Vogue, then Philips) were also instrumental in fabricating an American-style persona for him. (Looseley 2005, 193)

Hallyday quickly came to be linked with the rebellious image of rock and roll, something that is evidenced by Looseley, who says that when the singer toured France in 1961, 'the Mayors of Cannes, Strasbourg and Bayonne would not let him play, while in Montbéliard police used tear gas to control crowds' (2003, 26). It would certainly seem that Hallyday rapidly became associated with a rebel stance from early on in his career. At certain points, this association would be resurrected, to the extent that in the latter part of his career it was the 'rebel rocker' persona that would be most commonly associated with Hallyday.

By the late 1960s, Hallyday's star image was already undergoing significant change, reflecting the changes within youth culture. A consideration of his album covers in this period reveals an attempt to connect with the more psychedelic influences impacting on the French music scene. Whilst the back cover of *Johnny Au Palais Des Sports* (1967) contains photographs of the star smashing up the stage attired in a leather jacket, the front has a painted image of two Johnny profiles, one black one red with longer wavy hair and sideburns. The colourful image on the front offers a slight shift away from the bad boy Johnny on the reverse. A year later, with *Rêve Et Amour*, Hallyday's image seems to have undergone further revision, with a medieval-inspired drawing that creeps ever further towards the psychedelic imagery utilised by the likes of The Beatles. By 1969, in *Rivière ... Ouvre Ton Lit* Hallyday seems to have gone even further. The album's cover shows the singer with longer hair, a headband, a beard and sporting love beads. The inner image on the gatefold sleeve contains a photograph of Johnny and his band, the singer now wearing what looks like a native American inspired necklace, in an image that would not have been out of place in San Francisco's summer of love. Reflecting wider changes in the music industry, by the early 1970s, Hallyday's image as reflected on his album covers seems to have shifted to adopt the style of the singer-songwriter so popular in America at the time. On the inner sleeve of *Country-Folk-Rock* (1972), the star sits alone with an acoustic guitar. Similarly, on the cover of *Insolitudes* from 1973, he sits in the corner of a white room with the acoustic guitar leaning against the wall beside him. The next significant change in image that can be identified through these album covers is from *Rock'n Slow* in 1974, which sees Hallyday revert to the rock 'n' roll stylings that had helped him establish his stardom. Here he is back in a leather biker jacket, wearing aviator shades. The embracing of the rock 'n' roll image continued with *Rock a Memphis* (1975) and from this point on would become the default one for Hallyday whatever flirtations he had with contemporary trends. It would be these shape-shifting images that meant that Hallyday's star persona would be difficult to easily translate into cinema.

The changing cultural position of Johnny Hallyday within France can be traced through his parallel career as a film performer. Crucial here is the idea that Hallyday, to a certain degree, remains Hallyday whatever the role. As David Looseley suggests, 'Even in his numerous films, it is suggested, Hallyday does not act a part but, like the great Hollywood stars analysed by Edgar Morin (1972), he "contaminates" his roles with himself. Illusion, then, becomes reality in the postmodern myth of Johnny' (Looseley 2005, 197). What needs to be added to this equation is the idea that what constitutes Johnny Hallyday does not remain constant across his career. As his career progressed, Hallyday's star persona seemed to take on a sense of fluidity. Looseley noted this in terms of his appropriating American styles, stating that 'the methodical mimicry of successive Anglo-American styles was to become Hallyday's trademark for the next 20 years' (2005, 193), before reflecting after the performer's death that 'for the next 20 years, then, he became the "chameleon" the obituaries would speak of, embracing one pop styling after another, from power balladeer to Mad Max' (2018, 381).

Johnny Hallyday had first appeared in what were seen as throwaway vehicles designed to appeal and exploit his pop stardom such as *D'où viens-tu Johnny?* (Where Are You from, Johnny?) a 1963 French film that also starred Sylvie Vartan. Vartan was a *Yé-Yé* singer who had toured and recorded with Hallyday and by 1965 was married to the star. Their marriage was widely covered in the French media, creating something of a national event and indicating the impact of the pop stars of the era on French popular culture (Deluxe 2013, 70). This reflected a rather negative image of Hallyday and French music in the 1960s and 1970s. However, this began to change in the 1980s, and as Looseley has suggested, it was closely linked to the film roles he took that brought him into the orbit of respected practitioners in that field. He argues that 'it is also commonly accepted, not least by the performer himself, that, after his acting roles in Godard's *Détective* and Costa-Gavras's *Conseil de famille*, both in 1985, some intellectuals started to speak of him more favourably' (Looseley 2005, 195), with this shift in attitude indicating how popular culture may achieve legitimacy in contemporary France.

The 1969 release *The Specialists*, directed by Sergio Corbucci, offers an interesting example of an attempt to transpose Hallyday's image as France's premiere rock 'n' roller into the context of a European western. The ability of the makers of *The Specialists* to use Hallyday's star persona in the context of the western meant the film was a box-office success in France whilst it disappointed in other territories. From the outset, Hallyday's character, who wears an all-black costume that evokes the star's rebel rocker image later enhanced by a chainmail waistcoat, is presented in stark contrast to a gang of four exploitative young characters whose costume clearly signifies 'hippie'. The extent to which the filmmakers saw these young characters in this light is reflected in the English language dialogues for the film that Eureka published on their website to coincide with their Blu-ray release (https://eurekavideo.co.uk/wp-content/uploads/2020/06/TheSpecialistsEnglishScript.pdf), which simply calls the characters 'Hippies'.

The use of Hallyday's star image in *The Specialists* is further complicated by the fact that the anti-hippie, anti-hero the film creates is somewhat at odds to the singer's music persona at this historical moment. As his album covers indicate, Hallyday did have a flirtation with the psychedelic sound so loved by the hippies the film seems to despise, remoulding his image in a manner that reflects the fashions of this element of contemporary youth culture.

Over thirty years later, in 2002, Hallyday appeared as Milan, a world-weary bank robber, in *L'homme du train* (Man on a Train). Directed by Patrice Leconte from a script by Claude Klotz, of all Hallyday's film appearances, this one seems to have a clear understanding of the 'methodical mimicry' Looseley talks of regarding the fluidity of his star persona. Reviewing the film in the *New York Times*, Elvis Mitchell continually evokes Hallyday's popular music past, suggesting that 'Mr. Hallyday is ravaged, a pop ruin'. He continues his response to the film by continually evoking Hallyday's status as a pop star, going so far as to suggest that in his creation of the character of Milan he 'takes to the screen as if he were actually once a well-respected pop star'. The link between his character in *L'homme du train* and the un-fixed nature of his pop star persona is particularly strong.

For his introduction to the audience, a man sitting alone on a train, the camera spends time on Milan's appearance and attire. Particularly, his lived-in features and his worn leather jacket with its collar pulled up. The sequence contains a shot of the character's wrist watch, the cuff of his jacket and his hand, followed by one of his goatee-bearded chin and the collar of his jacket and denim shirt, then one of his head and shoulders, revealing Hallyday's familiar craggy features and blue eyes. This introduction seems to clearly draw on the 'bad boy' aspects of the Hallyday persona and fits the character of a thief well. However, as the film progresses, Milan is shown in a more complex light.

The story of *L'homme du train* involves Milan meeting and then staying with an aging teacher, Manesquier, played by Jean Rochefort. At a crucial moment in the middle of the film, Manesquier, who is increasingly obsessed by Milan, asks his barber to cut his hair like the criminal and tells him he is going to grow a similar goatee. The following sequence shows Milan shaving his goatee off, leaving a moustache like Manesquier, then emptying the contents of his cigarette into one of the teacher's pipes and smoking it. His flirtation with another identity, which had begun by his wearing a pair of the teacher's slippers, then extends to his talking to one of Manesquier's tutee's about literature when he turns up for a class. Given the shifts and changes of his star image that Hallyday had adopted across his – by 2002 – lengthy career, there is certainly an intertextual frisson as his character Milan tries on another identity for size.

In his review, Mitchell goes so far as to see Hallyday's star persona as something that bleeds more widely into the creation of the character in order to help inform the audience's potential reading of the film. He argues that 'Mr. Leconte has made a movie that functions as a series of laconic, bruised pop gestures, counting on the audience to bring a series of associations to close the gaps that *Man on the Train* refuses to'. These associations would certainly, within France – if not outside given Hallyday's different cultural status and meaning in varied national and sociocultural consumption contexts – offer resonance to a character whose identity is presented as both reflective, and as the film progresses, fluid.

If *L'homme du train* can be read as a sophisticated engagement with an un-fixed and changeable star persona, in many ways the Hong Kong film *Vengeance* (*Fuk sau* 2009) was something of a departure, even for Johnny Hallyday. He took the role of Costello, a French Chef who turns up in Hong Kong seeking revenge after his daughter and her family are killed by assassins, close to the start of production. Director To's first choice for the part was French film star Alain Delon, but he was forced to pull out of the part. To had long admired Delon's portrayals of gangsters and criminals in his collaborations with Jean-Pierre Melville, in particular *Le Samurai* (1967) and *Le Cercle rouge* (1970). Indeed, this is reflected in the name of Hallyday's character, Costello, which was the surname used for Delon's role in the former film. The choice of costume for Hallyday also has echoes of Delon as he sports a black overcoat and trilby hat, white shirt and black tie, and sunglasses creating a classic gangster look. This choice seems to blur the boundaries between Hallyday's star image – he is often seen in black, often leather, recalling his rock 'n' roll bad boy image – and that of Delon's gangsters. The lateness of his acquiring the role further suggests the possibility of a blurring of the two images.

However, when the film was released, critics seemed to warm to Hallyday's taciturn performance suggesting that he was an apt replacement for Delon. Kirk

Honeycutt (2009) stated that 'with his long, deeply etched face, lanky figure in dark suit and tie, sometimes accessorized with an overcoat and black hat, and slow, steady gate [sic], Hallyday perfectly fits the story's concept: A soft-spoken, deadly stranger in a foreign land who seeks the help of local assassins to take his revenge', whilst Roger Ebert (2010), who saw Hallyday as a 'French combination of Elvis Presley and Charles Bronson', said the performer 'could have been the first choice: He is tall, weathered, grim and taciturn'.

To's use of Hallyday's image in *Vengeance* is very different to how it informed *The Specialists* and *L'homme du train*. His costume in To's film reflects the director's evocation of Delon/Melville rather than the rocker Hallyday persona utilised by both Corbucci and Leconte. This reflects the complex potential for fluidness in Hallyday's persona. As with Yves Montand, his career had lasted so long that it was, certainly by the 2000s, possible to see a variety of moments within it that are encapsulated by differing, if crucially linked, star personas. This was very different to the more fixed personas of the Yé-Yé stars whose moment in the limelight was much shorter. Therefore, whilst both *L'homme du train* and *Vengeance* offered different takes on Hallyday, they both begin close enough to the core black clad, rock 'n' roll rebel aspects of his image to work effectively. Ultimately, whether it is a popular chanson singer like Yves Montand, a 1960s pop star such as Chantel Goya or a rock 'n' roller like Johnny Hallyday, the success of a French popular music star on film is often most apparent when the vehicle they appear in acknowledges an audience's ability to read their star persona across a variety of different media.

References

Austin, Guy (2003), *Stars in Modern French Cinema*, London: Arnold.
Barton Palmer, R. (2010), 'Introduction', in R. Barton Palmer (ed.), *Larger Than Life: Film Stars in the 1950s*, 1–17, Ithaca: Rutgers University Press.
Briggs, Jonathyne (2015), *Sounds French: Globalization, Cultural Communities, & Pop Music, 1958–1980*, Oxford: Oxford University Press.
Deluxe, Jean-Emmanuel (2013), *Yé-Yé Girls of 60s French Pop*, Port Townsend: Feral House.
Ebert, Roger (2010), '*Macbeth* meets *Memento* in Hong Kong', *RogerEbert.com*. Available online: https://www.rogerebert.com/reviews/vengeance-2010.

Honeycutt, Kirk (2009), 'Vengeance – Film Review', *Hollywood Reporter*, 17 May. Available online: https://www.hollywoodreporter.com/movies/movie-reviews/vengeance-film-review-93168/. Accessed 27 January 2021.

Looseley, David L. (2003), *Popular Music in Contemporary France: Authenticity, Politics, Debate*, Oxford: Berg.

Looseley, David L. (2005), 'Fabricating Johnny French popular music and national culture', *French Cultural Studies*, 16 (2): 191–203.

Looseley, David L. (2018), '"Une passion française": The mourning of Johnny Hallyday', *French Cultural Studies*, 29 (4): 378–88.

Melehy, Hassan (2018), 'Godard Gets the Blues: Movies, Music, and Baraka', *Esprit Créateur*, 58 (4): 149–67.

Mitchell, Elvis (2003), 'Take a Spaghetti Western, Add French Dressing', in *The New York Times*, 9 May. Available online: https://www.nytimes.com/2003/05/09/movies/film-review-take-a-spaghetti-western-add-french-dressing.html. Accessed 27 January 2021.

Montand, Yves, Hervé Hamon, and Patrick Rotman (1992), *You See I Haven't Forgotten*, London: Chatto and Windus.

Moores, Pamela M. (1991), 'Celebrities in Politics: Simone Signoret and Yves Montand', in John Gaffney and Eva Kolinsky (eds), *Political Culture in France and Germany: A Contemporary Perspective*, 130–54, London: Routledge.

Taylor, Lisa (2004), 'Baby I'm a Star: Towards a Political Economy of the Actor Formally Known as Prince', in A. Willis (ed.), *Film Stars: Hollywood and Beyond*, 158–73, Manchester: Manchester University Press.

Filmography

And God Created Woman (Et Dieu ... créa la femme) (1956), [Film] Dir. Roger Vadim, France: Iéna Productions.

Château en Suède (Nutty, Naughty Château) (1963), [Film] Dir. Roger Vadim, France/Italy: Les Films Corona/Euro International Film.

Conseil de famille (1985), [Film] Dir. Costa-Gavras, France: K. G. Productions.

Desperately Seeking Susan (1985), [Film] Dir. Susan Seidelman, USA: Orion Pictures.

Détective (1985), [Film] Dir. Jean-Luc Godard, France: JLG Films.

D'où viens-tu Johnny? (Where Are You from, Johnny?) (1963), [Film] Dir. Noël Howard, France: Hoche Productions.

Étoile sans lumière (Star Without Light) (1946), [Film] Dir. Marcel Blistène, France: Société Universelle de Films.

Goodbye Again (1961), [Film] Dir. Anatole Litvak, France/USA: Argus Film/Mercury Films.

La grande strada azzurra (The Wide Blue Road) (1957), [Film] Dir. Gillo Pontecorvo, Italy: G. E. S. I. Cinematografica.
La guerre est finie (The War is Over) (1965), [Film] Dir. Alain Renais, France: Europa Film.
L'avenu (The Confession) (1970), [Film] Dir. Costa-Gavras, France: Les Films Corona.
Le Cercle rouge (The Red Circle) (1970), [Film] Dir. Jean-Pierre Melville, France: Comacico.
L'homme du train (The Man on the Train) (2002), [Film] Dir. Patrice Leconte, France: Ciné B.
Le Joli Mai (The Lovely Month of May) (1963), [Film] Dir. Chris Marker, France: Sofracima.
Le Samurai (1967), [Film] Dir. Jean-Pierre Melville, France: Compagnie Industrielle et Commerciale Cinématographique.
Le Voleur De Tibidabo (The Thief of Tibidabo) (1964), [Film] Dir. Maurice Ronet, France/Spain: Les Nouvelles Editions/Jet Films.
Les Portes de la nuit (Gates of the Night) (1946), [Film] Dir. Marcel Carné, France: Société Nouvelle Pathé Cinéma.
Let's Make Love (1960), [Film] Dir. George Cuckor, USA: Jerry Wald Productions.
The Man Who Fell to Earth (1976), Nicolas Roeg, UK: British Lion Film Corporation.
Masculin-Feminin (1966), [Film] Dir. Jean-Luc Godard, France: Anouchka Films.
My Geisha (1962), [Film] Dir. Jack Cardiff, USA: Paramount Pictures.
On a Clear Day You Can See Forever (1970), [Film] Dir. Vicente Minnelli, USA: Paramount Pictures.
Paris chante toujours (Paris Still Sings) (1951), [Film] Dir. Pierre Montazel, France: Courts et Longs Métrages.
Paris est toujours Paris (Paris is Always Paris) (1951), [Film] Dir. Luciano Emmer, France: Omnium International du Film.
Pierrot Le Fou (1965), [Film] Dir. Jean-Luc Godard, France: Films Georges de Beauregard.
Saluti e baci (1953), [Film] Dir. Maurice Labro and Giorgio Simonelli, Italy: Athena Cinematografica.
Souvenirs perdus (Lost Souvenirs) (1950), [Film] Dir. Christian-Jaque, France: Gray-Film.
The Specialists (1969), [Film] Dir. Sergio Corbucci, Italy: Adelphia Compagnia Cinematografica
The Wild One (1953), [Film] Dir. Laslo Benedek, USA: Stanley Kramer Productions.
Unominie e lupi (The Wolves) (1956), [Film] Dir. Giuseppe De Santis, Italy/France: Titanus/Société Générale de Cinématographie.
Vengeance (Fuk sau) (2009), [Film] Dir. Johnnie To, Hong Kong: Milky Way Image.
What's New Pussycat? (1965), [Film] Dir. Clive Donner, USA: Famous Artists Productions.
Z (1969), [Film] Dir. Costa-Gavras, France: Valoria Films.

7

Adam Ant, John Lydon and Jordan: Punk stars on film

Rachel Hayward

> *No subculture has sought with more grim determination than the punks to detach itself from ... normalized forms, nor to bring down upon itself such vehement disapproval.*
>
> – Hebdige ([1979] 1998, 19)

The notion of a punk 'star' is somewhat antithetical, but for the purposes of this discussion will be used to signify international recognition for music; renown in terms of (anti-)fashion; and notoriety for punk acts. Adam Ant, John Lydon and Jordan had intertwined lives and careers in the 1970s; they were all influential icons of the punk experience, and they emerged from the punk scene in different ways. Each acted in films at different points in their careers, and this chapter explores the relationships between their acting roles and their punk and post-punk identities.

Jordan: Original punk star on film

With her distinctive rubberwear clothing and make-up, which she defined as Mondrian-inspired, self-described 'living work of art' (Mooney and Unsworth 2019, 317) Jordan is one of the most recognisable icons of British punk. She performed with the Ants, whom she also managed in the early days of their career, and was an essential part of the McLaren-managed anarchy surrounding early Sex Pistols gigs. As a Bowie-inspired youth, Jordan, who was born Pamela Rooke in Seaford, East Sussex, experimented with her physical appearance, creating striking outfits and attention-grabbing haircuts from a young age

(Mooney and Unsworth 2019, 30). Her experimentation with self-expression also extended to her name, and before becoming Jordan in summer 1973, she had been Jipper, chosen for its androgyny (Mooney and Unsworth 2019, 57), and for a time considered the moniker Riah, Polari slang for hair (Mooney and Unsworth 2019, 58). Jordan's fiercely individualistic identity would soon be influential in London's punk movement.

Originally a sales assistant in a boutique section of Harrod's where her sartorial experimentation was supported, Jordan became most well known as the face of Westwood and McLaren's King's Road clothes shop during its SEX and Seditionaries eras. The shop became the dark heart of the British Punk scene, and Jordan's role within SEX was more than that of sales assistant. She was a figurehead and a creator, assisting Westwood in making the clothes and simultaneously co-creating an ideology around fashion: 'The wrong person wearing it could bastardize the message, so the clothes couldn't go to just anybody' and 'beauty and style and originality shouldn't just be given away' (Baron 2016, 116). Jordan's punk style recalibrates definitions of beauty and is consonant with York's reading of the subculture in that 'the original punks were the most absolute works of art you ever saw' ([1980] 1983, 44). Importantly for this exploration of punk stardom, Jordan authentically embodied punk in her daily life; hers is not an adopted persona for public benefit. Baron uses photographer Nick Knight to illustrate the impact of Jordan's daily punk styling: 'Fashion was what you saw at gigs, or on the street. In that respect, she was one of the first great models, with her mile of catwalk along the King's Road' (2016, 116). The visibility of Jordan's street fashion, and her taking extremes of fetish-wear to an almost quotidian level, were a key part in her success as an early and enduring punk icon. Her approach to clothing demonstrates the punk aesthetic described by York: 'They're picking up the strangest things and changing the meaning of what they wear' ([1980] 1983, 42–3).

Derek Jarman was immediately smitten with Jordan when he first saw her in the mid-1970s, noting at the time, 'smudged black eye paint, covered with a flaming blonde beehive ... the face that launched a thousand tabloids' (Peake 1999, 242). This chance sighting on a railway platform would lead to an enduring friendship, an influential cinematic partnership, and became a popular anecdote to be reflected on many times by both Jarman and Jordan, although she wasn't aware at the time of the impression she had made (Mooney and Unsworth 2019, 104). Jordan's ideas, style and persona were so enticing to Jarman that he cast her in his first feature *Sebastiane* (1976), directed with Paul Humfress. In the brief moments she appears in the film, Jordan makes a memorable impression for she is dressed in one of her rubber outfits, which Jarman called her 'office clothes' (Mooney and Unsworth 2019, 371), while the rest of the cast are appropriately dressed for ancient Rome. This begins Jordan's extension of her persona into an on-screen version: one that looks very familiar, but with a notable exception.

The majority of Jordan's film work was with Jarman, she bookended his career with *Sebastiane* and a contribution to his final film, *Blue* (1993). In addition, she also played a receptionist in Robina Rose's *Nightshift* (1981), a rarely screened artist film. This work is noteworthy as the director deliberately plays with Jordan's established on-screen image. Here the director strips Jordan of the visual accoutrements of Jordan the punk icon: 'Without your make-up and without the hair standing up, wearing one of my beige dresses. It was a double mask and you were mesmeric' (Mooney and Unsworth 2019, 371).

Jordan's most iconic work is as Amyl Nitrate in *Jubilee* (1978), Jarman's nightmarish vision of 1970s Britain as seen by Elizabeth I via time travel with John Dee. Although not the leader, Amyl is a key player in the band of youths and also acts as a narrator for the audience; Amyl, and by extension Jordan, is our gatekeeper and the amateur documentarian of the current state of the world in the narrative. Jordan is also Jarman's inspiration for the film: he was planning to document the punk Zeitgeist on Super-8, in a similar way to Don Letts' *The Punk Rock Movie* (1978), but he would centre it on Jordan. Jarman's producers saw the financial potential for expanding his idea and suggested a feature (Peake 1999, 245). Jordan had assisted Jarman in his punk education and introduced him to many people in the punk scene ahead of shooting the film; he credits her with bringing both the Slits and Adam Ant to the *Jubilee* cast. Ant had already caught the director's eye when Jarman first saw him the street with the word FUCK carved into his back. Jarman would re-present this visceral moment in *Jubilee*, albeit in a more sanitised yet ironic way with LOVE replacing FUCK and the female characters claiming the action.

Jordan has two iconic vignettes in the film: *Rule Britannia* and *Jordan's Dance*, the latter so significant within Jarman's oeuvre that a stand-alone version is available to be exhibited in gallery installations. Its title is also significant, for it calls upon the audience to merge the identity of Jordan and her on-screen character, Amyl. This segment of the film was shot on Super-8 by Jarman. With both breathtaking beauty and stark brutality, it presents a dream-like vision as Jordan performs an improvised ballet on wasteland while masked naked men watch a bonfire, and the Union flag burns. While Jordan dances, the violence of the scene as experienced through Jarman's lens does not come from the punk herself, but from the environment she finds herself in. Jordan had spent many years training as a dancer and the scene confounds expectations of punk behaviour and punk dance, both of which were more usually understood as aggressive, alienating or inert (Hebdige [1979] 1998, 108–9). The scene also calls into question audience expectations of punk gender identity: Jordan's ballet performance in her handmade tutu plays with codes of femininity in a manner similar to Rose's 'double mask'. We are still within the realms of punk aesthetic in which 'conventional ideas of prettiness were jettisoned along with the traditional lore of cosmetics … make-up for both boys and girls was worn to be seen' (Hebdige [1979] 1998, 107), but the costume, made by Jordan herself, and her improvised movement assert Jordan's autonomy over her own image.

Jubilee can be seen as a punk star vehicle for Jordan – the role of Amyl was written for her – and even with its ensemble cast, Jarman firmly places Jordan as the star of the film, using her image from the *Rule Britannia* segment for its poster. Our punk icon already had a punk wardrobe, so Jordan was the cast member who was not provided with a costume, apart from the boiler suit to match Mad, played by Toyah, when the pair commit their revenge attack on a policeman.

Jubilee's place in punk history has since been reappraised, but it was not generally well received by some of the punks upon its release, and even this pedigree of Jordan and friends could not ensure the film was accepted as representative of the culture. In a public punk act, Westwood printed on a t-shirt a diatribe directed towards Jarman outlining what she saw as *Jubilee*'s flaws. This lengthy message to the director is included in full in Jordan's autobiography and includes comments such as, 'the most boring and therefore disgusting film I had ever seen' and 'as to the parts about the near future there were 2 good lines in it' (Mooney and Unsworth 2019, 125). This criticism was not Westwood's alone, for isolated negativity could be attributed to punk rivalries. Jordan notes how York, who had so astutely written about British subcultures, told Jarman of his feelings about the film and reflected on that with regret: 'I thought he'd got it wrong, he didn't get it and saw punk in this rather elaborate, historical, overworked way' (Mooney and Unsworth 2019, 261). Jarman was himself affected by the reactions, noting, 'For those who expected a punk music film, full of "anarchy" and laughs … it was difficult to swallow. They wanted action not analysis and most of the music lay on the cutting room floor' ([1984] 2010, 164).

Adam Ant: Punk star, pop star, film star?

In 1977 Adam Ant was a young punk singer heavily influenced by his art school studies, film stars and Jordan. He drew particular inspiration from the work of pop artist Allen Jones, being attracted to 'its shock value as well as the aesthetic' (Ant 2008, 75), stating that he 'began dressing in a Jones-inspired way, getting myself black leather trousers made' (2008, 75). It was the excitement of fetish-wear and the clothing that attracted Ant to punk, rather than the nihilism, violence or disavowal of societal structures which formed the wider politics and culture of punk. His initiation into punk music came, as it did for many others, via a Sex Pistols gig, although Ant states that 'there was no blinding flash of realisation like other people claimed' (2008, 79). Born Stuart Goddard, Adam Ant is his chosen name; a persona that came into being following his attempted suicide in 1976: 'I had killed Stuart Goddard. A handful of my mother-in-law's pills ... had done the job' (2008, 8). Ant's periods of mental ill health during his career have often been played out very publicly, and he is committed to destigmatising mental health conditions.

Jubilee was the first on-screen appearance from Ant, and although it features a performance with his newly formed band The Ants, he was disappointed the film did not have a more positive impact on his musical career (Ant 2008, 95). In *Jubilee*, he is Kid, an objectified and somewhat immature musician who is dominated by Little Nell's highly sexualised character, Crabs. As noted, Jarman uses the film to disrupt and challenge gender representation, and Kid is certainly part of this: 'Its amazons make men uncomfortable ... Its men are all victims' (Jarman [1984] 2010, 183). To begin with, Kid is an ingénue, his beauty revealed when Crabs removes his large glasses and declares, 'You're gorgeous!' His naïve innocence will be corrupted by his dealings with omnipotent media mogul, Borgia Ginz, and he is seen narcissistically licking and kissing a television screen whilst watching footage of the Ants' *Plastic Surgery*, yearning most of all, for fame. Kid is an exaggerated version of Ant himself, and as such, his on-screen performance here is the most closely aligned with his burgeoning punk star persona.

After making *Jubilee*, Ant continued to focus on his music, and following the band's 1979 debut album *Dirk Wears White Sox*, and some managerial advice from McLaren, he was set on a new path which would see him evolve from punk star to pop star with the next release. When stardom came to Adam and the Ants, the success was monumental. Ant became 'the first teen idol of the 1980s ... the first to engineer a self-conscious move from margins to mainstream' (Rimmer [1986] 2011). His 1980s image was very different from that of his younger punk days: he embraced the colour, fun and non-confrontational vibrancy of the new pop decade, as well as the opportunities for mass appeal afforded by the music video. Echoing scenes of *Jubilee* in his 1980s pop incarnation, Ant would develop a complex relationship with the media, making decisions on which media invitations to accept based on viewing figures or readership numbers. For example, Ant's 1980s fans were young, and he worked within their frames of reference to further his popularity, appearing on kids TV shows and choosing magazines such as Smash Hits or Look-in for interviews as well as the daily tabloids (Ant 2008, 146).

Ant began a pattern of recreating his own image with a series of meticulously researched and styled characters such as pirate, dandy, warrior, hussar and highwayman, and each new costume became highly anticipated by his fans. Ant produces a cohesive brand for his pop work, with carefully designed outfits, make-up, dances and live revues coalescing to form iconic pop moments for his fans. As part of this closely managed approach, Ant would storyboard the music videos himself as part of his wider vision: 'I'd written the song with the idea of the video in mind, which is probably why both were so successful. With "Prince Charming" I was moving closer to what I thought was my future' (Ant 2008, 165). Videos were treated as mini film productions, enlisting high-profile creative support from stars such as Diana Dors for *Prince Charming*, a video with enduring appeal. Its final montage sees Ant dressed as a range of other stars and some of his own personal favourites: Alice Cooper, Rudolph Valentino, Marlon Brando and Clint Eastwood from the *Dollars Trilogy*. Eastwood was among Ant's film heroes, and the song *Los Rancheros* from The Ants' second album is written about him and is one of the many film references in Ant's song writing.

After *Jubilee* and as his pop star status increased, further screen acting remained an option for Ant: 'Ever since *Jubilee*, producers had been sending me film scripts … Some I read, others I ignored, but the idea that acting would be a part of my future was firmly in my mind' (Ant 2008, 165–6). In early 1981, Jarman offered Ant another film role in his ultimately unrealised film *B-Movie*, but Ant's pop stardom and concern over his representation on screen influenced his decision to turn down the part in a letter to the director: 'I have to complete two world tours in 1981 … Also, I am not too sure about the type of film I want to take part in; if at all. I do not want to meddle or dabble or be considered another "singer cum actor" à la "Breaking Glass/Quadrophenia" … Much love,

Adam'. (Peake 1999, 550). The following year, at the time of recording his solo *Friend or Foe* album, Ant was again drawn to acting and maintained that he did not want to replicate his pop star persona. Recounting a conversation with Terence Stamp, Ant notes, 'I told him that I wanted to get into movies but didn't want to take the kind of parts I was being offered, most of which were parts as a pop star' (Ant 2008, 183). By January 1984, Ant's phenomenal music success was waning, and at this point he 'began to become obsessed with making it as an actor' (Ant 2008, 212). Ant started with a stint in *Entertaining Mr Sloane* at Manchester Royal Exchange Theatre in spring 1985, and as his music career continued to dip throughout the course of 1985 and 1986, his acting work would increase, and he ended up having a five-year hiatus in his musical career. Ant was selective with his roles, focussing on finding the right break to fit his vision.

In July 1985, just days before his Live Aid performance, Ant turned down a cameo on *Miami Vice*, a television show that he found to be 'too trashy' (Ant 2008, 222). Judgements on the quality of the programme aside, *Miami Vice* did have a custom of including celebrities, notably but not exclusively musicians, in acting cameos. Season 2 in 1985, which would have featured Ant had he accepted, included cameos from Gene Simmons, Miles Davis and famously, Phil Collins. Ant's contemporary and fellow punk scene to pop star convert Boy George took up a fun US television guest role, playing himself in the glorious *Cowboy George* episode of *The A Team* in 1986. These types of exposure would not fit the profile Ant was looking to achieve as an actor: he wanted to work in Hollywood. Ant did, however, take a dramatic role in *The Equalizer* as his first television role. The show also made use of cameo appearances, but these were more often guest actors. Working on *The Equalizer* was an immensely positive and formative experience (Ant 2008, 224) and would lead him to seek out further roles: 'By the end of the shoot I could no longer say, hand on heart, that music was my sole love anymore. Now there was something else' (Ant 2008, 224).

When Ant does embark on his film acting career with *Nomads* (1985), pop star vehicles such as Prince's *Purple Rain* (1984) and Madonna's *Desperately Seeking Susan* (1985) were having a significant impact on performers' popularity. Ant's music career had already hit its early 1980s peak, and repackaging the Ant Music of 1981–3 for the big screen would have been too stale for rapidly moving pop tastes. Instead, Ant seemed to be looking towards his Hollywood idols for an on-screen model to follow. With characteristic diligence, Ant approaches his first US film in a similar way to his music videos: researching details, displaying his love of film stars, curating his look and seeking out control of elements of the production beyond merely his own performance. In that respect though, navigating the conventions of a new artform would not be straightforward. He rejected the faux punk outfit selected by the wardrobe team and writes of how he instead assembled the costume for his character, including a duster coat Ant was told had been worn by Steve McQueen in *Tom Horn* (Ant 2008, 215).

Nomads is a psychological thriller featuring Pierce Brosnan in an early career performance and is the debut film from McTiernan who would go on to direct iconic action films including *Die Hard* (1988). Ant is 'Number One', leader of the eponymous nomads, a murderous punk-styled tribe who target anthropologist Pommier (Brosnan). Ant is joined in his punk gang by Mary Woronov who had numerous credits by that point, including in US punk classic *Rock 'n' Roll High School* with the Ramones. The punk gang remain silent and menacing throughout, their punk look designed to fuel fear but also, specifically in the case of Ant, presented in an eroticised way. In an interesting link to his pop star days, Ant's silent performance draws heavily on the on-screen persona of Ant's idol Clint Eastwood. This is a more mature extension to the pop homage seen in his dressing up as the Dollars-era Eastwood character, which we saw in the 1981 'Prince Charming' video. His more serious styling for the film sees Ant adopt Eastwood's mannerisms, such as his squint, and in a key scene of *Nomads* where Pommier first photographs the gang, Ant's positioning, facial expression and prop usage replicate in detail that of Eastwood in *For a Few Dollars More* (1965). In seeking to be a serious Hollywood actor, Ant draws heavily on his idol for his understanding of stardom in his first film role.

Although for Ant *Nomads* served to highlight how difficult breaking into Hollywood would be (Ant 2008, 215), he persevered with acting. He also remained committed throughout his film acting career to his assertion to not play pop stars, though he would take a role as a rock star in an episode of the US television programme *Northern Exposure*. Ant does not have any singing roles on-screen post-*Jubilee*, and only two of his US features are connected with the music industry; in both of these, he takes the role of the nefarious manager figure and not that of the pop star. In *Spellcaster* (1988), Ant is Diablo who orchestrates the schlock horror deaths of teenagers who are in search of fame and fortune. The film is summarised in rare Ant Sight and Sound coverage: 'standard fantasy movie ... camp cameo from Adam Ant as the devil ... and some nice creature effects, but otherwise unremarkable' (Kermode 1991, 60).

Unusually perhaps, for a musician who carefully managed and monetised his career and pop star persona,[1] Ant does not have his own songs featured in any of the scores for films he acts in post-*Jubilee*. In the early 1980s, punk songs were still part of the film/pop culture repertoire as former Sex Pistols Paul Cook and Steve Jones's work on *Ladies and Gentlemen, the Fabulous Stains* (1982) demonstrates. Ant recorded a track for Giorgio Moroder's 1984 re-presentation of Fritz Lang's 1927 classic *Metropolis* but did not contribute other Adam Ant material – punk or pop – to his films' scores. This furthers the notion that he sought to keep the two areas of work separate, not wanting to blend his pop persona with his acting roles. One film comes close to being an exception here. Ant's collaborator Marco Pirroni has a guest guitar appearance on the lead track 'Inseminator' for *Drop Dead Rock* (1995). This is a comedy about an aging British punk rock star, Spazz-O, which sees Ant playing the role of his ruthless manager and features Deborah Harry in one of her lesser-known film roles. Ant wrote and recorded the track *Lamé* for the film, but that song would be used for promotional materials only, not appearing in the final cut.

In a bid to keep working as an actor, Ant appeared in a number of films of varying quality, some with very low budgets; television programmes; and made-for-television films. He worked with fellow post-punk pop musicians Martin Kemp and Grace Jones on *Cyber Bandits* (1995), a tech *noir* derivative of *Blade Runner* (1982) in which he plays a ship crew member alongside Kemp. Kemp has the larger role and goes for an American accent, whereas Ant keeps his original accent as was the case with most of his films. Ant was regularly the British-accented villain in these films, most successfully perhaps as Derek in *World Gone Wild* (1988) in which he leads a gang of murderous teenagers in drought-stricken post-apocalyptic America.

The vampire comedy *Love Bites* (1993) is the film from Ant's body of work that is most reminiscent of his early 1980s pop star persona. Ant plays Zachary Simms, a non-threatening eighteenth-century vampire looking to 'rehumanize' in the 1990s. This similarity to Ant's pop image is not because the character of Zachary replicates one of Ant's various signature looks – dandy, pirate, warrior and so on – but rather because it embodies the essence of fun and light-heartedness that were central to his persona and that are not displayed in the

---

[1] Ant would attempt, but ultimately fail, to copyright one of his carefully constructed make-up configurations https://www.lawgazette.co.uk/news/intellectual-property-law/36663.article (Merchandising Corporation v Harpbond [1983] FSR 32). Accessed 21 January 2021.

various villains that make up a large part of his acting roles. In this film, there is also a key sequence where Ant is dancing at a party; a rare direct link to his own pop star status which brings together the two sides of Ant's career. The film's successful connection to Ant's pop persona could be attributed to Marmorstein's experience of appealing to young audiences. For the *Love Bites* script, he adapted one of his own plays and draws heavily on his work as a writer on the long-running hit US television programme *Dark Shadows*. In *Love Bites*, he applies Ant's talents as a showman and despite having a release that focused on home entertainment, including in the United Kingdom, *Love Bites* gives Ant one of his most memorable screen roles.

Ant's films failed to find traction with UK theatrical distributors, with Wayne Wang's *Slam Dance* (1987) and of course *Jubilee*, being notable exceptions. This, however, is in large part explained by the wider context of 1980s cinemagoing, with UK cinema box office hitting a nadir in 1984. Ant had exposure via UK home entertainment, with ten of his films being released. He was not able to achieve a level of cinematic success that matched his phenomenal chart-topping musical accomplishments of the early 1980s, but he remained true to his desire to carve out an acting career independent of his singing career. He did not transform from pop star to film star, and perhaps the less snappy 'pop star to regularly working actor' is more appropriate here.

Order of Death: Lydon's *Performance*?

In contrast to Ant, Sex Pistols and Public Image Limited (PiL) singer John Lydon has taken very few dramatic film roles. He has acted in just three features, with two of these films, *The Independent* (2000) and *Sons of Norway* (2011), each only having small Lydon cameos. He was offered other roles, such as in the 1980s comedy horror *Critters* (1986), but proved to be very selective in his work: 'I turned down *Critters*, which was a cheap and nasty knock-off version of *Gremlins*. I was really pleased – crisis averted!' (Lydon and Perry 2014, 284). Lydon's first, and most substantial, film acting role is in *Order of Death* (1983) an English language, New York–set psychological thriller from Italian director Roberto Faenza. His character is Leo Smith, a young man with a history of making false criminal confessions who claims to be the 'cop killer' responsible for a recent spate of murders. It is his desire to make this confession that draws Leo Smith to Lieutenant Fred O'Connor, played by Harvey Keitel. O'Connor is one of two corrupt policemen who jointly own a flat paid for with money from their illegal activities. This domestic set-up is a symbolic indicator of a clandestine relationship between the two policemen – a relationship that is violently disrupted by Smith's presence. O'Connor imprisons Smith in the bathroom of the flat following his confession of being the killer, initially keeping him bound and gagged in the bathtub.

The source material for *Order of Death* is a 1976 novel by British writer Hugh Fleetwood who also worked on the final draft of the film script and was present during the shoot, striking up a friendship with Lydon during the production. The novel *The Order of Death* (Fleetwood [1976] 2013) is used here as a comparison text as it offers insights into Faenza's decision-making during the production of the film. Very few details are altered in the adaptation of the novel, but those elements that are changed tend to be related to the casting of Lydon, and often, but not exclusively, with the purpose of magnifying his punk identity, in turn creating a more complex character for the audience to decipher.

The narrative of *Order of Death* revolves around questions of identity and characters swapping roles; on the surface that is between criminal and policeman, but also the roles assumed within the male relationships, and the male/female ones. As an additional layer of blurring identity, the casting of an established star plays with the audience's relationship to the film, as the star persona is likely to be conflated with the on-screen character. I agree with Prothero that this is to the film's advantage: 'What plagues the audience until the very last moment is how seriously to take Smith. Is he really the homicidal anarchist he claims, or merely a whining, over-indulged poseur? In other words, much the same question that hung over Lydon's head' (1999, 62). Faenza is complicit in this merging, inviting Sex Pistols or PiL fans to link Lydon the individual and Smith the character through the type of bag Smith uses – an Arsenal Football Club holdall – a team so dear to Lydon that he writes a whole chapter about supporting them in his 2014 autobiography. This detail, also noted by Prothero (1999, 62), could be expected to be recognised by many Lydon fans, but for audiences who don't spot the reference, it could simply mark the character as having connections with English football. But crucially for Faenza, the connection between star and character works for both punk fans and for people outside the subculture who would have a strong understanding of Lydon's star persona, perhaps through the filter of British tabloids, and I am herein focussing on Lydon's punk star persona rather than Lydon the individual. As Johnny Rotten he was notorious for his snarling vocals; for spitting; for his fixed stare; for his aloof mannerism with press and interviewers; for goading his audience, 'clap you fuckers' (Ingham 1993, 241); and for his aggressive and unnatural performance style based, in part, on Sir Laurence Olivier's Richard III (Mooney and Unsworth 2019, 125). So reviled were the Sex Pistols that they toured under false band names such as S.P.O.T.S, Sex Pistols on Tour Secretly (Lydon and Perry 2014, 167). All of these well-publicised traits imbued the Rotten–Lydon persona with an enduring sense of volatile danger. His international fame with the Sex Pistols and position as a de facto figurehead for the UK punk scene make Lydon an interesting film casting case study.[2]

There are two functions of punk identity within the film: firstly, in generic terms, as a visual style, punk is a synecdochic representation of danger and a symbol of deviance; secondly, as a star with an identity inextricably linked to punk, Lydon brings specific significance to the role of Leo Smith.

We are given insight into Smith's psychology when O'Connor searches Smith's room at his grandmother's house. O'Connor does so with the aim of protecting himself by locating and removing evidence that could incriminate him in a future investigation. As he scans the bedroom, we see posters in a typical punk style: in one, a naked man wearing a gas mask, a stark and sexualised example of punk appropriation of war objects; and in another, a cut-out of Lydon's (Smith's) head stuck on a naked male body that has been shot through with arrows. This imagery of pierced flesh which Smith has personalised draws on references to iconography of the Christian Saint Sebastian and the sadomasochistic homoeroticism this has come to represent. Film audiences may also recall the final scenes of Jarman's *Sebastiane*, with both sets of allusions serving to reinforce the information from Smith's grandmother that young Leo is a masochist. This interplay with punk imagery is an important marker to the audience, encouraging us to continue making those connections during the film. There is also a practical element to this technique, for the visual economy of the film-making replaces Smith's 'repulsive' first-person pornographic stories which O'Connor finds in the source novel (Fleetwood [1976] 2013, 98) as a signifier of deviance. The visual images indicate Smith's position as an outsider to be feared. Similarly, when a nervous

---

[2] It is worth noting here that overly symbolic readings of the film's listing of Lydon as 'John Lydon', using his birth name, and not 'Johnny Rotten', are to be avoided: 'After a drawn-out legal case against Malcolm McLaren, 1986 rightfully saw John reclaim the name "Rotten" and win a deal which gave control of the Sex Pistols assets back to the band themselves' (http://www.johnlydon.com/biography/) (accessed 7 September 2022).

O'Connor travels on public transport, it is a punk-styled woman who most fuels his fears and paranoia.

Leo Smith is not specified as being a musician, nor part of any counterculture in the source novel, and indeed in the film, Faenza does not identify Smith as a musician and only elements of his clothing could be labelled punk. To focus on the plot or costume specifics, however, would be oversimplifying the potential impact of star casting. Faenza's choice of a punk icon as Smith offers a sense of lingering fear, an element of doubt and ambiguity of character. In a similar casting choice, Don Letts, Joe Strummer, Mick Jones and Paul Simonon are given fleeting seconds-long cameos playing the Street Scum in Scorsese's *The King of Comedy* (1982). Members of the public, and occasionally punks, would attack Johnny Rotten, unable to disassociate the stage persona from the private persona. Talking about himself, Lydon says, 'Am I a walking contradiction? … Oh yes, I'm not' (Lydon, Zimmerman and Zimmerman 1994, 309).

Lydon's international profile and reputation serve to bring a level of media and fan attention to the film, feeding into an economic interpretation of cinematic stardom. Writing about the casting of the film, Fleetwood notes that drama student Mark Rylance was lined up for the role of Leo, but 'Faenza's view was that we had to have "a name"' ([1976] 2013, 'Introduction'). Lydon takes this casting point further, detailing that a musician was specifically required: 'Bonnie [Timmermann], a casting agent, was looking for an actor for Italian director Roberto Faenza. He wanted a young Englishman, preferably a rock singer, for the role of Leo Smith in *Order of Death*. She had contacted Sting, and Elvis Costello. Both too busy' (Zerbib [1983] 1993, 606). Prior to taking on the role of Leo Smith, Lydon had not acted before, though in 1978, after the Sex Pistols had split up, he auditioned for the role of Jimmy in *Quadrophenia* (1979), which eventually went to Phil Daniels. Lydon says 'I'd have needed some coaching … as to how a film was put together at that point, and I just wasn't prepared to listen to anyone about anything' (Lydon and Perry 2014, 229–30). It can be assumed that five years later Lydon was ready for the acting challenge of *Order of Death*. 'The casting agent rang me up and said: there's a part. I went there and I thought it would be a good laugh. Then I read the part and thought, ah ha! I'd better take this one seriously!' (Zerbib [1983] 1993, 599*)*.

It was not usual practice for Faenza to cast musicians or singers, and his casting preference was for established television or film actors. His comments on casting Lydon are reported in *The Face*: ' "of course I'd heard about the Sex Pistols," says Faenza. "But I liked his personality very much. And his face …

John has a great face"' (Zerbib [1983] 1993, 607). The casting of singer Lydon in his first acting role is significant, and here it would be especially valuable to take wider pop culture relations with cinema into account. Faenza's film regularly elicits comparisons to the 1970 Mick Jagger star vehicle, *Performance* (Cammell, Roeg), with Lydon and Perry stating that there was 'clearly meant to be a *Performance* thing of role reversal going on in the film' (2014, 282). This is in part due to the similarities in the identity swap thematic of the two films but also with the use of high-profile rock singers in debut roles, something that was particularly important in *Performance*, with Jagger essentially playing a version of his own pop star persona. *Performance* was a significant cultural phenomenon, which, in large part through the use of its star casting, captured the psychedelic and sexual excesses of the swinging sixties. It can be posited that through a similar star deployment strategy, Faenza is attempting to capitalise on the star effect of the earlier film.

Faenza directly references *Performance* by replicating Jagger's tailored look and slicked back hair from the iconic *Memo from Turner* song sequence within *Performance* when Lydon dresses up as Smith's grandfather. The reference, if noticed, takes the viewer out of the filmic world and into intertextual references. It serves to acknowledge to the viewer the similarities in casting a star in the two films, and it is fun for the punk-minded viewer that Lydon as Smith is dressing as Smith's grandfather who happens to be styled on Jagger. The Rolling Stones and their counterparts were for punks emblematic of 'old guard stars more motivated by making money than making music' (Coon 1993, 192).

While there are similarities between the two films, crucially, *Order of Death* differs in the use of its star and is not presented as a John Lydon star vehicle. Notably, there is no musical section that would correspond to the *Memo from Turner* sequence, with its song that was released as a solo track by Mick Jagger, nor is there involvement in the film from Lydon or PiL in a musical sense. Faenza enlists Ennio Morricone to compose the score. The film has striking aural motifs, most notably the diegetic and non-diegetic use of the song *Tchaikovski's Destruction*, but music does not occupy the same role in *Order of Death* as it does in *Performance*. In his autobiography, Lydon recounts the production team's reaction to the work PiL offered up for the *Order of Death* score: 'They were wary that Johnny Rotten and his band would take control of the film if it went too far and none of our music was used in the end' (2014, 284–5). He continues by saying in his usual tongue-in-cheek sardonic manner, 'They didn't want an upstart like me who can't act stealing the scenario' (2014, 285).

Lydon's lack of acting experience results in an unpolished interpretation of Smith, which in Sight and Sound was described, rather ambiguously, as 'a studied non-performance' ('On Now' 1983, 76). The rough-hewn nature of Lydon's on-screen presence works for the character, and in the early scenes of the film, he presents a twitchy performance that suits Smith so well. His voice is recognisably Lydon's, with his idiosyncratic cadence coming through at points of the performance. His British accent, which is a large part of his star persona, was written into the narrative of the film with some simple dialogue:

O'Connor:	You British?
Smith:	I'm as American you are
O'Connor:	Don't give me any shit.
Smith:	I was just brought up in England

Prothero frames Lydon's acting as 'that kind of classic rock star performance which entails the occasionally clumsy importation of on-stage traits' (Prothero 1999, 62) and notes the positive impact on the film this can have: 'Lydon manages to up the tension by leaving us unsure as to whether its Smith or the man who plays him who has the penchant for amateur dramatics' (Prothero 1999, 62).

With examination of the source novel, Lydon's Rottenesque delivery of the dialogue can be read as less accidental than Prothero's reading. Lydon's vocal delivery in the film matches the description in the source material, with Fleetwood describing how Smith 'whispered in his flat voice, "Have you killed him?"' ([1976] 2013, 107). As Smith and O'Connor's dynamic switches in the second half of the film, Lydon's voice and movement become more assured. This switch is symbolised in a key sequence of Lydon dancing light-heartedly down the hallway of the flat while wearing a bathrobe which had been previously worn by O'Connor's flatmate, now deceased. In the later sections of the film, Lydon commands his performer's vocal dexterity with flashes of rage as he shouts, 'By going you've made her suspicious', and by employing, albeit sparingly, a menacing sing-song voice with characteristic Johnny Rotten intonation.

The physical nature of Lydon's performance is noteworthy, and sees Faenza drawing on the punk star's persona. Lydon fans are rewarded in the film with instances of the singer's intense stare, for example, when Smith and O'Connor come face-to-face for the first time, or when Smith interrogates O'Connor and Lydon's face is half in shadow and half lit by an Anglepoise lamp. He is often seen semi-naked and tied up, but also when clothed in a dressing gown, arms crossed around his body, the costume mimics the straitjacket bondage wear of his punk days. Perhaps this also serves a practical purpose of giving the performer who is used to working with a microphone something to occupy his hands. The singer's physique is contrasted with Keitel's, and here the punk body is presented as sickly and uncared for, which corresponds with Fleetwood's original text: 'The boy naked was even more weak and thin than he had seemed dressed' ([1976] 2013, 61). This is in direct contrast with the model-like posing of the alluring yet threatening beauty of Ant's punk styling in *Nomads*.

For all the noted successes, Lydon's portrayal of Smith does have limitations, and this could have influenced Faenza's decisions with the concluding scenes of the film. Towards the end of the novel, Smith has an extensive elucidatory monologue, but this is omitted from the film. Perhaps this is indicative of Lydon's ability to perform such a lengthy text. However, despite Faenza's casting of a 'name' for the role of Smith, Keitel's elevated status within Hollywood firmly places him as the film's star. It is, however, Lydon's face reflected in the window of the flat that remains on screen as the film's credits play out, with his iconic stare looking back at his audience throughout.

Fleetwood comments that Lydon was 'extremely nice and intelligent', 'wonderfully professional', 'on set at 8am and always knew his lines' ([1976] 2013, 'Introduction'), so it seems that the punk star was ready for the new challenge of acting. However, *Order of Death* did not spark a completely new career direction for Lydon, for he struggled with the processes of film-making: 'I couldn't accept that the film, as it would be seen in cinemas, was uncontrollable by me. What ends up on the cutting room floor could be my best bits ... I have to be involved in all of it' (Lydon and Perry 2014, 284). It would be a further seventeen years before Lydon would appear in a film again.

Ahead of its UK release in November 1983, Lydon took part in the promotion for *Order of Death* and was as direct and obstreperous as ever with the UK media, using the expected Lydon tropes of communication, as these extracted comments from an interview for *Thames at Six* demonstrate:

Rainbow: It was a very violent book, and it's a very violent film. What was in it that appealed you then?
Lydon: Guilt, greed, confusion, just humanity. Just average people, I suppose.
Rainbow: The transition from being a punk rock singer to a film actor, was that an easy one for you?
Lydon: same thing innit?

...
Rainbow: Are you going to make more films?
Lydon: Probably, I hope so, decent ones. All violent.
Rainbow: Is that what makes a decent film then?
Lydon: Well, that'll do for me. Alright, cheers. [he walks off] I can't be bothered.

As Fleetwood concluded, 'when there was an audience around him he would put on more of an act, like all of us, perhaps' ([1976] 2013, 'Introduction').

The punk persona, whether performed or authentic, is so visible and often divisive in its deliberate unlikability, that mass stardom itself becomes problematised. The three punk stars' on-screen careers have each played out very differently, with Ant, Jordan and Lydon enjoying varying degrees of success. Jordan did not seek a long-term career in stage or screen performance, but she does note, 'I enjoyed all my dalliances with film and theatre because they were so unconventional' (Mooney and Unsworth 2019, 373). Jordan's transition from punk figurehead to enduring icon on film is arguably the most successful of the three examples explored. This is in large part due to her on-screen performance aligning closely with her punk persona and her striking appearance, as well as the increased appreciation for Jarman's work. The timing of *Jubilee*'s production within the UK's core punk period sets apart Jordan's acting career from the later work of Lydon and that of Ant in the US. Here, both youth and fidelity to punk also come into play regarding successful switching from punk star to film star. At this time, punk performers had not become stale, as the 1960s rock icons had been to 1970s British youth. British punks were not out of reach from their fans or fellow punks, so Jordan's authenticity, as previously described, translates well on-screen for her portrayal of Amyl.

> The punk ethos shook up the UK music scene, giving voice to musicians with varying talent levels:
>
> Everything changed, quite suddenly, when punk kicked off ... this hitherto unknown, scruffy, xeroxed *unofficial* lot were storming our office and our awareness. It was a proper counterculture in action, injecting unpredictable fizz into a stale scene. Punk was music for and by outsiders (emphasis in original). (Goldman 2019, 6)

The transition to film star is more complex, and not only because a higher degree of talent is required. There is an inherent tension between the pop punk do-it-yourself approach – which Jarman was working within for *Jubilee* – and the stricter requirements of more mainstream film stardom, which Ant was seeking when looking to establish his US acting career. With *Order of Death*, Lydon was also working within established US star structures, albeit in an Italian production. In this film, his star status is deployed by Faenza as part of the film's casting strategy.

Regardless of year or country of production, the most engaging film work from these three punk icons is seen when they either confirm or confound audience expectations of their pop culture personae. Such engagement with their star status can be seen as crucial. The middle ground of forging a new career path and discarding both a punk and pop identity, as attempted by Ant, proved to be a challenging tactic.

References

Ant, Adam (2008), *Stand & Deliver*, London: Pan Books.
Baron, Katie (2016), *Fashion + Music: Creatives Shaping Pop Culture*, London: Laurence King Publishing Ltd.
Coon, Caroline (1993), 'Rebels Against the System', in C. Heylin (ed.), *The Penguin Book of Rock Writing*, 190–8, London: Penguin.
Fleetwood, Hugh ([1976] 2013), *The Order of Death*, London: Faber and Faber Ltd.
Goldman, Vivien (2019), *Revenge of the She Punks*, Austin: University of Texas Press.
Hebdige, Dick ([1979] 1998), *Subculture: The Meaning of Style*, London: Routledge.
Ingham, Jonh [sic] (1993), 'The Sex Pistols (are four months old)', in Clinton Heylin (ed.), *The Penguin Book of Rock Writing*, 239–45, London: Penguin.
Jarman, Derek ([1984] 2010), *Dancing Ledge*, Minneapolis: University of Minnesota Press.
Kermode, Mark (1991), 'Spellcaster', *Sight and Sound*, 1 (8): 60.
Lydon, John with Andrew Perry (2014), *Anger Is an Energy*, London: Simon & Schuster.
Lydon, John with Keith Zimmerman and Kent Zimmerman (1994), *Rotten: No Irish, No Blacks, No Dogs*, London: Plexus Publishing Limited.
Mooney, Jordan with Cathi Unsworth (2019), *Defying Gravity. Jordan's Story*, London: Omnibus Press.
'On Now' (1983), *Sight and Sound Winter 1983/84*, 53 (1): 76.
Peake, Tony (1999), *Derek Jarman*, London: Little, Brown and Company.
Prothero, David (1999), 'Copkiller', in Jack Hunter (ed.), *Harvey Keitel Movie Top Ten*, 57–66, London: Creation Books.
Rimmer, Dave ([1986] 2011), *Like Punk Never Happened: Culture Club and the New Pop*, London: Faber and Faber Ltd.

York, Peter ([1980] 1983), *Style Wars*, London: Sidgwick and Jackson Ltd.
Zerbib, Patrick ([1983] 1993), 'Situation Vacant', in Clinton Heylin (ed.), *The Penguin Book of Rock Writing*, 599–611, London: Penguin.

Filmography

Blade Runner (1982), [Film] Dir. Ridley Scott, USA: The Ladd Company, Shaw Bros., Warner Bros.
Blue (1993), [Film] Dir. Derek Jarman, UK: Channel 4 Television Corporation, Arts Council of Great Britain, Opal, BBC Radio 3.
Critters (1986), [Film] Dir. Stephen Herek, USA: New Line Cinema, Sho Films, Smart Egg Pictures.
Cyber Bandits (1995), [Film] Dir. Erik Fleming, USA: Cyberfilms Inc., IRS Media, Lumière Pictures.
Desperately Seeking Susan (1985), [Film] Dir. Susan Seidelman, USA: Orion Pictures.
Die Hard (1988), [Film] Dir. John McTiernan, USA: 20th Century Fox.
Drop Dead Rock (1995), [Film] Dir. Adam Dubin, USA: Spazz-O Productions.
For a Few Dollars More/Per Qualche Dollaro in più (1965), [Film] Dir. Sergio Leone, Italy, Spain, West Germany: Produzioni Europee Associate, Arturo González Producciones Cinematográficas, Constantin Film Munich.
Jubilee (1978), [Film] Dir. Derek Jarman, UK: Megalovision.
Ladies and Gentlemen, the Fabulous Stains (1982), [Film] Dir. Lou Adler, USA: Paramount Pictures.
Love Bites (1993), [Film] Dir. Malcolm Marmorstein, USA: Waymar Production.
Nightshift (1981), [Film] Dir. Robina Rose, UK: Robina Rose.
Nomads (1986), [Film] Dir. John McTiernan, USA: Cinema VII.
Order of Death [alternative titles *l'assassino dei poliziotti, Copkiller, Corrupt*] (1983), [Film] Dir. Roberto Faenza, Italy: Aura Film, Cooperativa Jean Vigo, RAI Radiotelevisione Italiana.
Performance (1970), [Film] Dirs Donald Cammell and Nic Roeg, UK: Goodtimes Enterprises.
Purple Rain (1984), [Film] Dir. Albert Magnoli, USA: Warner Bros., Purple Films.
Quadrophenia (1979), [Film] Dir. Franc Roddam, UK: The Who Films, Polytel.
Rock 'n' Roll High School (1979), [Film] Dir. Allan Arkush, USA: New World Pictures.
Sebastiane (1976), [Film] Dirs Paul Humfress and Derek Jarman, UK: Megalovision, Cinegate, Disctac.
Slam Dance (1987), [Film] Dir. Wayne Wang, UK, USA: Zenith Entertainment, Island Pictures, Sho Films.
Sons of Norway/Sønner av Norge (2011), [Film] Dir. Jens Lien, Norway, Sweden, Denmark, France: Friland, Götafilm, Nimbus Film Productions, Les Films d'Antoine.

Spellcaster (1988), [Film] Dir. Rafal Zielinski, UK, USA: Empire Pictures, Taryn Productions Inc.
The Independent (2000), [Film] Dir. Stephen Kessler, USA: United Lotus Group.
The King of Comedy (1982), [Film] Dir. Martin Scorsese, USA: Embassy International Pictures.
The Punk Rock Movie (1978), [Film] Dir. Don Letts, UK: Notting Hill, Punk Rock Films.
World Gone Wild (1988), [Film] Dir. Lee H. Katzin, USA: Apollo Pictures.

Television

Dark Shadows (1966–1971), [TV programme] ABC.
Miami Vice (1984–1989), [TV programme] NBC.
Northern Exposure. Heroes (1992), [TV programme] CBS, October.
The A Team. Cowboy George (1986), [TV programme] NBC, February.
The Equalizer. The Lock Box (1985), [TV programme] CBS, October.
Thames at Six (1983), [TV programme] Thames ITV, November. Available online: https://www.youtube.com/watch?v=u3X847BTEP8 (accessed 12 January 2021).

8

From the street to the dance floor: Political imaginings of the pop star in popular Indian cinema

Omar Ahmed

Pop stars in Indian cinema have often materialised in the larger-than-life performances of major film stars. Beginning in the early 1960s, it was probably with Shammi Kapoor in the film *Chinatown* (1962), singing *'Baar Baar Dekho'* ('Look Again and Again') with his floppy quiff and wild dancing, where we first saw the omnipresent influence American pop stars like Elvis Presley would have on the vernacular of song and dance in popular Indian cinema. Pop stars have often been part of a wider political discourse, but sometimes they can take on an apolitical public persona, rendering them ineffectual. Zoya Akhtar's *Gully Boy* (2019), a recent success and a cultural phenomenon in India, which charts the rise to fame of a street rapper from the slums of Mumbai, adopts a narrative parallel to that of *Disco Dancer* from 1982, in which an angry street kid grows up to become an unlikely star for a marginalised underclass. Along with *Secret Superstar* (2017), this group of mainstream films, largely contemporary, imagine variations of the pop star through an indefinite political prism. This chapter will explore the ways in which shifting representations of the Indian pop star is a site for negotiating the politics of class (proletarianism), religion (Muslim identity) and gender (women), coming to function as a counter-narrative to the broader contrasting sociopolitical and historical contexts of India in the 1980s and the ongoing rule of mob law, racial hatred and sectarian divide that characterises Modi's India.

The proletarian eroticism of *Disco Dancer*

It is not that class has never existed in India cinema. It has always been there. Ever present. But it has often been rendered invisible in films, particularly the lives of working-class people, dubiously titled the subaltern,[1] and superseded by the oppressive hierarchy of caste. A significant shift in making class far more evident, although momentary, did take place in the late 1970s, much of it accelerated by Parallel Cinema[2] and the steady, open politicisation of Indian cinema. The Angry Young Man, arguably a derivative of the anti-hero trope from films like *Ganga Jumuna* (1961) emerged against the backdrop of an uncertain 1970s political landscape in which radical oppositional forces were repressed through the deployment of state apparatus,[3] machinations that would have a long-term traumatic impact on the psyche of the nation. In his monograph,[4] Indian comedian Anuvab Pal (2011) argues that *Disco Dancer* (1982) essentially reworks *Deewaar* (The Wall 1975), the quintessential Angry Young Man film. *Deewaar* was part of a cycle of films released in the 1970s in which the eponymous figure of Vijay, essayed by Amitabh Bachchan, was reincarnated on multiple occasions as a brazen symbol of anti-establishment rhetoric and proletarian imagining. In *Disco Dancer*, Jimmy's mother has been wronged by society, branded a thief and effectively ostracised to the margins, a wrong that Jimmy is determined to overturn, and which he succeeds in doing, not through violence but music. In the 1980s, the craze of disco-themed soundtracks in Indian cinema was triggered by the success of *Qurbani* (Sacrifice 1980). It was the talented Pakistani singer Nazia Hassan, catapulted to fame with her brother Zoheb, who voiced the hit song '*Aap Jaisa Koi*' (Someone Like You), popular even today with audiences. The soundtrack of *Qurbani*, a fusion of Disco and Hindi music, a creative hybridity that characterised the work of influential composer Biddu 'remains India's first truly international sound in music' (Bhattacharjee and Vittal 2015, 253). Much of the commercial success of *Disco Dancer* was

---

[1] In postcolonial theory, the term 'subaltern' is used to describe the oppressed lower classes, expressly peasants and Dalits.
[2] Parallel Cinema (1969–95) was a radical state-led film alternative to the mainstream that lasted over three decades in India.
[3] In 1975, Prime Minister Indira Gandhi suspended basic rights and democracy, leading to a 21-month period of internal repression and dictatorship that would have a long-term impact on the constitutional make-up of India.
[4] Anuvab Pal's monograph is an irreverent take on the film and formed the basis for his stand-up show *Democracy and Disco Dancing*, which he performed at the Edinburgh Fringe in 2019.

down to the memorable soundtrack by Bappi Lahiri, a Bengali born composer, who would become famous for his eclectic sampling, some of it bordering on outright plagiarism. In fact, the music of *Disco Dancer* was representative of a 'musical practice ... shamelessly promiscuous in its borrowings' (Sen 2008, 88), with music sampling overwhelming the Indian music industry through much of the 1980s and 1990s.

The international success of *Disco Dancer* was unexpected, transcending the limitations of the Hindi language to emerge as a cultural phenomenon in the Soviet Union:

> Disco Dancer became a landmark film in the Soviet Union, comparable to Awaara in its wide appeal there ... the film drew 60.9 million Soviet viewers in 1984, the highest turnout for any film that year. (Rajagopalan 2008, 93)

The enormous success of Raj Kapoor's *Awaara*[5] (The Vagabond 1951) in the 1940s captivated audiences in the Soviet Union and the Eastern Bloc, and the popularity of popular Indian cinema would remain so with Soviet audiences for years to come. Critics in the Soviet Union with high-art cultural tastes derided the escapist trappings of *Disco Dancer*, overlooking how it was the music and dancing that struck a chord with audiences. The euphoria around *Disco Dancer* in the Soviet Union transformed Indian actor Mithun Chakraborty into a legend in the eyes of film audiences who became enamoured by his sensual and tragic performance as Jimmy, the disco king of Bombay. Turn to social media in Russia today and you will find a subculture of memes, supercuts and homages that celebrate *Disco Dancer*, expressly the signature song 'Jimmy Jimmy Jimmy Aaja'; a strong cult following that has only increased exponentially over the years.

Disco Dancer is primarily a critique of stardom, following the rise of a street performer to a major pop star. And while *Disco Dancer* is often dismissed as popular escapism, the cultural significance of disco and its relationship with the latent proletariat political undercurrents are worth discussing further as it is arguably one of the first and few attempts in popular Indian cinema that imagined the figure of the pop star as a political symbol, referencing class and situating Jimmy as a musical proletariat. This calls for a consideration of what disco signified and stood for politically in the 1970s and how Jimmy's body and

---

[5] *Awaara* was one of the first mainstream Indian cinemas to enjoy international commercial success, with audiences abroad, notably in the Soviet Union, and would make Raj Kapoor a major international star in the Soviet Union for many decades.

dancing is open to a political reading in relation to Richard Dyer's discussion of eroticism in his seminal article 'In Defence of Disco' (1990).[6]

Disco (1970–9), a cultural and musical concept and lifestyle, emerged from the American urban night clubs in the 1970s and was a modern fusion of funk, soul, jazz and Motown with a predominantly electronic rhythm and often upbeat lyrics. Tim Lawrence maps the political significance and roots of disco as a safe space for marginalised groups:

> Lacking alternative social outlets, gay men and women of colour, along with new social movement sympathisers, gathered in abandoned lift space … and off-the-beaten-track discotheques … to develop a uniquely affective community that combined sensation and sociality. (2006, 129)

If disco was about escape and community for the marginalised from the wretched gloom of the 1970s, it only arrived in India after we had seen the death of disco in 1979. In this respect, the idea of disco that circulated in popular Indian cinema was largely decorative and devoid of the broader oppositional sociopolitical dimensions of what disco had stood for ideologically in America through much of the 1970s. However, in *Disco Dancer*, the political is a tangible representation, contestably translated through the way in which Jimmy's social and political oppression is visualised repeatedly through the eroticism of song and dance. Oberoi (Om Shivpuri), a derisive property magnate who has wronged Jimmy's mother, forbids his daughter Rita (Kim) from associating with Jimmy because he is from the slums and goes to great lengths to try and sabotage Jimmy's career, including the horrific electrocution of Jimmy's mother, a scared threshold that Oberoi transgresses. Whereas the cultural elite deride Jimmy as abhorrent and cheap, nothing but a street ruffian, song and dance for him becomes a space for resistance, subversion and empowerment. Even when he achieves success, Jimmy holds on to the memories of his days as a street performer, a concrete link to the real. Although Jimmy tries his best to upend the imaginary construction, David Brown (Om Puri), Jimmy's manager who launches his musical career, first sees Jimmy dancing in the streets at night. The dislocated style in which the sequence is edited suggests that neither Jimmy nor David occupy the same space. It is as if David conjures Jimmy from his imagination, reiterating a cultural notion that pop stars are ultimately constructs, unreal and can materialise instantaneously.

---

[6] First published in *Gay Left* magazine, Summer 1979.

What makes Jimmy particularly unconventional and political is the ways in which he uses his body on the dance floor. Much of the discourse on *Disco Dancer* glances over the strong political connotations and history of disco that gets translated through the eroticism of Jimmy's dancing. Perhaps this explains why the film gained such a strong foothold in the consciousness of Soviet audiences because they understood how the erotic can and is political. Writing in 1979, Richard Dyer describes the eroticism on display in disco as a 'whole body eroticism' (1990, 353) and argues that what made disco unique in terms of the erotic was a refusal to deny physicality, something that Dyer reasons popular song often does. Dyer identifies a number of ways in which eroticism is performed and articulated in disco, including 'the willingness to play with rhythm' and 'the range of percussion instruments used and their effect' (1990, 353). Most critically, Dyer posits that all of these features 'restores eroticism to the whole of the body ... and leads to the expressive, sinuous movement of disco dancing' (1990, 353). In the context of *Disco Dancer*, Dyer's reading of disco as erotic is substantial because I don't think up to that point in popular Indian cinema an Indian film actor had danced in such an openly sexual style, and while the eroticism on display in many of the song and dance numbers may have been new to Indian film audiences, it was the norm in disco culture. And in this respect, *Disco Dancer* stays true to the origins and roots of true disco, an idea that is articulated most vehemently in the song and dance sequences.

The first major song and dance sequence in the film, titled '*Ae Oh Aa Zara Mudke*' ('Please turn back'), marks the arrival of Jimmy as a bright new star in the world of Indian pop music, and sees him dressed in all white, gyrating his hips and encircled by enthusiastic spectators. The song is really about Jimmy trying to win over Rita, someone who is sceptical about his unfamiliar talents as a singer. A roaming handheld camera tracks the movements of Jimmy very closely, relaying an intimacy that augments his sexualised dancing, much of which is centred on the signature gesture of the arched back and outstretched arms. Since this is a televised performance, the handheld camerawork is best suited to capturing the spontaneity on display, and in a key moment, Jimmy falls to the ground and begins dancing on his back and feet, creating a chaotic rhythm that mirrors the frenzied beat of the synthesiser. In this particular moment, the eroticism of Jimmy's body is very animalistic, primal even, and as he continues to perform, he does so that everyone around begins to mirror his expressive actions and gestures with a synchronic harmony. While this is the birth of Jimmy the pop star, his overtly sexualised dancing conjectures a heightened physicality that sets the tone for the remainder of the songs that is also open to a queer reading of the pop star in Indian cinema since not only does the erotic complicate normative interpretations of sexuality, but the repeated focus on the body of Jimmy also becomes a symbol of fetishised pleasures. Since disco harbours a political resonance, Jimmy's impasse at the end in the climactic song titled '*Yaad Aa Raha Hai*' ('I am remembering') is representative of a traumatised state. He can't dance any more because the trauma of his mother's dance is too much. It is Rita who sings to Jimmy and coerces him to dance again. Moreover, Jimmy's traumatic state is an overt allegory of the ways in which an underclass is constantly subjugated, whereby they become resigned to an inert political state. What we witness in this climactic song is the transformative power of music and how *Disco Dancer* politicises the figure of the pop star with his erotic physicality – a major political signifier.

Whereas *Disco Dancer* imagines the pop star in popular Indian cinema as a queer proletarian messiah-type figure with erotic overtones that are readily overstated on the dance floor, contemporary films, including *Secret Superstar* and *Gully Boy*, politicise the pop star through an alternate prism of religion and gender, interrelated in some respects, and against a backdrop of Modi's Hindutva, a brand of Hindu nationalism that today shapes the very fabric of Indian culture, society and politics. Both *Secret Superstar* and *Gully Boy* are framed centrally by Muslim protagonists and demonstrate the significance of new media technology and expressly social media in granting anonymity and the limelight to self-made rags-to-riches pop stars.

Gender and Muslimness in *Secret Superstar*

Just like *Disco Dancer*, *Secret Superstar* was also a cultural sensation outside of India, expressly in China, where it broke box office records and reiterated the growing popularity of Indian superstar Aamir Khan with Chinese film audiences. *Secret Superstar* narrates the story of teenage singer-songwriter Insia (Zaira Wasim) who lives in a patriarchal middle-class Muslim family and is subjected to domestic abuse by an overbearing father. When Insia begins uploading songs to YouTube, her videos become a viral sensation, transforming her into an online pop star. *Secret Superstar* brings together two very prescient sociopolitical themes of the present day in India – the repression of women at home and the representation of Muslims. Although *Secret Superstar* does not directly deal with the rise of anti-Muslim sentiments and Islamophobia, the focus on a lower-middle-class Muslim family with a teenage girl at the centre of the narrative is unconventional for popular Indian cinema. Moreover, writer Ajaz Ashraf argues that the choice to set the film in Gujarat carries deeper political connotations and 'nudges the Hindus of Gujarat to reassess their perception of Muslims' (Ashraf 2017). This is significant because the film draws the explicit link to a BJP Hindutva context since Modi was Chief Minister in Gujarat when he oversaw a pogrom that led to the killing of Muslims in 2002. However, this is as far as the film goes in referring to the ongoing persecution of Muslims in India today and which has arguably accelerated under the polarising reign of Modi.

It was Theresa Senft, in 2001, who coined the idea of the 'micro celebrities' as ordinary individuals who use social media to 'create audiences for themselves' (Baym 2012, 289) through self-branding, something which has become ubiquitous with YouTube influencers and the extraordinary reach they have cultivated through their channels and related outlets. In 2015, NME asked the question: 'Are YouTubers the New Pop Stars?' One could argue that when NME posed this question back in 2015, they were in fact behind the curve since YouTubers had already claimed a new audience and digital space that marked them out as micro celebrities with millions of subscribers. In *Secret Superstar*, Insia's transformation into a viral pop star comes about through the liberating force of technology – specifically a laptop, a prop and symbol that carries with it great political weight. Whereas in *Disco Dancer*, Jimmy's pop star status is politicised through the cultural associations of disco, in *Secret Superstar*, it is YouTube that grants Insia an anonymity whereby she can claim a type of personal freedom. When Insia uploads her first video to YouTube, it is her mother who gives her the idea to use the niqab to conceal her identity. The niqab and burqa, symbols of Muslim female identity, have over the years become an increasingly contentious source of cultural debate concerning oppression, identity and gender politics. It could be argued that the image of the niqab as something quite negative, often demonised by the mainstream media, is subverted in this context where it is used creatively and becomes a source of empowerment for Insia.

As Insia records her first video, she gets lost in the moment, and we cut to a dream sequence. Escaping from the misery around her, a fade to black segues into Insia the pop idol on a brightly lit stage singing freely, an imaginary enactment of her desire to participate in reality talent shows on television. In some respects, the absence of the niqab also suggests the refusal to be tied down by identities imposed upon her by tradition, culture and religion. The song titled '*Main Kaun Hoon?*' which directly translates as 'Who Am I?' narrates the anxieties of breaking free from constraints in the hope of realising your dreams – an adolescent longing that underpins a great many traditional pop songs. As the dream sequence ends, the camera swings back round revealing that there is no audience in front of Insia, only a sea of darkness, underlining an uncertainty she feels about her future. At first, Insia is dismayed by the lack of views for her video, but an unexpected interest in her song leads to many users leaving comments of encouragement and appreciation. This culminates in a wide shot in which Insia is framed on the sofa on her laptop while the space around her becomes taken up with comments from YouTube users, a metaphorical translation of the new connection she has forged with an audience and signifying her emergence as a micro celebrity.

While it is in essence new media technology and expressly the laptop that opens up this new world for Insia, it is also important to recognise the role gender and specifically the mother plays in this regard, adopting an interventionist role in the face of patriarchal violence.[7] It is worth turning here to ask to what extent Najma and Insia are representative of the New Woman, a relatively new trend that has emerged with the rise of Indian independent cinema. In her article on 'The New Woman in Bollywood', Nandita Dutta (2018) places a noted emphasis on the significance of the laptop and the threat it poses to the power of the father in the domain of the family and home: 'He commands his daughter to destroy the laptop … ending their temporary access to the world and its potential for desire and freedom'. The destruction of the laptop, 'enabler of dreams' as Dutta describes it, shatters Insia's status as a micro celebrity and curtails her pop star aspirations, reiterating the fragility of technology. Of the films (*English Vinglish*, *Tumhari Sulu*) she looks at, Dutta reasons *Secret Superstar* 'provides the most radical break' because 'Najma decides to break out of the hetero-patriarchal family'. Conversely, Dutta later goes on to argue that the representation of the Muslim woman is flawed since Najma is ultimately 'framed as a backward, uneducated, oppressed figure'. Scholar Maidul Islam is also critical of the film's representation of Muslim women, criticising the use of the burqa, which he says 'is the only

---

[7] If anything, the critical examination of patriarchy comes to stand in for the gradual shift to a broader orthodoxy apparent under Hindutva, but also prevalent in religions including Islam. The representation of the patriarch as an overbearing and violent figure is an archetype not uncommon to the Indian melodrama and I would argue is problematic when it comes to the Muslim male who yet again is framed as not normal, thereby undermining the film's desire to give agency to the Muslim characters.

hindrance that the Muslim woman has to overcome' (Islam 2019, 132) in society while ignoring the wider nexus of social and economic obstacles like 'health, education and employment' (Islam 2019, 132). The question of employment and economic independence is an important one because as Dutta suggests, Najma takes the decision to break free on the basis that Insia 'has risen to fame and will be able to provide for the family'. Since stardom and fame inevitably brings with it money and the opportunity for social mobility, something that Jimmy is able to experience in *Disco Dancer*, the likelihood of Insia emerging as the breadwinner seems pure wish fulfilment in a contemporary reality in which many stateless Muslims in India are some of the poorest citizens and with high rates of unemployment.

In spite of such political oversights, the representation of Insia as an Indian Muslim girl who transcends her social limitations is significant in the landscape of popular Indian cinema since it is an empowering one and rare in many ways. Moreover, the connection with music and Insia's gradual status as a pop star is confirmed in the final sequences when she attends an award ceremony with her mum and is finally recognised for her musical talents. In this respect, technology and YouTube act as a libertarian force that affords Insia instant status as a pop star, an idea that also resonates in *Gully Boy*, the latest entry in the shifting politicisation of the pop star in popular Indian cinema.

Political ambiguities of the Mumbai rap star in *Gully Boy*

Released in 2019, director Zoya Akhtar's[8] *Gully Boy* is the rags to riches story of Murad Ahmed (Ranveer Singh), a young Muslim youth who finds a way out of the slums through the power of rap music. The screenplay is based on the true story of two Mumbai-based MCs, Naezy and Divine, who broke into the Mumbai rap scene in 2014. Unlike *Disco Dancer* and *Secret Superstar* that conjure the pop star as a fictious concept, Murad's character is grounded in the real world and imbued with a greater degree of authenticity. Murad lives in the slums of Dharavi[9] in a cramped shanty house in an extended family and supplements his

---

[8] Zoya Akhtar is one of the few women film-makers working in the Indian film industry who has enjoyed unprecedented critical and commercial success.
[9] Located in the state of Maharashtra, Dharavi is one of the largest slums in the world and home to over one million people.

educational aspirations with a job as a driver chauffeuring around the privileged youth of the Mumbai elite. *Gully Boy* is closer to *Disco Dancer* than *Secret Superstar* since Murad's attempts to escape social and economic deprivation and the connections with hip hop culture and rap music, a double bind, bring with it very strong political connotations. While music for Murad becomes a form of political resistance (the overt affiliations with the subversive and outspoken underground rap scene in Mumbai), his transformation into a rap star is an equivocal political act that on the surface appears to lack any kind of reference to the current Modi regime in India.

It does seem a bit odd that all the way through the film, Murad never questions if his status as a Muslim might be one of the reasons why he is living in the slums. The film codifies Muslims through recognisable stereotypical imagery that has often circulated in popular Indian cinema; Muslimness is merely decorative and not an ideologically substantial subtext. For instance, the subplot of Murad's father, who marries for the second time and perpetrates acts of domestic abuse, bears some similarities with *Secret Superstar*, suggesting that the portrayal of the Muslim patriarch as a dysfunctional, violent figure is perhaps an unavoidable caricature when representing Muslim families on screen. In a 2019 interview[10] with film writer Ankur Pathak, when asked why *Gully Boy* does not address the political realities of India today, director Zoya Akhtar reasoned that that would have made for a completely different film. Sadly, this sounds like the familiar reactionary capitulation and conformity that prevails in the face of Hindutva's right-wing nationalist propaganda machine. The near absence of any kind of overt critique of Modi and the apolitical status of Muslims is particularly complicated by the problematic casting of Alia Bhatt and Ranveer Singh, both of whom were part of an Indian film delegation that met with Modi in 2019, resulting in a shameless narcissistic selfie that merely confirmed the sycophantic political sympathies of the Bollywood elite.

The lengths the film goes to avoid politicising Muslims is not altogether totalising, and contradictions remain. For example, the dire social conditions of Muslims are highly visible in the slum milieu, with the cramped living conditions and lack of jobs mapping a contemporary economic reality, questionably situating Murad as a far greater political construct and symbol of the underclass than he first appears to be. Additionally, Murad's job as a driver reiterates the

---

[10] This candid interview with Zoya Akhtar raises many other questions about the film particularly the 'browning up' of Ranveer Singh for the role of Murad.

menial low-paid frontline jobs many Muslims are forced to take on, while his near invisibility to the Mumbai elite that he chauffeurs around carries with it substantial political symbolism. Cocooned in the car, Murad may as well not exist. In one scene, as he passes by a nightclub, hesitating whether or not to go inside, a bouncer manning the doors gestures to Murad with his hand for him to leave. It is a micro gesture that harbours a refrain of hatred, amplifying Murad's exclusion from mainstream society. The refusal to engage in dialogue with Murad, reminding him of his marginal unimportance, is a particularly revealing ideological gesture that can be interpreted as a rejection that takes place on two levels – first as a Muslim and second as part of a marginalised underclass, both posing a threat to the norms of Modi's India. In terms of the politics of Muslim identity, where this is most clearly delineated is in the character of Safeena (Alia Bhatt), who can be read as a counter-Muslim representation, challenging the stereotype of the submissive Muslim woman (Islam 2019, 129) often perpetuated in popular Indian cinema. Unlike Najma in *Secret Superstar* who is literally imprisoned by her husband's violent and repressive behaviour, Safeena is situated as someone who navigates and negotiates the complicated life of a Muslim girl in Mumbai, wearing the hijab with pride while remaining firmly in control of her identity. The casting of Alia Bhatt, who has taken on unconventional roles in off-centre films while cultivating the star image of a neo-feminist warrior, is critical in this respect.

Music as a form of resistance is encapsulated in Murad's rise to fame as a rap star from the slums of Dharavi. In her discussion of rap music and Black politics, Lakeyta M. Bonnette argues that rap 'music offered a safe space among a marginalised community to assert fears, concerns, attitudes and dissatisfaction' (2015, 84). Moreover, rap has often served as a means of protest, platforming a counter to the mainstream media. Although Jayanti Datta labels the rap of *Gully Boy* as 'Dharavi Rap' (2020, 238), attempting to make a distinction from rap music in America, the performance of the first major song in the film titled '*Meri Gully Mein*'[11] shot in the slums of Dharavi projects Murad (and his partner MC Sher) as an undeniably political entity that inadvertently harks back to the streetwise political rap of the 1980s and arguably reconnects Murad with the latent anti-establishment leanings of Jimmy in *Disco Dancer*. The backdrop of Dharavi[12] in the song is critical to the way we read Murad's representation

---

[11] Based on the original song 'Meri Gully Mein' by MC Divine and Naezy.
[12] The film was partly shot on a set, including this sequence.

as someone who subverts his lowly social and economic status, taking on the persona of 'Gully Boy' to speak for his community in an unfiltered way. The Indian government's ongoing attempts to redevelop Dharavi is something the settlers have resisted, and in this broader context of land rights, displacement and forced slum clearance, the staging of the song in the milieu of Dharavi can be interpreted as a form of political resistance, a retort that the song '*Meri Gully Mein*' heralds, celebrating the streets of Dharavi as resilient and inimitable in the face of globalisation. Jayanti Datta (2020) argues that Mumbai rap is political activism in which critical intervention has seen different rap groups take on caste, gender and environmental issues. However, the political anger about Modi's reign is far less pronounced in Murad and MC Sher's streetwise lyrics, and points to the political compromises popular Indian cinema often has to make in fear of irking the establishment. And in this context, Murad's status as a political rap star is somewhat diluted and disingenuous, reiterating that the imagining of the pop star in popular Indian cinema has often been characterised by political ambiguities.

Shweta 'Sky' Mehta (Kalki Koechlin), a savvy musician who recognises the potential of Murad and MC Sher, takes the lead on shooting the video in Dharavi, and before the filming commences, Sky zips down Murad's adidas tracksuit top so we can see his vest. This gesture of manipulating and controlling the reality of the slums by outsiders, effectively the middle classes of India, demonstrates the ways in which mainstream creative industries exploit new ideas and make them palatable for audiences, which seems to be the case with Murad's rise to fame as a rap star. The approach to '*Meri Gully Mein*' is resolutely self-reflexive, whereby the camera crew are altogether transparent, weaving through the cramped spaces of Dharavi and reminding us that Murad's stardom is merely a construction, a fabrication of reality. As Murad and MC Sher begin to rap into the camera with lines like 'The entire city echoes in my street', the acrobatic freestyling body poppers around them are bathed in a golden light that makes everything appear romantically alluring. However, the lyrics to the song expressing toughness, solidarity and guile are enough to counter the altogether familiar accusations of poverty porn when choosing to shoot in the slums. Damini Kulkarni argues that *Gully Boy* 'is able to represent a spatial imaginary which facilitates – and even encourages – individuals from oppressed communities' crafting and perfecting embodied performances of their own cultural capital' (2020, 92). The song '*Meri Gully Mein*' draws extensively from the cultural capital of life in the slums of Dharavi, and Murad's hyperbolic performance, witnessed by his friends and family, frames him as ubiquitous whereby he freely enters and exits the homes of his community, prancing through the streets and dancing on the rooftops. This symbolic celebration of Dharavi, the authentic site for Murad's stardom, is anchored in the brazen streetwise attitude of Murad and MC Sher who exude a relentless energy, their bodies liberated by rap music and moulded into a politically subversive cultural form that is defiant and playful. Later, Murad's stardom is validated through the popularity of '*Meri Gully Mein*' on social media, restating the centrality of technology as a means of empowerment, an idea that not only reconnects with the laptop in *Secret Superstar* but is indicated earlier in the film when Murad uses an iPad to record his first rhymes.

Rap music and hip hop culture are relatively new ideas to Indian cinema, and in *Gully Boy*, the imagining of the rap star, an updating and evolution of the traditional pop star, is reasonably subversive, although lacking in political antagonism when it comes to critiquing the contemporary landscape of Modi's deeply right-wing Hindutva project. However, it is the song '*Apna Time Aayega*' (Your Time Will Come), the anthem of *Gully Boy*, and which is used to close the film, where the film seems to draw its greatest political power from. It is a rap anthem sung angrily by Murad that is clearly an ardent warning about social oppression, prophesying that the marginalised will one day rise up and claim their rightful position in society. '*Apna Time Aayega*' is performed by Ranveer Singh in a brazen cathartic exhortation, with the crowd of revellers reacting in sync to his every rhyme and gesture. The lyrics to the song '*Apna Time Aayega*' are profoundly subversive, specifically the following verse (translated into English):

> This fire of my words,
> Will break my chains
> The seed you have sowed
> So, shall you reap
> I have a dream
> That makes fear fear
> And it is alive
> You can't bury it

The belief that music will liberate people like Murad is symbolised in the imagery of enslavement, while the popular proverb of reaping what you sow implies the long-term consequences of the oppression of an underclass, and the growing hostility towards Muslims, will naturally lead to an uprising that cannot be contained or suppressed by the establishment. And Murad's status as a Muslim makes this prophecy altogether prescient and the rage veritably transparent, concretising the ways in which his final transformation into a contemporary rap star is a very political act indeed.

Conclusion

Unlike the West which has produced a litany of pop stars from all walks of life, the pop stars of India have largely emerged from the sphere of playback singers, an art that has often helped to elevate the stature of many famous Indian film stars on screen. This dominant trend was countered in the 1990s with the launch of MTV and Channel V, leading to 'Indi-pop' and new pop stars like Alisha Chinai, Sonu Nigam and Daler Mehndi, many of whom would also go on to work in the Indian film industry. Pop stars in the Indian films I have looked at tend to be vehicles for ideological expression, coming to function as genres, reflecting deeper social and political anxieties which are contested through contradictory imaginings and representations. The choice to imagine two of the most visible pop stars in Indian cinema as Muslims is a welcoming sight, carrying with it a subversive political undercurrent while reiterating the plural and syncretic ideals that have been core to Indian culture and film for many decades. Undeniably, Jimmy's dancing, Insia's singing and Murad's rhymes draw out the value of using music to protest injustice, remain defiant in questioning the status quo and disrupt a dominant state-controlled narrative in which an underclass of Indian citizens remain invisible, kerbed and disenfranchised from the mainstream. As Murad exclaims in the anthem '*Apna Time Aayega*', 'I have no fear left. I'll find my own path, I'll steal success if I want, I've earned what I have' – an explicit riposte of self-determination and resistance to Modi's Hindu-first India.

References

Ashraf, Ajaz (2017), 'Secret Superstar: How Advait Chandan's Film Critiques Saudi Arabia, and Nudges Hindus of Gujarat', *Firstpost*, 3 November. Available online: https://www.firstpost.com/entertainment/secret-superstar-how-advait-chand

ans-film-critiques-saudi-arabia-and-nudges-hindus-of-gujarat-4190637.html. Accessed 17 November 2020.

Baym, Nancy K. (2012), 'Fans or Friends?: Seeing Social Media Audiences as Musicians Do', *Participations*, 9 (2): 286–316.

Bhattacharjee, Anirudha and Balaji Vittal, eds (2015), *Gaata Raha Mera Dil: 50 Classic Hindi Film Songs*, Noida: HarperCollins.

Datta, Jayanti (2020), 'Mumbai Rap – A New Sense of the Sacred', postScriptum, 5 (2): 234–45.

Dutta, Nandita (2018), 'Between the "Home" and the "World": The "New Woman" in Bollywood', *Café Dissensus*, 25 November. Available online: https://cafedissensus.com/2018/11/25/between-the-home-and-the-world-the-new-woman-in-bollywood/. Accessed 17 November 2020.

Dyer, Richard (1990), 'In Defence of Disco', in Simon Firth and Andrew Goodwin (eds), *On Record: Rock, Pop, and the Written Word*, 351–8, London: Routledge.

Islam, Maidual (2019), *Indian Muslim(s) after Liberalization*, New Delhi: Oxford University Press.

Kulkarni, Damini Rajendra (2020), 'Appropriation and Articulation: Mapping Movements in *Gully Boy*', *Cinergie – Il Cinema E Le Altre Arti*, 17: 87–96.

Lawrence, Tim (2006), 'In Defence of Disco (Again')', *New Formations*, 58: 128–46.

M. Bonnette, Lakeyta (2015), *Pulse of the People: Political Rap Music and Black Politics*, Pennsylvania: University of Pennsylvania Press.

Pal, Anuvab (2011), *Disco Dancer: A Comedy in Five Acts*, New Delhi: HarperCollins.

Pathak, Ankur (2019), 'Gully Boy: Zoya Akhtar on Her Politics, Alia's Violence & Ranveer's Brown-Face', *Huffington Post: India*, 22 February. Available online: https://www.huffingtonpost.in/entry/zoya-akhtar-gully-boy-interview_in_5c6e3a56e4b0e2f4d8a2a6d4. Accessed 17 November 2020.

Rajagopalan, Sudha (2008), *Indian Films in Soviet Cinemas: The Culture of Movie-Going after Stalin*, Bloomington: Indiana University Press.

Sen, Biswarup (2008), 'The Sounds of Modernity: The Evolution of Bollywood Film Song', in Sangita Gopal and Sujata Moorti (eds), *Global Bollywood: Travels of Hindi Song & Dance University*, 85–204, Minneapolis: University of Minnesota Press.

Filmography

Awaara (1951), [Film] Dir. Raj Kapoor, India: R. K. Films.
Chinatown (1962), [Film] Dir. Shakti Samanta, India: Shakti Films.
Deewaar (1975), [Film] Dir. Yash Chopra, India: Trimurti Films.
Disco Dancer (1982), [Film] Dir. Babbar Subhash, India: B. Subhash Movie Unit.
Ganga Jumuna (1961), [Film] Dir. Nitin Bose, India: Citizen Films.

Gully Boy (2019), [Film] Dir. Zoya Akhtar, India: Excel Entertainment/Tiger Baby Films.
Qurbani (1980), [Film] Dir. Feroz Khan, India: F. K. International.
Secret Superstar (2017), [Film] Dir. Advait Chandan, India: Zee Studios/Aamir Khan Productions.

ptg# '… and presenting JUANITA MOORE as Annie Johnson and MAHALIA JACKSON as Choir Soloist' … singing 'Trouble of the World' in *Imitation of Life*

Benjamin Halligan

Yo – turn my music up.
Up some more.
Up… some more.
Up a little bit more.

– Aaliyah, '4 Page Letter'[1]

Frantz Fanon closes *Black Skin, White Masks* – his 1952 exploration of the subjective conditions engendered by colonialism, on both oppressed and oppressor – with a consideration of an abstract ideal, or utopic condition, that is post-oppression, or post-racism. *Black Skin, White Masks* opens with an engagement with a kind of neurological contagion that endangers the African in Europe: the 'black man entering France' (2008, 5) who then exits as, in terms of aspirations, language, thoughts, something else altogether, via a 'change of personality' (2008, 8). In terms of the psychoanalytical framings that exerted a major influence on Fanon's writing, thinking and clinical work, this phenomenon is quite recognisable: a reinvention requiring a rigorous self-oppression of the undesired elements and attempts to blot out (one could say bleach out) the elements of shame – the blackness itself. But this seems a relatively minor, even manageable, disorder or neurosis, in Fanon's thinking – albeit one that chafes against traditions (also for Fanon; see Nielsen 2013) of Négritude – and

---

[1] Atlantic: AT 0010 T, UK, 1997.

so the lesser of two evils: accept this manageable fate rather than psychiatric incarceration (as the greater evil). The condition is akin to that which Fanon refers to as 'the birth of conflicting knots in the ego, stemming on the one hand from the environment and on the other from the entirely personal way in which this individual reacts to these influences' (2008, 62). The self, with its conflicting ideas, is then knotted into tight stasis: difficult to unpick, and risking a tightening of that ball of enmeshed tensions for anyone who attempts this unpicking. Indeed, R. D. Laing's book of poems/dialogues, exploring interpersonal and psychological tensions related to barely sketched characters, was called *Knots* (Laing 1972). And that 'worse' was Fanon's major concern: the 'psychiatric phenomena entailing disorders affecting behaviour and thought', to the extent that 'the truth is that colonialism in its essence was already taking on the aspect of a fertile purveyor for psychiatric hospitals' (Fanon 1983, 200).[2] Fanon's 'white mask', adopted by the knotted 'black man entering France', allowed, or gave access to, a measure of freedom and a semblance of outward psychological normality, at least.

So what is this coda of an abstract ideal or utopic condition that is post-oppression, or post-racism, that closes *Black Skin, White Masks*? Fanon decries 'subjugation of man by man', of course, but also the very imbibed behaviours that prompt such a reading of life: man is merely man – essentially beholden to a radical equality disinterested in skin colour (and, one must add, gender) – so 'the black man is not. No more than the white man'. (2008, 206). Fanon dismisses the lived experience of oppression as arising from little or nothing more than contingency: 'At the start of his life, a man is always congested, drowned in contingency. The misfortune of man is that he was once a child' (206) – historically, then, contingencies contaminated from the point of infancy (and the formation of the superego). Step one in the breaking of his logic is to unceasingly challenge it – and Fanon's 'final prayer', ending *Black Skin, White Masks*, is 'O my body, always make me a man who questions!' So: 'it is through self-consciousness and renunciation, through a permanent tension of his freedom, that man can create the ideal conditions of existence for a human world'.

From here, step two:

Superiority? Inferiority?

---

[2] For further information on psychosexual disorders from a post-colonial perspective, see Sankara (1990, 32–7). I acknowledge, with gratitude, Richard Pearce, former Head of Religious Doctrine at Stonyhurst, for the formative exposure to Fanon.

Why not simply try to touch each other, feel the other, discover each other? (2008, 206)

This chapter concerns some of these tensions, in respect to one film: more particularly, how the reaching for something that might tentatively suggest 'ideal conditions' (in a vision of wealthy and liberal 1950s North American society) or reasonable attempts to negotiate the prospects of the 'white mask' at that point (attempting to literally achieve whiteness, via passing, or gaining entry to the ideal condition via domestic servitude) exacts a price. I wish to understand that price as exacted psychologically, pace Fanon, but also, arguably, as exacted on, and hindering, a wider African American community. The 'white mask' immobilises that simple operation of Fanon's – 'try to touch each other, feel the other' – so that challenges (overcome or failed) around empathy and awareness become the entire life experience. And that realisation of a price exacted, at any rate, only finally comes in a couple of minutes of the film – minutes which are my primary focus (and so lent a textual analysis, in this consideration). The belated realisation of the importance of that human interaction (of touching, of feeling), I argue, cannot occur in – or will not let itself be confined to – the limits of the melodrama itself and seems to need to break free of that vernacular. How this is done is through music, and the figure of the (actual) musician, stepping into the frame – and with music that, roughly, was understood as within a slavery tradition, so linking the experience of this vision of affluent post-war America to the experience of the colony and the diaspora.

To strengthen this linkage, I will note one more connection: Fanon was received, not so many years after, as an interpretative grid for militants critiquing and usurping that same white, American society – as revealing Global South–type oppression located within the First World and that must engender solidarity and joint action between township and ghetto. For Stokely Carmichael and Charles V. Hamilton, writing in 1967,

> Black Power means that black people see themselves as part of a new force, sometimes called the 'Third World'; that we see our struggle as closely related to liberation struggles around the world. We must hook up with these struggles. We must, for example, ask ourselves: when black people in Africa begin to storm Johannesburg, what will be the role of this nation [i.e. the United States] – and of black people here? ... There is only one place for black Americans in these struggles, and that is on the side of the Third World. Frantz Fanon, in *The Wretched of the Earth*, puts forth clearly the reasons for this and the relationship

of the concept called Black Power to the concept of a new force in the world. (Carmichael and Hamilton 1971, 14–15)

(The 'begin to storm' would occur most notably with the Soweto uprising, in 1976 – the year Hirson (1981) calls 'year of fire, year of ash'.) That internationalism is clearly expressed in the slogan of a 1969 Black Panther poster, designed by Emory Douglas (their Minister for Culture): 'Afro-American solidarity with the oppressed People of the world' above a graphic of a determined-looking African American woman wielding a pen- or staff-like weapon, sun rays emanating behind her.

My approach to *Imitation of Life* – Douglas Sirk's 1959 remake of John M. Stahl's 1934 film – is therefore via Afro-European post-colonial thought, rather than in respect of African American history and thought.[3] My consideration is of the situation of the African American maid, in a film set in the years before the emergence of Black Power – so that a latter-day Négritude seems the correct contextualisation of the maid's lot, bolstered by the way in which her requiem service incorporates Spirituals, and that her position within white society is one of Fanonian knots rather than psychiatric disorders.[4] What was new, in Sirk's *Imitation of Life*, was a fledgling sense of dignity, arising from the structure of the film: the presentation of the African American 'house servant' is in a more equitable balance with the WASP-like house owner.[5] Or, put another way, the film seems as interested in Annie, if not more so, than in the nominal star of the film – and so seems to spend more time with Annie. If considered in respect to comparably mainstream and notable depictions from the two decades prior – as with Mammy (Hattie McDaniel) of *Gone with the Wind* (1939) or Uncle Remus (James Baskett) of *Song of the South* (1946) – *Imitation of Life* seems defiantly

---

[3] The films themselves are based on Fannie Hurst's 1933 novel; the screenplay of Sirk's film was by Eleanore Griffin and Allan Scott.

[4] Négritude, deployed in a very general way here, is identified by Jones as a sense of a 'black ancestral myth' towards re-establishing a 'familial group', through work to 'reawaken a latent feeling of affinity with the common descent of all Africans who had long become separated into seemingly independent groups' (2010, 129). The cultural project of Négritude represented 'an attempt to plunge deeper than the reactive identity that blacks had formed in response to colonial humiliation and recover a vitalist and romantic personality putatively common to those who understood themselves as Guadeloupians, Martinicans, Senegalese, Malians, and other African groups' (130–1). Négritude does not directly feature in the film, nor did Sirk seem aware of it (as per the early 1970s interviews with Halliday 1997); Annie herself briefly articulates prosperity theology as her code for living.

Although the term 'Négritude' is used in this chapter in a number of variations, this does not reflect a sentiment that the term is readily available for a general applicability. It does, however, signal to a desire to see further scholarship engaging with American post-war cinema and the legacies of Négritude.

[5] WASP: White Anglo-Saxon Protestant.

modern. Indeed, part of the subversion of the film is that this structural balance renders the travails of the glamourous home owner as trivial, even ridiculous, when contrasted with the quiet dignity of the everyday struggles of Annie (Juanita Moore).

But that 'seems' – of the film seeming more interested in Annie than the star – is difficult. The opening credits of the film are late to note Juanita Moore and Mahalia Jackson – but that lateness allows for a greater build-up of tumbling diamonds to fill the screen, and affords them a bit more information too (see Figure 9.1). The closing credits place (and interlock) these two emergent figures only at the very end of the roll call (and after listing the most minor of roles too):

> and presenting JUANITA MOORE as Annie Johnson and MAHALIA JACKSON as Choir Soloist.

Is this exclusivity, for the real main attractions here – that the grandest entrance is always last? Or is this yet further relegation – of the African American presences – to the back of the bus? (The US release poster tends to the latter reading: Moore at the back of the row of cast members, and the most diminished in physical size accordingly). Or is this unresolved ambiguity (exclusively best *and* coming last) also something that can be recognised in Fanon: the ontological uncertainty of Black skin, white masks?

Without announcement, or even intimation of as much, *Imitation of Life* introduces a wholly new character in its final few minutes, in the midst of family tragedy, and affords this interloper foremost prominence. As friends and adopted family grieve the passing of Annie, the saint-like African American 'house maid', the Gospel singer and Civil Rights activist Mahalia Jackson appears. She sings 'Trouble of the World' from the pulpit of the Baptist church – a song which would have been known from the 1956 album *Bless This House*, by Jackson and the Falls-Jones Ensemble.[6] This sudden introduction of Jackson is a deus ex machina. Sirk uses her to brutally re-orientate the film's trajectory, making for the finale of *Imitation of Life* and, indeed, the very last minutes of Sirk's commercial or Hollywood career.[7] The narrative shock of this moment

---

[6] Columbia: CL 899, 1956 (although the anonymous liner notes cited below are from a 1963 reissue: CBS: 62319). The album is sometimes held to be Jackson's most immediate work – undiluted by later attempts to appeal to wider audiences.

[7] Sirk (1897–1987) would have creative involvement in three short films beyond *Imitation of Life*, once back in West Germany – most notably *Bourbon Street Blues* (1979), which included a performance from the most prominent figure of the New German Cinema, Rainer Werner Fassbinder, who considered himself a protégé of Sirk's and reworked Sirk's *All That Heaven Allows* (1955) as *Angst*

Figure 9.1 Details from three opening credit titles, from *Imitation of Life* (1959).

is that Sirk seems to suddenly reveal the film to have been – or, to rethink-on-the-spot the film as, in fact, having been – a hagiography of a character that the viewer could have assumed, in the shuffling of various narratives, or by dint of her ethnicity, to have been minor. Once the film hits its stride, four essential narratives emerge.

---

essen Selle auf (*Ali: Fear Eats the Soul* 1974). In this, Fassbinder's engagement with Sirk suggests a reading of Sirk other than that of camp, which has been a, or even the, major mode of consideration of Sirk's films, once rediscovered – perhaps via echoes of Sirkian melodramatics in Andy Warhol's film projects, and then those of John Waters. One thinks of *Poor Little Rich Girl* (Warhol 1965) or *Polyester* (Waters 1981), respectively.

Firstly, and most generically, the film seems to concern the rags-to-riches story of Lora Meredith (Lana Turner), who becomes a notable theatre actress and then an international film star. The film suggests elements of pure talent, propelling her, even as a single mother, from very modest circumstances into a world of artists and intellectuals. A sojourn to Italy to make a film suggests elements of Ingrid Bergman's work with Roberto Rossellini might be a template, with the actress willing to court scandal and art. But her appearance is of the Marilyn Monroe template: the blondeness and WASP whiteness of GI pin-ups of the Second World War. At the same time, other elements of the film suggest opportunism on Lora's part and a willingness to embrace a 'casting couch' culture to ensure stardom. The slight mystery surrounding her origins – her personality seems to arrive fully formed – raises the suspicion of someone who performs a bright and resilient personality, in the face of adversity, as much as performs as an actress. A few slips here and there, as with her disengagement with her growing daughter and ignorance of the life of Annie, despite the decades-long service, could be read as indicative of the overwhelming effort she channels into performing the glamorous role of Lora Meredith.[8]

Secondly, and seemingly demanding the most engagement from the audience, comes a liberal's morality tale, concerning the behaviour of Sarah Jane (Susan Kohner), Annie's increasingly estranged daughter. The engagement is needed since Sarah Jane embraces her 'passing': that is, a light-skinned African American who can be mistaken for white. Even in terms of contemporary considerations of this – from Philip Roth's novel *The Human Stain* (2000) to Mariah Carey's autobiography (2020) – the way in which both versions of *Imitation of Life* deal with passing is admirably complex. The daughters' desire for whiteness is such that it propels them to abandon and then hide from the sole parent, and move away from the comfort of biracial, upper-class existence into very much less-salubrious environs. In a series of Judas-like betrayals, Sarah Jane (in 1959) shuns the mother, who tries to enact discrete missions of mercy

---

[8] The most immediate parallel in terms of the idea of the lauded star as essentially fake is from another of Sirk's effective protégés – and also a European *auteur* who worked subversively in Hollywood film-making – Paul Verhoeven. His *Showgirls* (1995) features a protagonist who has reinvented herself (even renamed herself) in order to start afresh in Las Vegas – almost a remake (via writer Joe Eszterhas) – of my second identified narrative of *Imitation of Life*, discussed below. But this idea of fakery is the flipside, in general, of misogynistic tales of the casting couch: the female as willing victim (to enable her career) – with a slyness and dishonesty, and sexual availability, that allows a negotiation of both roles (quasi-prostitute, film star). For a tawdry 'exposé' of such notions, see *The Casting Couch* (Ford 1990), by British soft porn director Derek Ford and his associate Alan Selwyn.

to her troubled daughter – even into a seedy burlesque club. Sarah Jane's entry into the world of Greenwich Village seems only to deliver her into ever further circles of exploitation – and even violence (a suitor, discovering her ethnicity, presumably dashing his dreams of perfect teen coupledom, violently assaults her and leaves her bleeding in the street). By the time she has gained employment in the upmarket Moulin Rouge club in Hollywood, passing seems more of an economic necessity – to remain in employment and to hope for romantic patronage. (The club was an innovation, when it opened in 1954, in terms of entertainment: a resolving stage and a choreographed, French-themed show; a restaurant and bars; notable clientele; and attempts to establish itself via the quality control of the 'lavishly dressed showgirls'; see Mallory 2018.) The club is shown as functioning as a conduit for showgirls to businessmen, and the effective required whiteness of mainstream showgirl/glamour culture of this moment might have marginalised Sarah Jane had her biracial status emerged again – potentially returning her to the humble social status of her mother. (*Playboy*-calibrated lifestyle culture only began to 'diversify' in the mid-1960s; see Johnson 2017.) When Annie visits this world, she is initially mistaken for a chambermaid by a fellow dancer of Sarah Jane's. Sarah Jane's Damascene conversion comes too late: the mother has died, just before being able to hear the daughter's plea for forgiveness, which undoubtedly would have been immediate and unconditional on Annie's part. Sarah Jane, guilt-racked and hysterical, crashes the funeral and nearly throws herself into the hearse.

Thirdly, even if only provisionally, since perhaps this was true only for some viewers of the time, the film offers vignettes of romance – strands of narratives involving glamorous men who come into Lora's orbit and distract her from the one honest man who has been her suitor, who eventually proves himself to be a constant. Some familial tension occurs, with both mother and daughter attracted to him. It is difficult to remember much of the detail of these strands, in casually recalling a viewing of the film, but they would be the required mortar for a film that, as per any Hollywood melodrama of this period (sometimes referred to as 'women's pictures'), is essentially a romance. (I pick this up again below, in a brief consideration of footage of the film's opening night.)

Fourthly, Annie's story, where Sirk makes a notable change to Stahl's adaptation of 1934. In the earlier version, the shared fortune arises from a jointly owned pancake business, between WASP Beatrice Pullman (Claudette Colbert) and African American Delilah Johnson (Louise Beavers), with Beatrice taking Delilah's secret family recipe first to a café and then to packs of pancake flour (branded with an image of Delilah). Delilah still chances her way into being Beatrice's maid, Delilah's daughter Peola (Dorothy Black, and then Fredi Washington) still aspires to whiteness and the family still wind up as fabulously rich. Sirk observed that this change in the origins of fortunes (from pancakes to film stardom) makes more sense of the flight of Sarah Jane; Delilah would not have been able to buy her own home, whereas Annie would have been able to, so something more to propel Sarah Jane away was necessary (Halliday 1997, 148). And Lora's airless, tasteless house – brilliantly floodlit, like the stage of a Noël Coward domestic drama, and full of ornate bric-a-brac and mock-historical fittings, and looking like no one actually lives in it – provides more reason to flee. Every meal seems a semi-formal dinner party; all the food seems presented; for Handzo, all this was 'Intimations of Lifelessness' (1977–8). In this, Sirk's mise en scène is the ambience and evidence of an overwhelming condition of an ever-heightened imitation of a life, and one that seems to be acted out by all involved. Initially, this contrasts with the happy bustle of the cheek-by-jowl existence in tenement buildings of the pre-fame life. But these later interiors seem disinfected or sanitised to clinical levels: Fanon's psychiatric hospital disguised but nevertheless *within* the home – cushioning (and accommodating) the knotted condition, even anaesthetising the patients. Unlike Sirk's earlier *All That Heaven Allows* – with its cross-generational, cross-class romance shattering the intimations of a respectable, small-town life – no explosion occurs during Annie's life. Even her death is a matter of domestic chore and structure, as she explains the funeral plan to those at her deathbed, and outlines arrangements she has already made and where they are to be found.

The stage-like space of the house allows for the white mask performance. But this is not Fanon's African ingénue in France – it is the (African) American in America, post-slavery, post-colony. And the mask seems more like a skin here – indeed, as with Sarah Jane's light skin salvation strategy, white skin so fully enabling, even naturalising, the white mask: a becoming-white at the behest of the other. Achille Mbembe, writing on Fanon, on the origin of this force of self-reinvention, 'For everything, or nearly everything, encouraged colonized people to inhabit as their skin and their truth the fiction that the Other had produced in their regard' (2019, 5). The damped-down, non-exploding, domestification still then requires this will-to-be-white, but with a more complicated nexus of performances (for a social status quo, and one that would hold for a few years at least, prior to Black Power). That is, each performance is understood as verifying the imagining of the other, in proximity to the other – a 'double image' at work (to borrow the title of a Miles Davis composition): Lora plays the film star, and plays the film star as she imagines others, such as Annie, would see the film star; Annie plays the maid, and plays the maid as she imagines others, such as Lora, would see the maid. (How else could Lora remain so ignorant of Annie? Sirk expands this question to the point of seemingly condemning the film as flawed by such an absence, in his white protagonist: 'This is the best thing Lana Turner does, saying that 'No!' [when Annie dies] – because she [Lora] is nothing ... I couldn't overcome the material. As you can see, now you know me, I'm not a weepie man. I don't really like this kind of picture'; quoted in Halliday 1997, 153.) Thus, white creates the idea of Black, and Black, in turn, for Mbembe, writing of 'The Black of the White and the White of the Black', spurs the creation of the idea of whiteness:

> Fanon was right [in *Black Skin, White Masks*], however, when he suggested that the Black Man was a figure, an 'object', invented by Whites and as such 'fixed' by their gaze, gestures, and attitudes. He was woven 'out of a thousand details, anecdotes, and stories'. We should add that Whiteness in turn was, in many ways, a fantasy produced by the European imagination, one that the West has worked hard to naturalize and universalize. Fanon himself said of the two that Blackness did not exist any more than Whiteness did. (2017, 43–4)

So for Annie, the condition is naturalised too: on the one hand, a becoming-Black, in the sense of becoming a code that others would recognise and, on the other, the white mask passport or permissions (for limited access to the white environs of Sarah Jane) and maid performance. But this becoming serves Annie too: even in the most desperate of situations, when spurned by her sinking daughter, she can remain pragmatic, stoic and thinking, finally, of the other's wants – agreeing to leave, after one final embrace, and with Sarah Jane's flatmate mistaking Annie for a maid, which is graciously laughed off by Annie. In her life, until its end, the knot holds fast. Melodrama, then, in its splintering from naturalism, becomes, appropriately, a stage of or for mutually verifying, mutually reinforcing performances. Characters, occasionally, seem to recognise the price demanded by such reinvention: that Fassbinderian shot of the woman, gazing at herself in the mirror – most notably (and problematically) the trans protagonist of *In einem Jahr mit 13 Monden* (*In a Year of 13 Moons* 1978); or Cary Scott (Jane Wyman), in Sirk's *All That Heaven Allows* (1955), catching her reflection looking back at her, from the grey, mirroring screen of the new television set – a gift of companionship ('the last refuge for lonely women') from those who would rather lock her into isolated widowhood, such as her departing children, than see her find love or sensuality again.

This reading of *Imitation of Life* then considers the life situation portrayed as one of mutually enforced self-repression. This is the condition that Sirk then explodes in the final minutes of the film.

But before moving to this moment, I want to briefly return to the seedy nightclub (of my identified second narrative strain) to note Sarah Jane's performance of the song 'Empty Arms'. This is in the basement of Harry's Club, which, next to a cleaner's and a grocery shop and over the road from overflowing litter bins, is no Moulin Rouge. And the performance is seen, unbeknownst to Sarah Jane, by Annie – who slips by the distracted bouncer to gain entry. Sarah Jane grinds against the wall, flashes her behind to the jazz band, vamps on the rim-shots, displays her cleavage to the audience (seen in partial profiles in the foreground, and rendered grotesque), caresses one elderly man in the front row and reclines in front of another (and so on) while singing 'an empty purse can make a good girl bad … you hear me, Dad?' (Another front row audience member seems to be an elderly Madam, who enters with Annie – the association threat of this intruder whose intentions for Sarah Jane are the opposite to Annie's.) The club is shot in dusky purples and reds, with light diffused through smoke, and plenty of disinterested background business kept in focus, including another dancer at a table chatting with a guest – marking the venue as a knocking shop. Sarah Jane's showgirl performance is incidental, bar to a few watching it, with the blonde dancer (for variety, against Sarah Jane's brunette looks) waiting for her turn in the dim spotlight. The image is obscured by plumes of cigarette smoke and also foregrounds, arrestingly, jezebel-red candles (from the bottles on the tables), while the singing is interrupted by raucous, drunken laughter. (The world-weary voice itself belongs to JoAnn Greer.)

The moment is an extension of performing a role for others, as activated by a series of looks or glances, motivated by desires (see Figure 9.2): Sarah Jane, 'brazenly', to the guests (for money or romance), the guests at Sarah Jane (for sex or titillation), and Annie at the spectacle unfolding (as part of her journey to find and recover her daughter). The camera is levelled horizontally accordingly, paralleling these glances, and pans rather than tracks (imitating head movement, to keep the desired dancer in the field of vision) – and reverse angle cuts back to Annie. She is behind wooden slats which seems, incredibly (since the implications are so uncomfortable), to cage her – as she watches her daughter snatched from her and disappear into this white realm of exploitation. So the

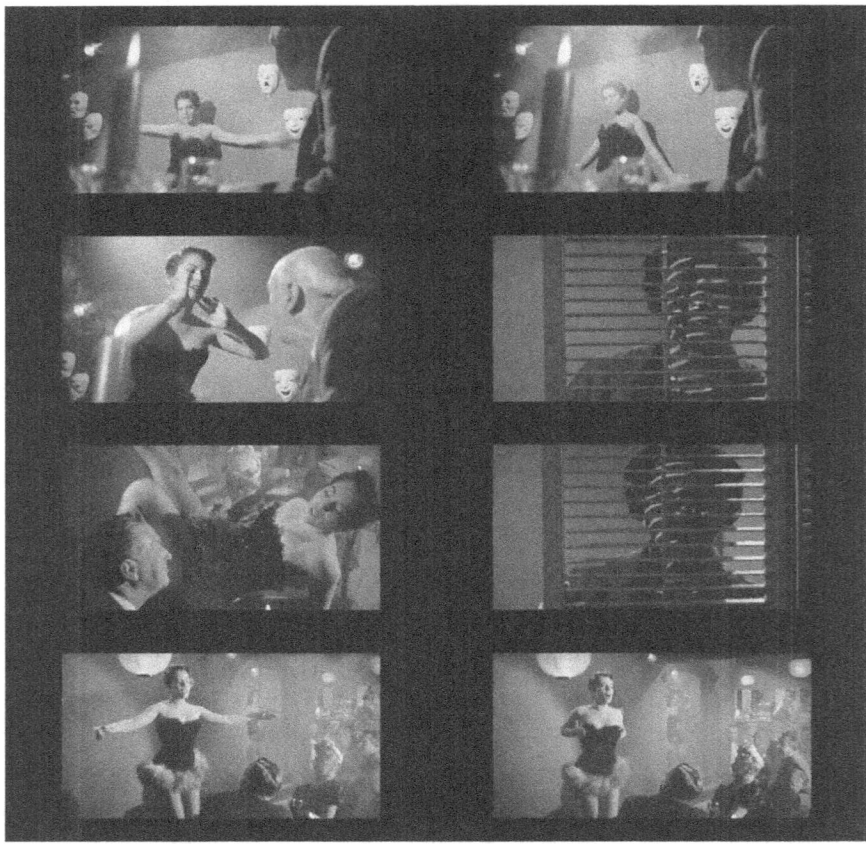

Figure 9.2 Sirk juxtaposes open gazes of desire from free white men with a hidden gaze of horror, for which bars cage the face of the on-looking African American: Sarah Jane's performance of 'Empty Arms' in Harry's Club.

sequence is entirely secular, in the amoral sense of the pleasures of the flesh on offer, but also in the material sense of a rational reality, and of figures interacting with each other in this cramped space and nothing else, pulling the camera down to exist on that level alone, in with them, in the tight spaces between them.

The sequence (and indeed Sarah Jane herself) then needs redemption, with a reversal of this philosophical position, for the second song performance of the film: Annie's funeral service. Sirk lap-dissolves from the framed picture of Sarah Jane by Annie's bed, at the moment of Annie's death, to the church and its clear, dawn-blue light, through a stained-glass window. For this, it is Mahalia Jackson who is now singing. And now the camera angles are diametrically different: the spaciousness of the stone interior (in deep focus), looked up-and-at by the camera – the chamber allowing the acoustic, Spirituals-swelling of the choir voices – which then pans down to frame Mahalia against (church-white) candles and bouquets, and cuts to her against a plain cross. The movement is repeated for the Gospel choir, framed between two candles – and this time pans down to the front row of the congregation, with Lora seemingly mid-breakdown. The cut back to Mahalia projects another glance – via Mahalia's eyes: back upwards, heavenwards. The movement here can be read as pre-secular: the soul of the departed drifts upwards, as if aided or guided onwards by Mahalia's voice, and the camera follows, to a measure, but ultimately seems doomed to remain on earth. Here, it looks at those who are left, and is freed from any one particular point of view, capturing the event and crowd. But in that grounding, in what appears to be cutaway shots, then comes the image of the milkman (David Tomack) – first seen (it seems) hours ago, and only briefly too, visiting the tenement flat – who had extended Annie credit. He is mentioned by Annie before she dies as deserving one final tip – and that she had, in fact, sent him 'a little something' every Christmas (perhaps a fifty-dollar note, as this is what she suggests now), 'in both our names': that is, Lora and Annie's names. (Part then of Annie performing maid Annie for others incorporates needing to also perform an element of film star Lora, for others.) The milkman looks crushed at the funeral, and bows his head. While the household may have moved on to then-unimaginable fortunes, Annie has clearly never forgotten those who once afforded small kindnesses when they were most needed, and perhaps redistributed her wealth accordingly. When he is first encountered, he seems little more than a comical bit part, but now his grief places him before more substantial characters (those of Lora's theatre years, seen after). And another flank of unknowns appear, and the crowds outside consist of hundreds of unknowns too – to, that is, the viewer of narratives one, two and three. The crowd continues to swell and more people arrive. They must be those who crowded Annie's life, as unseen in narrative four, and then their friends and associates, or passers-by: the neighbourhood itself aware that a significant event is occurring. Indeed, even the sudden presence of Annie's church friends and associates towards the end of the film suggests elements of a hidden life – and a life of Annie's doing good for so many others, even when in adversity herself. Beneath the self-repression, outside of the airless house, life itself had occurred.

Mahalia, singing to all of them, not only vocalises and expresses the woes that Annie kept hidden, but seems to be those woes too – that is, to switch from a performance of servitude (the labour of the body, the life of the maid, of propriety and politeness and control), to the performance of emotion (the soulfulness of the music, shaking the body, degrading control). The woe now breaks surface and overwhelms the film: the raw emotion, in the unmodulated intonation, jarring against the courtly language of the melodrama; the reorientation of the film from white to Black skin; to culture as the preservation, fortification and transmission of life experience of the oppressed, rather than culture as a glitzy career option; the shift from mannered, actor-ly perform*ance* to 'untrained', musician-ly perform*ing*. In short, Jackson lends Annie, and maybe even Mammy and Uncle Remus, their unmediated voices. Such a move, from a textual point of view, would seemingly be impossible with just another actor-performer on screen.[9] Mahalia then is alien to the film: she is not incorporated as another actress, but as an actual singer – her raptness, the very wide-openness of her mouth, the closeness of the camera to her as it films, documenting the singing, breaks with melodrama, in favour of cinéma-vérité. Indeed, this sudden switch to musician, from actress, seems to trigger such freed emotional expression – as, finally, voiced by another, on behalf of the departed Annie. It also, ontologically, correctly aligns the singer and the song, the voice and the body – unlike the dubbing of 'Empty Arms', which also seems to suggest the unlikelihood that Sarah Jane can sing a bit like Billie Holiday of 'Summertime' (see Figure 9.3).

Annie's troubles are universalised in this contextualisation, and historicised: hers is *the trouble* of *the world* itself – a Black consciousness drawing on, and contributing back to, the diaspora. Her line of flight, now to the heavens – to be united with God ('to live with God!', 'to live with My Lord!'), to be reunited with her mother ('I want! See my mother!') – streams the diaspora upwards into the afterlife. In terms of the way in which the film seems now at the point of hagiography, and the sudden nexus of rhizomatic connections to innumerable strata of the African American community that has emerged, as if summoned, and the achievement of peer regard and dignity, as evidenced

---

[9] Since this chapter parallels elements of *Imitation of Life* and *All That Heaven Allows*, one further comparison seems appropriate. The latter ends with the sudden appearance of a baby deer – seen previously, fed grain by Ron Kirby (Rock Hudson). With the appearance, Kirby gains consciousness (he is recovering from a near-fatal accident), and seemingly awakens back into a possible future with Cary Scott who, guilt-stricken, is attending to him. In this way, nature seems to return the favour: nurturing Kirby in turn. Sirk here offers a Green deus ex machina: Kirby within the wider ecosphere, and perhaps that as the key to his vitality, and his shunning of the trivialities of the white society of the small town – which is just as sleazy in its own way, albeit in the setting of a cocktail party, as Harry's Club.

Figure 9.3 Unfamiliarity, jarringly, crowds the frame – unknowns and, outlandishly, a bit-part player, indicate that another life was lived, as Mahalia Jackson sings at Annie's funeral.

by Lora and family and associates, one wants to add to 'contextualised' and 'historicised'. Annie's troubles, via Mahalia, are Négritudinalised. And Annie's sanctification, via Mahalia, and the crowding African America unknowns, is Négritudinalised. This funeral may be read, for better or worse, as a reawakening of that 'latent feeling of affinity with the common descent of all Africans' (Jones 2010, 129).

It is in the audio mixing that this process occurs too. I have noted the music, above, as both Gospel and Spiritual. I rest the vagueness or even inaccuracy of this association of the rendition of 'Trouble of the World' on the vagueness of associations that would be the common currency for such a film of white romance – the screen time, and star billings, given to narratives one and three; Annie and Mahalia in the 'and presenting' end credits category, as essentially appended, therefore. The LP liner notes of *Bless This House* make such vague associations too: 'gospel singing', 'early Negro spirituals and Protestant hymns', and jazz, and blues and, via Enrico Caruso, opera. Another small fragment of circumstantial evidence for this vagueness is found in a 16-mm promotion film, presumably made as a newsreel trailer for the film. The credit is to Universal-International News, with Fred Maness (who often voiced Universal newsreels) credited as commentating, and the title is '*"Imitation of Life"* Has Gala Preview'. Figure 9.4 contains screengrabs of the entirety of the meagre crowd shots as the performers arrive and walk up the red carpet. The crowd could be said to consist of exactly the kinds of figures one would suspect a studio would imagine for a 'woman's picture' or 'weepie' – perhaps these women were hired, or won a competition to attend, or were gala regulars, and seem dressed up for the occasion, with husbands or fathers confined to the second row. But, with fitting irony, a lone African American suddenly appears, for under one second, as the camera tracks right – stepping slightly out and peering over the shoulder of a woman in her Sunday best. He alone, jacketless, seems genuinely there – perhaps by happenstance, or perhaps by talk of a picture with African American performers (although Juanita Moore and Mahalia Jackson are not filmed as being at this event). Whereas the others dress in the finery one associates with the post-war years (fur coats and gloves, poodle clip or bob hairstyles), our interloper seems to sport the sharp light shirt of a Miles Davis and the fedora of a Lester Young of this era – this was the year of release of *Kind of Blue*.

One could talk then of the 'white ear' (as well as 'white gaze') of 1959: trying, crudely, to interpret something that is not WASP hymnal. And that vagueness would relate the culture of the Spiritual to Gospel, thence to the diaspora, thereafter to the history of slavery, outside America and within. This funeral, in the 1934 film, also mixes tones of Gospel and Spirituals into the soundtrack – but balanced tastefully with other audio elements, so little more than a theme mixed into the sound-bed. The maximal use in Sirk's film pushes this context into the foreground: the mixing forces in the meaning – as per the Aaliyah of my epigraph: that insistent, repeated instruction, 'turn my music up. / Up some more. / Up… some more. / Up a little bit more'. In this respect, this switch from actress to musician also seems unavoidable if such a realignment of meaning is to occur in the final moments of the film: the white masks have smothered the Black skins – but a voice, for the voiceless, can and will still emerge.

'Trouble of the World' in Imitation of Life 163

Figure 9.4 The crowd shots from the 1959 newsreel '"*Imitation of Life*" Has Gala Preview'.

The limits of efficacy of this emergence also seem apparent in *Imitation of Life* too. Annie has been subsumed into a heaven for the humble, the victims and the fundamentally good. Such selfless qualities, however, seem passive. In a short, post-funeral scene, indications are given that life will go on – perhaps (as Sirk himself reads this scene) unchanged.[10] Where, then, is the legacy? To return to Carmichael and Hamilton, Black Power represented that way in which 'black

---

[10] For Sirk, on this 'very bare and brief little scene afterwards [where] the happy turn is being indicated', 'everything seems to be OK, but you know it isn't … [t]hey're all sitting in the limousine together – until everything starts to go wrong again, which it would for sure' (quoted in Halliday 1997, 151–2).

people see themselves as part of a new force' (1971, 14). Here, Négritudinally, Annie returns to, or becomes part of, an *old* force. And 'Trouble of the World' maps this direction of travel (away from life, the world, and its attendant troubles) with precision: 'Soon I will be done / [with the] trouble of the world'; 'I'm going home / to live / with God', where there will be 'no more / weeping and wailing'. The old force offers therapy (via a removal of the white mask?), staying the weeping and the wailing of the world. But the potentials of weeping and wailing are needed, for Carmichael and Hamilton, for the coming insurgencies and future martyrs of a new force.

References

All That Heaven Allows (1955), [Film] Dir. Douglas Sirk, USA: Universal Pictures.
Angst essen Selle auf/Ali: Fear Eats the Soul (1974), [Film] Dir. Rainer Werner Fassbinder, West Germany: Filmverlag der Autoren GmbH & Co. Vertriebs KG.
Bourbon Street Blues (1979), [Film] Dir. Douglas Sirk, Hans Schönherr and Tilman Taube, West Germany: Independent Film School Project.
Carey, Mariah, with Michaela Angela Davis (2020), *The Meaning of Mariah Carey*, London: Macmillan.
Carmichael, Stokely, and Charles V. Hamilton (1971), *Black Power: The Politics of Liberation in America*, London: Pelican Books.
Fanon, Frantz ([1952] 2008), *Black Skin, White Masks*, trans. Richard Philcox, New York: Grove Press.
Fanon, Frantz ([1961] 1983), *The Wretched of the Earth*, trans. Constance Farrington, Middlesex: Penguin Books Ltd.
Ford, Selwyn ('Selwyn Ford': pseudonym of Derek Ford and Alan Selwyn) (1990), *The Casting Couch: Making It in Hollywood*, London: Grafton Books/Collins Publishing Group.
Gone with the Wind (1939), [Film] Dir. Victor Fleming, USA: Selznick International Pictures, Metro-Goldwyn-Mayer.
Handzo, Stephen (1977–8), 'Intimations of Lifelessness: Sirk's Ironic Tear-jerker', *Bright Lights*, Winter: 20–2, 34.
Hirson, Baruch (1981), *Year of Fire, Year of Ash: The Soweto Revolt: Roots of a Revolution?*, London: Zed Books.
Halliday, Jon (1997), *Sirk on Sirk: Conversations with Jon Halliday*, new and rev. edn, London: Faber and Faber.
Imitation of Life (1934), [Film] Dir. John M. Stahl, USA: Universal Pictures.
Imitation of Life (1959), [Film] Dir. Douglas Sirk, USA: Universal Pictures.

In einem Jahr mit 13 Monden/In a Year of 13 Moons (1978), [Film] Dir. Rainer Werner Fassbinder, West Germany: Tango-Film.

Johnson, Scott (2017), 'Playboy's First Black Playmate Reflects on Hugh Hefner's Legacy', *Hollywood Reporter*, 4 October. Available online: https://www.hollywoodreporter.com/news/playboys-first-black-playmate-reflects-hugh-hefners-legacy-1045838. Accessed 30 August 2022.

Jones, Donna V. (2010), *The Racial Discourses of Life Philosophy: Négritude, Vitalism, and Modernity*, New York: Columbia University Press.

Laing, R. D. (1972), *Knots*, New York: Vintage Books.

Mallory, Mary (2018), 'Earl Carroll Puts Swank into Sunset Boulevard', *The Hollywood Partnership*, 1 November. Available online: https://hollywoodpartnership.com/post/earl-carroll-puts-swank-sunset-boulevard#:~:text=Built%20by%20renowned%20musical%20revue,entertainment%20venue%20for%20eight%20decades. Accessed 30 August 2022.

Mbembe, Achille (2017), *Critique of Black Reason*, Durham: Duke University Press.

Mbembe, Achille (2019), *Necropolitics*, Durham: Duke University Press.

Nielsen, Cynthia R. (2013), 'Frantz Fanon and the Négritude Movement: How Strategic Essentialism Subverts Manichean Binaries', *Callaloo*, Spring, 36 (2): 342–52.

Polyester (1981), [Film] Dir. John Waters, USA: New Line Cinema.

Poor Little Rich Girl (1965), [Film] Dir. Andy Warhol, USA: Film-Makers' Cooperative.

Roth, Philip (2000), *The Human Stain*, London: Jonathan Cape.

Sankara, Thomas (1990), *Women's Liberation and the African Freedom Struggle*, London: Pathfinder Press.

Showgirls (1995), [Film] Dir. Paul Verhoeven, USA: Carolco Pictures, Chargeurs, United Artists.

Song of the South (1946), [Film] Dir. Harve Foster and Wilfred Jackson, USA: Walt Disney Productions.

10

Cinema, jazz and representation

Daniel Graham

'Does Louis XIV still live here?'
'No! He died a long time ago'
'Are you sure?'
'Yes'

– *Conversation between Dale Turner and Francis Borel in* 'Round Midnight

Cinema and jazz share a unique and distinctive history that is chronologically concomitant yet dissimilar in social reach and method of representation. Both cinema and jazz can rightly claim to be invented and pioneered in America at the beginning of the twentieth century. Both cinema and jazz reacted to, reflected and assuaged that century's cataclysmic social changes by using the time-honoured convention of *telling a story*. This was done from a unique point of view using a codified method of expression – a language if you will. Not a language as rigid and protected as French but a fluid and adaptable one such as English that is now understood across almost the entire world thanks to the pervasive influence of commerce and trade. In fact, it was their protean nature that made cinema and jazz a universal language by virtue of an adaptability born out of tradition (a survival instinct perhaps), something like the British Royal Family only a lot more fun, relevant and communicative.

The most significant point of departure between cinema and jazz could be identified as their method of production and cost of distribution. More pertinent, however, is the difference in their racial origins. Jazz, unmistakably, was born from the experience of the Black American who at that time in the history of the United States suffered a blatant and subhuman prejudice almost without exception. Their attempts to promote their own music and have it disseminated widely was, therefore, beholden to the white male power structure of the recording industry and night club circuit.

Cinema in Hollywood, in stark contrast, was conceived very consciously from its inception (with rare, notable exceptions) to be an all-pleasing form of mass entertainment, heavily influenced by European émigré film-makers and businessmen who brought with them an uncanny commercial sense and a solid grasp of the time-honoured tenets of storytelling. Adolph Zukor (Paramount Pictures), William Fox (20th Century Fox), Carl Laemmle (Universal Pictures) and the four Warner Brothers were the founding fathers of Hollywood. Their influence and legacy could not be more different to that of the great pioneers of jazz, including Louis Armstrong, Duke Ellington, Coleman Hawkins, Charlie Parker, Dizzy Gillespie and Thelonious Monk. Hollywood was all about giving the people what they wanted whilst jazz was about creating a distinctive musical identity outside of the mainstream as a form of rebellion and an affirmation of their right to a dignified and creative life.

Movies were vastly more expensive to produce than jazz records, therefore the imperative to entertain very much dictated both its style and content. Where these two uniquely American forms of art and entertainment crossed paths is also where their dissimilarities became most apparent. If American cinema was ultimately a representation of a way of life via the great genre of the Western, the Film Noir and the Gangster Film for example, then jazz was invariably presented by Hollywood as something Afro exotic, forbidden, drug laden, sexy, beatnik or romantic/tragic, but very rarely as a triumphant 'overcoming of the odds' type experience so cherished by studio chiefs, screenwriters and cinema owners. Bertrand Tavernier's 1986 paean to jazz, 'Round Midnight, was a rare (and late) exception in that Tavernier is a genuine authority on jazz as well as one of France's most distinguished, intelligent and consistent film-makers. More of that later.

We should also talk about the very different means by which cinema and jazz are conceived, developed, executed, distributed and maintained as part of an ongoing legacy. Cinema, as we know, remains a heavy industry in that it employs several hundred people, requires a great logistical effort and cost that involves fabrication, construction and transport and is very heavily accountable to its financial backers. Like any similar material production, it is intended to reach as wide an audience as possible relative to its production costs. Jazz, on the other hand, can be created and delivered (i.e. rehearsed, performed and recorded) at a fraction of the cost of film production, which therefore allows a far greater creative control for the artist. Its technical means can be as elementary as a saxophone, double bass and drum kit, although the training and preparation required to perform it are, arguably, far more intense and arduous than the training required to work in cinema.

Allow, if you will, for this argument to be put more bluntly. Cinema is far more accommodating, even welcoming, of the fast rise to fame by an unskilled, technically limited performer. Jazz, in stark contrast, gives extremely short shrift to the one-note show pony no matter how pretty or fresh looking they first appear or sound. You simply do not get onto a bandstand with seasoned jazz musicians if you haven't first mastered your instrument, if not your craft. Even a genius like Charlie Parker was sent offstage by a crashing cymbal (courtesy of drumming legend and Count Basie alumnus Jo Jones) when still a nascent improvisor. Times have moved on from Kansas City in the 1930s, but the principle remains the same: learn your craft properly or don't even pretend to call yourself a jazz musician. There was, however, a time in the late 1960s in the wake of Albert Ayler and John Coltrane's innovations in avant-garde jazz that did see a bit of a surge in some unconvincing technicians getting serious attention in the jazz field, especially amongst critics who were a little too eager to discover the new thing. Even undisputed giants of the music like Ornette Coleman rather erred on the side of untrammelled expressionism when he unwisely picked up a trumpet and a violin in addition to his home instrument of alto saxophone.

There were several students of Ornette's saxophone language, but there were virtually none of his trumpet or violin playing. This aberration of unskilled players, outside of Ornette Coleman, was a soon to be a forgotten bump in the road. The rigorous integrity of jazz wouldn't allow for phonies or flash in the pan charlatans for very long. Soon enough the 'screamers' and the 'howlers' were relegated to the latrine of music history. Making uninformed noise on a trumpet or saxophone was never going to make a serious mark in jazz music. Those kinds of kindergarten antics were best left to other, less-demanding, music genres.

Cinema, at least in front of the camera, has a much wider tolerance for unskilled newcomers provided they carry a certain ingénue quality that can be moulded to one's satisfaction. Many of the most successful cinema actors, especially American, became famous through a methodical and judicious process of typecasting. The more pragmatic and prudent actors recognise their limitations and are more or less content to build a long-lasting career on this. We love them because they play minor variations of the same type in every movie they make. In the classic Hollywood star system familiarity doesn't breed contempt, it encourages idolatry. Europeans, especially the French, have historically been ardent supporters, followers and exponents of jazz, relatively unencumbered by the kind of historical racism that continues in 2020 to stain America's national fabric with its enviable (but lost) dream of unity. The Europeans consider jazz, rightly so, as American art music and not the product of a ghetto culture soaked in narcotics. Tavernier's *'Round Midnight* was the most serious attempt, up to that time, by a film-maker to depict the life of a noted American jazz musician – in this instance, one living in exile in Paris. Shielded from the racism of the New York City he left behind, our jazz hero somehow looked like a melancholic saint left forlorn and homesick, ambling through a smoky, dimly lit Paris.

What happens when the Hollywood dream factory, run largely by accountants and assembly line storytellers (which is not necessarily a bad thing), brings its long and varied skill set and financial resources to the strongly idiomatic world of the jazz musician – the African American jazz musician to be exact, as told by a French film director who knows as much about cinema as he does about jazz. In 1986, when Bertrand Tavernier's *'Round Midnight* was released, the jazz movie up to that point had long perpetuated the image of the African American jazz musician as someone invariably hip, dependent, doomed yet brilliant. Audiences had not yet enjoyed a jazz movie that treated the music as a serious art form, never mind the musicians themselves. It is perhaps the greatest myth of all that jazz musicians are not trained at the level of symphony orchestra musicians or that they simply peel off random series of notes in the hope that it will all come together in the end, hidden under a frenzy of arbitrary sounds and rhythms. Hollywood representation of jazz did little to change this misperception.

Before Miles Davis attended The Juilliard School in 1944, the large majority of jazz musicians had not attended higher education music schools or conservatories – they instead learned their craft through extensive practice, jamming with fellow musicians and by listening to records. Pianist Cedar Walton, who features in *'Round Midnight*, has recounted in interviews how this approach helped inform a musician's individuality, a musician's distinctive and personal sound. Very gradually, however, this ebbed away as the decades passed to the point where a musician like Wynton Marsalis appeared to immense acclaim around 1980, delivering a kind of academically polished neo-bop. Keith Jarrett was unsparing in his criticism of Marsalis's style by remarking that he sounded like a very precocious high school trumpet player. The inference was that Marsalis had arrived at his style through arduous, academic study (born out of a natural and prodigious talent nonetheless) rather than the old school method Cedar Walton spoke of. Indeed, when Miles Davis felt The Juilliard School became too stifling an influence, he abandoned his studies to play with Charlie Parker, the greatest genius jazz has ever known.

Similarly, no amount of film school tuition about how a movie is made can adequately prepare a student for the material world of film-making, especially when it comes to writing and directing. Whilst the origins of this aphorism are hard to determine, the expression that best encapsulates the movie-making process is this: 'You make a film three times. Once when you write it, once when you shoot it and once when you edit it.' Cinema is heavily predetermined at concept stage yet evolutionary and plastic in execution, by necessity more than by design. Jazz on the other hand, whilst also heavily informed by preparation, almost entirely relies on the nature of spontaneity to gauge its success. Jazz is a truly collaborative art form as opposed to the Harry Cohn*esque* definition of the word, which reads something like 'this is my vision and you agree with it. That's collaboration'.

In jazz you simply don't create collaboration by way of dictatorship or coercion. It is about preparing, listening, reacting and feeling with the group next to you. It is a conversation with a shifting orator, rooted in predetermined material (even in free jazz) that encourages both individual expression and group interplay. Movie making doesn't like on-the-spot surprises that take the ship off course. It functions in a determinedly schematic way. Jazz does not. How then does one marry these two creative forces in a way that remains loyal to each party without compromising the lesser partner. It's worth pointing out here that generalities are being made to assert a finer and more universal point. How do two vital cultural forces find common ground to create a film as sensitive and as dreamlike as Bertrand Tavernier's *'Round Midnight*, warts and all.

Let's start with the source material, which in this case was the book *Dance of the Infidels* by Francis Paudras, a moving and candid account of his friendship with American bebop jazz pianist Bud Powell during his years as an exile in France. Paudras was a struggling graphic designer in Paris in the 1960s when he befriended the jazz legend. A meaningful friendship ensued, and Paudras became Powell's most active supporter, even tending to Powell's medical needs with the help of jazz saxophonist Johnny Griffin. Powell's wife Altevia Edwards entered into a contentious custody battle with Paudras over the troubled pianist, the inference being that Edwards mistreated Powell in some way, whether directly or by way of neglect.

Powell, who suffered mental problems as well as a debilitating alcoholism, was perhaps jazz's most unpredictable and doomed genius. His startling creativity, when in full form, seemed unstoppable. According to alto saxophonist Jackie McLean, Bud Powell could even outplay Charlie Parker on a really good night, no small feat by any measure. By the time Powell was resident in Paris, he had lost much of his earlier genius. Paudras, who was a devoted jazz aficionado of the highest order, knew all of Powell's records by heart, which put him in a unique position of empathy and understanding. One can imagine Bertrand Tavernier, a bona fide jazz expert, becoming excited by the dramatic potential of Paudras's memoirs, especially as it was a story set in France at a time when he was in his early twenties and taking his first steps towards a career in cinema.

When Tavernier looked for a screenwriter to bring Paudras's story to the screen, he enlisted David Rayfiel, best known at the time as Sydney Pollack's writer on films such as *Three Days of the Condor* and *Out of Africa*. Initially, Tavernier faced considerable resistance from Warner Bros executives to his idea of casting real-life saxophone legend Dexter Gordon in the lead role of Dale Turner. Gordon, who had never acted in a wide release movie before, was sixty-two years old at the time and would effectively be carrying the film. There was clearly no question of authenticity on Gordon's behalf. Their concern was more his ability to appear natural and credible on screen as a fictionalised version of himself, or close to it. Dale Turner was an amalgam of Bud Powell and tenor saxophone innovator Lester Young, who was known to be a direct influence on the architect of bebop, Charlie Parker. For Dexter Gordon to be playing Dale Turner made a whole lot of sense, regardless of his acting experience.

Despite this initial reluctance from the Studio, Tavernier was determined to achieve maximum authenticity in a way that had eluded earlier jazz movies. The French director went several steps further to this end by hiring real jazz musicians to fill out the supporting cast. Herbie Hancock (who would win an Oscar for Best Music, Original Score), Wayne Shorter, Billy Higgins, Bobby Hutcherson, Tony Williams, Freddie Hubbard, Pierre Michelot and John McLaughlin had all played or recorded with Dexter Gordon before and helped to bring an authenticity to the film that would become one of its greatest legacies. However, the real innovation was Tavernier's insistence that all the diegetic music in the film be recorded live, as they shot, a totally unheard-of request up to that point. Jazz, being improvisatory in nature, is never played the same way twice; therefore, Tavernier knew the only way to do the music justice was to record sound and picture at the same time. Not only was this a technical tour de force, it helped make clear to an audience just how creative jazz musicians were. It was a case of Tavernier making cinema come to jazz and not the other way around. This was already a huge step towards changing the representation of jazz in cinema as well as a sign of Tavernier's great respect and admiration for the music.

So where then might we detect in *'Round Midnight* the negatively stereotypical portrayal of Black American jazz musicians that so riled jazz legend Max Roach, who himself had played with Bud Powell on many occasions? Can it be attributed to the white, male film-makers who created the movie? Is it that Max Roach wasn't in the film or is it motivated by the fact that a Jewish writer, David Rayfiel, wrote the script and not a Black American writer. Let's look at the movie itself scene by scene and delve into its structure, content, execution, inference and effect to try to understand why. The movie opens in a shabby-looking apartment where Dale Turner, played by Dexter Gordon, stands with his back to camera gazing out a window as he recalls the semi-fictionalised saxophonist Hershell (played by Hart Leroy Bibbs and based on musicians Herschel Evans and Lester Young). We then flash back, in a seamless single take that shifts from black and white to colour, to Hershell lying in bed in his pyjamas in the middle of the day as he and Turner discuss the merits and demerits of bebop. Hershell chastises Turner when he asks him 'Still playing those weird chords? Drives people wild, can't follow the tune!' to which the unflappable and taciturn Turner replies 'Yeah, I know'.

When Dale Turner arrives in a jazz-friendly Paris, things seem to have not actually improved that much as we find ourselves in another crummy apartment with dirty dishes piled up in a hand basin and stained pots and pans hanging from the wall. It isn't long before Turner vomits into the toilet, a result of his rampant alcoholism (a direct reference to Bud Powell here). The very next scene sees Dale Turner playing *As Time Goes By* (from *Casablanca*) to a very appreciative Paris jazz club audience (the Blue Note), who are all suited and booted to hear an American jazz legend in the flesh.

The screenwriter is clearly showing us here the contrast between a sordid, subsistence-level private life and the elevated art form the very same man creates on stage every night. Moments later we meet Ben, the red-shirted club owner counting dollars in his eyes as Turner and his bandmates (including Herbie Hancock and John McLaughlin) spin gold on stage. We look into the local Parisian audience – it is a sea of (white) faces. Is this what bugged Roach? Underpaid Black musicians performing great music for greedy white club owners and spoilt brat, White Parisians? Even as an outsider, one can feel his indignity if not entirely share it from a first-hand perspective. Indeed, Max Roach and Charles Mingus (another pioneer in jazz and in civil rights) formed their own record label in 1952, Debut Records, to avoid this very problem. Roach was one of the most effective, committed and persuasive of all jazz musicians, whose music was strongly political in content and execution. His criticism of the film was rooted in real life. Selective representation was clearly the issue for him.

In light of this, do we level criticism against a 'portrayal' of a race/wealth/cultural disparity or do we level criticism against the disparity itself? Is the portrayal perpetuating the disparity or merely recording it? By eradicating such portrayals, do we eradicate the problem itself or merely deny its existence? These are questions worth asking if we're to do the subject full justice. One thing that cannot be disputed, however, is just how seriously *'Round Midnight* treats the subject of American jazz and how respectful it is of its creators and its creative process. Even Clint Eastwood's 1988 Charlie Parker biopic *Bird* barely made mention of the actual creative process in the way *'Round Midnight* did. Eastwood's film seemed more concerned with Charlie Parker's downward spiral into drug dependency and debilitation than it was with his monumental contributions to music. Parker was virtuosic, innovative and forward thinking – perhaps the most influential jazz musician of all time – but we see little of this in *Bird*. Here's another example of Tavernier's approach in *'Round Midnight*. In one scene, Dale Turner talks in some detail of how bebop, probably the most technically challenging form of jazz, was created. He says,

> The swing band used to be straight time, and then there was the Basie band and I heard Lester Young … he was playing all the colour tones, the sixths, the ninths and major sevenths … like Debussy and Ravel. Then Charlie Parker came on and he began to expand … he went into 11ths and 13ths … luckily I was going in the same direction already.

This level of technical dialogue is simply astonishing to hear in a studio film with a not insignificant budget. It is very hard to imagine a movie about jazz made in 2020 going to these lengths to discuss the purely technical innovations of the music. If there is one thing studio executives really hate, it's dialogue they feel will confuse or frustrate the least curious possible person in the audience. Turning the critical metre back again in the direction of the movie, there are questions of gender relations one could ask with some justification. Apart from Dale Turner, whose 'partner' Buttercup is a bossy mother type, all the girlfriends we see of the Black American jazz musicians in the movie are much younger, pretty, white, demure French ladies who barely manage a single line of dialogue throughout. Is this an issue if we're assessing the movie's authenticity or system of representation? Was this casting choice based on reality, or did it perpetuate the idea that jazz musicians get only the best-looking women on their arm? Do we prefer perception over reality when reality makes us feel uncomfortable?

Interestingly, we next have the appearance of a bigoted, white, male French neighbour who appears in his underwear, angry and aggressive, at the door of Dale's Paris apartment as he and his friends enjoy a house party. 'Close the door! This isn't the Casbah!' he shouts in his absurd French indignity. The racist, colonial implications of his outburst are clear. Even in jazz-loving France, racism abides. Despite this, Turner and his friends laugh off his stupidity – they've heard it all before. Next, we see Dale Turner practising his tenor saxophone in a back alley amidst a disgusting pile of rubbish and refuse. Although this scene in particular may be historically accurate in some sense, its representation of a great Black American musician plying his craft amidst stinking rubbish seems a bridge too far. By this juncture in the movie, the point has been made abundantly clear that Dale Turner suffers for his art. Did we really need to see such an elegant and brilliant man sitting amidst rubbish bins playing his saxophone?

The fact that these questions can be asked only serves to remind us of just how influential movies are over our perception of real life. We invariably want movies to be an improved version of our own mediocre existence and feel let down when they fail to flatter, placate or feed this desire. This writer, for one, could have done without the humiliating imagery of Dale Turner (Dexter Gordon) playing his music in such a squalid setting. Given this, one can only imagine the anger that the movie provoked in its detractors. *'Round Midnight* is a movie with scenes of squalor and alcoholism followed immediately by a justified glorification of jazz that has no equal in cinema history. Perhaps then, it is actually about the human struggle more than it is about the race/class/culture disparity as noted above. I write this piece at the *same time* as I am watching *'Round Midnight* in an attempt to react to it in real time, just as the jazz musician must. There is a scene where Turner (Gordon) plays *Body and Soul*, a classic ballad much covered by jazz musicians. As we know, the music was recorded at the same time as the picture; we are therefore seeing and hearing exactly what the musicians played as the cameras rolled and therefore are witnessing the reactions of the musicians accordingly. As Turner (Gordon) plays his cadenza at the end of the song, he spins out a glorious eight-note ascending pattern as the beautifully legato camera stays on guitarist John McLaughlin and drummer Billy Higgins as they wait for Turner's (Gordon's) final phrases. The real beauty of this cinematographic approach lies in this very moment as we witness the tremendous level of empathy and listening that takes place on a bandstand with musicians as great as this. This surely must be the greatest achievement of 'Round Midnight. Tavernier said himself that he wanted to see the musicians react to what was actually being played as they rolled the camera, and this is only one such example of his unique achievement.

Mention must be made of the acting performances in 'Round Midnight. Dexter Gordon, who was Oscar nominated for his performance alongside Paul Newman and William Hurt, had not acted before in a major motion picture, and yet he exudes the grace and charisma of a veteran actor like Robert Mitchum or Burt Lancaster. Gordon's reactions are 100 per cent authentic 100 per cent of the time. True, he was playing a variation of himself in Dale Turner, but unlike his contemporary Miles Davis, who also acted in movies, Gordon is never caught posturing, projecting or indicating or hiding behind a bogus tough guy image. Gordon's comic timing, a skill that requires both natural ability and training from any actor, is immaculate. In a now famous and oft-quoted scene, an elegant French drunk takes one last drink at the bar of the Blue Note jazz club before collapsing. Turner looks on nonchalantly before turning to the barman with the immortal quip, 'Sil-vous plait, I'll have what he's having.' The cast also includes the likes of jazz legends Herbie Hancock, Bobby Hutcherson and Wayne Shorter, who also play slight variations of themselves with an effortless elan, charm and good humour. The brilliant Sandra Reaves-Phillips plays Buttercup, based heavily on Bud Powell's partner/manager, and demonstrates an unwavering instinct reminiscent of Anna Magnani in Rome, Open City. Lonette McKee plays a Billie Holiday modelled singer called Darcy Leigh, who is the former lover and acolyte of Dale Turner. McKee brings a dazzling feminine charm and grace to the movie, and her chemistry with Gordon plays like one of the great Hollywood love stories from the 1930s. They are simply magical together, so magical that their time on screen seems destined not to last, like a green ray at the end of a Hermosa Beach sunset.

A special paragraph should be reserved for the great French actor François Cluzet who plays Francis Borler, that is, Francis Paudras. Cluzet is an actor with a tremendous inner energy, focus and intensity (that you might normally see in an American method actor) that belies his modest frame especially when placed next to the gigantic Dexter Gordon (198 cm). In the one instant Cluzet seems ready to explode with rage, in the next he is all tenderness and sensitivity. The chasm that exists in between these two extremes is where Cluzet's most interesting acting happens. Dale Turner and Francis Borler are each other's ballast in this movie. One is unsure as to whether or not François Cluzet is a real-life jazz fan, and perhaps it's better this way. He is so convincing as Francis Borler that it matters not where reality lies. When we see Cluzet stand outside the Blue Note jazz club in Paris at the beginning of the movie in the lashing rain, penniless and unable to afford entrance, every inch of his body conveys a burning love of the music, a messianic belief in every segmented sound wave. Where it is unacceptable for an actor to pretend to be a jazz musician, it is somehow okay for a great actor to play a jazz fan even when he isn't one in real life. Perhaps this is because of the universality of the passion for listening to music as opposed to the very technical demands of playing it. Being a jazz fan is certainly not the same thing as being a jazz musician – however, one could not exist without the other.

There is also Martin Scorsese who commits his finest ever performance as R. W. Goodley, the manager of Birdland in New York City, based on his real-life counterpart Oscar Goodstein. Goodley (or is it Scorsese) is a bundle of New York City nerves, humour and charm who says the word 'great' six times in the space of fifteen seconds. As they pass Calvary cemetery in Brooklyn, Dale Turner asks ruefully, 'I don't remember all these people being here when I left.' 'Oh they were here ... they were here', replies R. W. Goodley, grinning characteristically. This isn't the first reference to mortality in *'Round Midnight*. Turner's tongue-in-cheek reference to Louis XIV encapsulates the movie's nonchalance in the face of death. As Turner and Borler arrive in Turner's shabby hotel room, even grubbier than his Paris digs, Turner turns to his French friend and phlegmatically opines, '*SOS ... same old shit*'. Disused fire extinguishers, in-house prostitutes, fading paint, drug dealers – this, we are told, is the lot of the jazz man in the 1960s whether in America or in France. Instant coffee and peanut butter is about all the motor-mouthed R. W. Goodley can offer Dale Turner as a way of recompense.

And so Dale Turner, our Olympian hero who swings from rubbish bins to dank hotels to swank New York City jazz clubs, approaches his end, an end that is both unknowable and predestined.

'There's not enough kindness in the world', Turner tells his friend Francis as he heads back to Paris. A cliché on paper but when delivered by an actor and musician as great as Dexter Gordon, it becomes an aphorism of stunning dignity. A tragic coda to this story is that Francis Paudras committed suicide in

1997. Opposites attract but the like-minded do so even more, especially when artistic impulses steer the ship. If someone ever wrote a biography of Francis Paudras, it could feasibly be titled *Dance of the Believers*.

How then do we reconcile the great beauty, dignity, respect, understanding and craftsmanship of Bertrand Tavernier's *'Round Midnight* with the criticisms levelled against it by Max Roach and others? How would *'Round Midnight* be treated in 2020 in the midst of the Black Lives Matter movement? Would it be called racist for depicting a Black American man as a hopeless alcoholic dependent on a caring, earnest white man? Quite possibly. Would this be justified? I think largely it would not be. I think such a criticism would be intellectually unsound to say the very least and entirely insensitive to the kind of subtleties of human relations that can transcend race. For example, many White jazz musicians were also alcoholics and drug addicts at the same time as Bud Powell such as Gerry Mulligan, Chet Baker, Stan Getz, Bill Evans and Art Pepper. It goes without saying that those very great musicians had people who helped them through the tough times just as Bud Powell did; so if a movie were made about their stories, would we be applying the same critical criteria? If a film were to be made about the special friendship between the White Baroness Pannonica de Koenigswarter and the Black jazz great Thelonious Monk (the Baroness was unofficial patron and benefactor of Monk), would this also be called racist?

In 2016, the decision to cast Zoe Saldaña (who has Puerto Rican and Dominican parents) as Nina Simone was heavily criticised by the late singer's estate, eventually leading to the actress apologising, presumably for not being Black enough given she had to wear make-up to bring her closer to Simone's skin tone. Initially, Saldaña had been more defiant but presumably caved in under pressure from agents, publicists, producers and the trial-by-execution monstrosity known as social media. Will this sensibility scare off future film-makers from making movies about jazz musicians if they do not have an identical skin tone or physiognomy? This may be a victory in the eyes of some (or many) but would surely make it even harder than it already is to get these kinds of movies financed, produced and released. I don't think anyone would argue that we need more movies about the Black experience and not less.

Let it be said clearly – the creation of jazz music by Black Americans is one of the greatest contributions to music and art the world has ever known. Cinema should be used as an aid to make this fact more widely known. It won't always get it right, but let's not shut down the process before it has a chance to take full flight.

I cannot imagine a movie like *'Round Midnight* being made in 2021 the way it was in 1986. Time, sensibilities and sensitivities have changed radically since then even if Paudras's story remains unchanged. Therefore, it is his story that would be rejected in 2020, his subjectivity. Is this a wilful, collective cherry picking of what is a shared cultural and racial history? The uncomfortable truth that has to be accepted, regardless of who is telling the story, is that hardship, dependency (emotional, financial or chemical) and suffering is universal. Princes can become paupers and vice versa. Material surroundings fluctuate but art remains, and it is art that nourishes us most ardently when watching *'Round Midnight*. The fact that Bud Powell's art (channelled via Dexter Gordon) rose out of such dire circumstances (being racism, mental illness and alcoholism) only highlights its preciousness. If *'Round Midnight* achieved only one thing it was to remind us of this.

References

Bird (1988), [Film] Dir. Clint Eastwood, USA: The Malpaso Company.
Casablanca (1942), [Film] Dir. Michael Curtiz, USA: Warner Bros.
Out of Africa (1985), [Film] Dir. Sydney Pollack, USA: Mirage Enterprises.
Rome, Open City (Roma, città aperta) (1945), [Film] Dir. Roberto Rossellini, Italy: Excelsa Film.
'Round Midnight (1986), [Film] Dir. Bertrand Tavernier, USA/France: Little Bear.
Three Days of the Condor (1975), [Film] Dir. Sydney Pollack, USA: Wildwood Enterprises.

11

Ryuichi Sakamoto: Behind the mask

Jason Wood

One of the biggest and most critically acclaimed global stars to emerge from Japan – if not the biggest – Ryuichi Sakamoto is undoubtedly a pioneering figure. As a keyboardist and songwriter in Haruomi Hosono's Yellow Magic Orchestra (YMO), Sakamoto helped set the stage for synthpop and inspired a generation of hip-hop, techno and electro artists. Fusing global genres and close studies of classical impressionism, Sakamoto is equally entrenched in cinema, scoring over thirty films, including Bernardo Bertolucci's *The Last Emperor* (1988) – for which he won an Academy Award, a Grammy and a Golden Globe – and *The Sheltering Sky* (1990), John Maybury's *Love is the Devil* (1998) and more recently Alejandro González Iñárritu's *The Revenant* (2015). His acting appearance in Nagisa Ôshima's *Merry Christmas, Mr. Lawrence* (1983) both built upon and significantly increased his profile both within Japan and internationally. Sakamoto also composed the film's score, delivering a complete and highly exportable package, and winning a Best Film Music BAFTA into the bargain.

Sakamoto has developed a polymath status, a Bowie-like figure who has used his success as a springboard to pursue deeper intellectual pursuits, stimulate creative development and map out esoteric personal journeys. His more recent work is marked by an interest in the relationship between space and sound: how the one reflects and refracts the other is something that Sakamoto has also explored both in his compositions and in his collaborations with visual artists, including Nam June Paik (*All Star Video* 1994) and *LIFE* (1999) with Shiro Takatani. Nature and the passing of time are also themes that anchor the composers work, as evidenced by 2017's *async*, made whilst in recovery from throat cancer, and the 2017 Stephen Nomura Schible–directed documentary *Ryuichi Sakamoto: Coda*, in which Sakamoto travels to the Arctic to record the sound of melting snow. In another scene, Sakamoto plays a 'drowned' piano that

Figure 11.1 Ryuichi Sakamoto.
Source: Getty Images

was found in the Miyagi Prefecture during the aftermath of the 2011 earthquake-tsunami that triggered a nuclear disaster in Fukushima, Japan.

These sonic observations are not just aesthetic; they run in parallel to Sakamoto's environmental and activism work. He is an anti-nuclear campaigner and the founder of the more trees project, which is involved in reforestation and carbon offsetting. The veins that connect Ryuichi Sakamoto's music, art and activism are his meditations on the ever-evolving nature of life.

For many, Sakamoto's stardom and presence is undoubtedly synonymous with cinema and is perhaps crystallised in time by his aforementioned acting debut as the taciturn and sexually conflicted prisoner of war camp commander Yonoi in Ōshima's radical adaptation of the 1963 novel *The Seed and the Sower* by the South African novelist Lauren van de Post. A film that explores issues of Japanese identity and taboo attitudes to sexual preference, the film built on Sakamoto's success with the YMO in Japan (and the presence of co-star Takeshi 'Beat' Kitano, a hugely popular comedian at the time[1]) and achieved global

---

[1] Known in Japan as a TV host, Takeshi Kitano rose to prominence in the 1970s as one half of the comedy duo Two Beat, before going solo and becoming one of the three biggest comedians in the country.

recognition, thanks also in part to the appearance in the film of David Bowie as the rebellious Western prisoner of war, Major Jack Celliers.

It's a film that reflects and refracts Japanese culture, fetishising Sakamoto's beauty and code of honour whilst also inviting a more Western interpretation and consummation of these elements, as evidenced by *Forbidden Colours*, the Sakamoto and David Sylvian penned and performed pop single that preceded the film. As the lead singer of Japan,[2] Sylvian had long indulged his obsession with all things Japanese. Japan invited Sakamoto to play keyboards on 'Taking Islands in Africa' from the band's *Gentlemen Take Polaroids* (1980) album, and then Sakamoto and Sylvian collaborated more fully on the 1982 single *Bamboo Houses/Bamboo Music*. The two would continue to orbit around each other.

Before we return in more detail to *Merry Christmas, Mr. Lawrence*, it is worth looking more closely at YMO and the role that the band played in securing Sakamoto's renown, popularity and willingness to engage with and interrogate his cultural heritage.

Solid State Survivors

Formed in 1978 by Haruomi Hosono, Ryuichi Sakamoto (who prior to the group's formation had been experimenting with electronic music equipment such as the Buchla synthesiser at the Tokyo National University of Fine Arts and Music) and Yukihiro Takahashi, YMO are one of the central figures in the techno/new wave movement of the late 1970s. Contemporaries of Kraftwerk and DEVO, the band have exerted a seismic influence on techno/hip-hop and rock music and also helped usher in the J-Pop phenomenon that overtook Japan in the 1990s.

---

[2] Formed in South London in 1974 by David Sylvian, Steve Jansen (drums), Mick Karn and Richard Barbieri, Japan were an influential New Wave British band that morphed from alternative glam-rock beginnings to incorporate electronic influences. Enjoying critical and commercial success, the band's international success enabled them to indulge their love of foreign cultural elements, particularly from Japan and the band's aesthetic fetishised Japanese traditions. During the early 1980s, Sakamoto collaborated with the band and formed a lasting alliance with Sylvian. Similarly, Steve Jansen was influenced by YMO's drummer Yukihiro Takahashi, subsequently joining him on several of Takahashi's solo projects and tours of Japan, along with additional full collaborative works between the two. The band split in December 1982, though they re-formed briefly in the early 1990s under the name Rain Tree Crow, releasing an album in 1991.

Initially conceived by Hosono as a one-off exploration of computerised exotica and a parody of Western conceptions of the orient (an element also meditated upon in Ôshima's drama), the disparate elements that were pulled into their sphere of influence included science-fiction writing and cyberpunk culture, the electronic music of Isao Tomita, Japanese traditional music, arcade games and the disco productions of Giorgio Moroder. The band's self-titled debut album released in 1978 spawned a global hit in *Computer Game*, a hugely influential single that reached the UK top twenty and sold 400,000 copies in the United States. Marketing tie-ins with Japanese electronic brands such as Fuji spread the popularity of YMO's technopop in their homeland and saw the hysteria surrounding the band reach Beatles-like proportions.

Solid State Survivor (1979) continued the excursion down electronic highways and upped the interest in alienated, dystopic visions. *Behind The Mask* would prove another international hit (it was later covered by Eric Clapton), and the album would go on to sell over two million copies worldwide. Frequently joined by other musicians such as Hideki Matsutake, the band consolidated their success with the studio album *Multiples* (1980) and the live recording – and revealingly titled – *Public Pressure* (1980), which sold a record 250,000 copies in its first week in Japan. Feted by the likes of Afrika Bambaata and enjoying sell-out international tours and performances on *Soul Train*, the band released a number of other equally successful and acclaimed recordings before pausing their activity in 1983, when they announced that they would *sankai*, or 'fan-out'. YMO reunited in 1993 with performances which drew 100,000 people to the show in Tokyo and included The Orb as their opening act.

During the period 1993–2002, the group members continued to focus on their solo careers but reunited when Hosono and Takahashi formed Sketch Show and invited Sakamoto to contribute on tracks on their releases *Audio Sponge* (2002) and *Loophole* (2003). Sakamoto joined Sketch Show for the Sonar Festival in 2004 for a performance under the name Human Audio Sponge (or HAS), a name inspired by the writings of UK-based writer, musician and curator David Toop. The band considered HAS to be a completely separate entity from YMO and embodied this idea in their performance style, shying away from live instruments. HAS was a name that reflected the musical direction of the three members at the time, absorbing various musical elements and converting these ideas in their original way to create a totally new sound. Amalgamating the two band names and appearing as HASYMO, the original YMO appeared together as part of Massive Attack's 2008 Meltdown, even performing two new songs.

Working with new collaborators, including Christian Fennesz and Cornelius, the band performed together as recently as 2011; the band have seen their back catalogue remastered, re-imagined and sampled and continue to see their name cited as influential by a plethora of contemporary music artists from the world of hip-hop, twenty-first-century electronica, ambient, acid house, Detroit, pop and mixers and DJ figures such as Kieran Hebden.

Forbidden colours

The incredibly prolific Ryuichi Sakamoto would of course go on to make a number of acclaimed records under his own name, both while YMO were on active duty and while they were on hiatus. At the time of the production of *Merry Christmas, Mr. Lawrence* they were very much a going concern, and their popularity and that of Sakamoto, as well as his compositional skills and his representation of a modern Japan, would no doubt have been a factor in casting him. Having him appear alongside David Bowie, a global star about to unleash the behemothic *Let's Dance* on the world, who had also displayed a prior fascination with Japanese culture, would have been simply too cute to resist and would have accentuated the Eastern/Western dichotomy. Director Nagisa Ôshima stated from the outset that he intended to cast two pop stars in the central roles, one to represent the East and one to represent the West. Bowie was a renowned Japanophile who adopted and indulged many elements of Japanese culture. Working with the designer Kansai Yamamoto on his early-stage outfits, Bowie also displayed a fascination with Japanese Kabuki theatre from his time studying under Lindsay Kemp. An admirer of the writer Yukio Mishima, whom he also painted, Bowie also dotted his music with references to Japan, from the use of the koto in 'Moss Garden' from *Heroes* (1977) to the lyrics of 'Move On'[3] from 1979's *Lodger*. Even in retrospect, Bowie largely avoided accusations of cultural appropriation (an indictment that Sylvian and his cohorts had to endure), and this was certainly a charge the artist never faced in Japan.[4]

---

[3] 'Spent some nights in old Kyoto. Sleeping on the matted ground.'
[4] 'Bowie was born to be the ultimate diplomat and artiste', comments Helene Thian. 'He took his creativity and fused it with his impulses to meld East and West and come up with a healing of the world in this post-war period. This was a homage to Japanese culture and the Japanese loved it as Bowie challenged the tendency of Western fashion at the time to lump all Asian styles together as "Orientalism"' (quoted from Wong (2016)).

Merry Christmas, Mr. Lawrence did not emerge from a vacuum. It was the work of an incredible influential figure in post-war Japanese cinema and a leading member of the Japanese *nuberu bagu* (new wave) movement. One of Japan's most renowned directors, Nagisa Ôshima's bold portrayals of turbulent post-war Japanese society, sociopolitical disaffection and sexual desire courted controversy throughout his distinguished career.

The Ôshima gang

Ôshima studied law at Kyoto University and joined in the student protest movement sweeping the country. After his studies, he joined Shochiku Film Company's Ofuna Studio as an apprentice and assisted a number of directors before debuting with *Tomorrow's Sun* (1959). Featuring a number of first-time actors, the film marked Ôshima as a director to watch. His first full feature, *A Town of Love and Hope* (*Ai to kibô no machi*) followed in 1959. A story of the relationship between a poor pigeon vendor and a bourgeois girl, the film's final scene outraged Japanese audiences (and Shochiku's studio head), leading to limited screenings after Shochiku withdrew its support. Ôshima started to gain popularity with his next feature, *Naked Youth* (*Seishun zankoku monogatari* 1960), boldly portraying disaffected Japanese youth in an adult's world. It won Ôshima the Director's Guild of Japan's Best Newcomer Award. Ôshima continued to expose the contradictions in post-war Japan with *The Sun's Burial* (*Taiyô no hakaba* 1960), a film about gangs in the Osaka slums.

The next film would see Ôshima depart from a traditional narrative and identifiable genre: *Night and Fog in Japan* (*Nihon no yoru to kiri* 1960) is a powerful memory piece about the agitated protests in the 1950s and 1960s. Intensely political, the film was banned after only four days on release amidst concerns about social stability after the assassination of the socialist leader Inejirō Asanuma.[5] Furious, Ôshima left Shochiku to set up his own production company Sozosha with his wife, the actor Akiko Koyama. After an adaptation of Kenzaburo Oe's novel *The Catch* (*Shiiku* 1961) and several television

---

[5] The leader of the Japan Socialist Party, Asanuma became a forceful advocate of socialism in post-war Japan and was noted for his support of the Chinese Communist Party. His criticisms of US–Japanese relations proved controversial, and he was assassinated in graphic fashion on live television by the ultranationalist Otoya Yamaguchi.

documentaries, Ôshima directed, amongst others, *Pleasures of the Flesh* (*Etsuraku* 1965), the surreal *Death by Hanging* (*Kôshikei* 1968) and *The Ceremony* (*Gishiki* 1971), which attracted interest in the West after it was selected for Director's Fortnight at Cannes.

In the 1970s, the director began accepting foreign financing in order to make films that reflected his militant refusal to fit in, films many of which 'focus on characters who either find themselves marginalised or choose to opt out. Ôshima himself was neither dissolute nor criminal, but he identified sex and crime as the twin fault-lines in Japanese society and explored both in almost everything he made, hoping always to shock his audiences into seeing themselves more clearly'.

In 1976, Nagisa Ôshima enjoyed a major international breakthrough with Western audiences with *In the Realm of the Senses* (*ai no corrida*), a turbulent tale of the pursuit of sexual satisfaction. Based on the true story of Sada Abe, a 1930s Geisha, the film, which won the 1976 Sutherland Trophy at the London Film Festival, was instantly hailed as a masterpiece and as one of cinema's great erotic films. Banned in Japan, the film became a major fixture on the international arthouse circuit. Ôshima followed it up with *Empire of Passion* (*Ai no bôrei* 1978), which focused on an adulterous couple who plot to murder the woman's husband. The director's critical stock was elevated still further when the film won him the Best Director prize at Cannes.

> You are the victim of men who think they are right ... Just as one day you and captain Yonoi believed absolutely that you were right. And the truth is of course that nobody is right.[6]

After suffering a series of strokes in the 1990s, Ôshima's output was limited, with *Gohatto* (1999), his take on the Samurai film, being his final work. A study of homosexual desire in an intensely coded masculine world, in the continued tradition of Ôshima's work, it exposed the contradictions in Japanese culture in a way that is ceaselessly provocative and compelling. There is a circularity to *Gohatto* that links it to *Merry Christmas, Mr. Lawrence* not only in a thematic sense – homosexuality and male Japanese cultural tradition – but also in terms of the director's collaborators. The mercurial Jeremy Thomas was one of the film's producers. The score was again composed by Sakamoto, and Takeshi Kitano, by

---

[6] Line spoken by Colonel John Lawrence, played in the film by Tom Conti.

now firmly established as a significant Japanese export for his work as an actor and as a director,[7] took the starring role.

Ôshima's English language debut, *Merry Christmas, Mr. Lawrence*, was a high-profile and extremely prestigious international production that was at the time controversial, especially within Japan, for its exploration of racism, unwritten desire and the sparks that fly when cultures collide. For Ôshima, that attraction lay in questioning, 'Is it possible in the cruellest of situations, such as war, for enemies to understand each other?'[8]

Adapted by the director and screenwriter Paul Mayersberg (whose screenplay credits include Nicolas Roeg's *The Man who Fell to Earth*, 1976, and *Eureka*, 1983), the film concentrates on a war of wills between enigmatic and rebellious prisoner of war Jack Celliers and coldly efficient camp commandant Captain Yonoi. Intelligently exploring the psychology of its characters, the clash between two cultures and traditions (British and Japanese) and two styles of military service (patriotic and pragmatic), the film makes for an audacious and original addition to the prisoner of war genre. Critically well received – despite some reservations about contrasting acting styles (surely intentional) and an unfortunate flashback sequence in which Bowie – then in his forties appears as a schoolboy – the film has become one of the foundations of both Bowie and Sakamoto mythology.

The queer element of the narrative was an invention on Ôshima's part and does not appear in the source novel.

> Our attitudes toward gender have changed very much since the war. I put a homosexual aspect between Yonoi and Celliers and also I clearly wrote a homosexual relationship between a Dutch prisoner of war and Kanemoto in the script. Van der Post made a very wry face when he saw this as there was no such homosexual episode in his book. He didn't dare to write about a homosexual love between Yonoi and Celliers either. But I felt that if he wrote the book now he would depict it as homosexual love, as I thought clearly the standard of expression had altered.[9]

---

[7] Takeshi Kitano's films as director include *Takeshis* (2005), *Zatôichi* (2003), *Dolls* (2002), *Brother* (2000), *Kikujiro* (1999), *Hana-Bi* (1997), *Kid's Return* (1996), *Getting Any* (1994), *Sonatine* (1993), *A Scene at the Sea* (1991), *Boiling Point* (1990) and *Violent Cop* (1989). *Hana-Bi* won the Golden Lion. Kitano won the Silver Lion for best director for *Zatôichi*.
[8] Interview with the author, 2005.
[9] Ibid.

Sakamoto arguably delivers the finest performance in the film and represents the moral and sexual complexity at the heart of it. His exterior sense of calm and regimental composition hides an inner raging torment, and once the mask of respectability has slipped, there is no return for him.

'Ryuichi Sakamoto is everything in the film. I am very satisfied with him. The beauty of Yonoi does not exist without him', commented Ôshima.[10] Sakamoto's score, his first for cinema, is also exquisite, and its use of Gamelan music particularly pleased its director as it referenced the murder scene of *The Son's Burial* (*Taiyo no hakaba* 1960).

A pop star both acting in a film and contributing its score has a long tradition in cinema. Bowie himself did it of course with both *Absolute Beginners* (1986) and *Labyrinth* (1986), but the tradition also includes the likes of Whitney Houston (*The Bodyguard* 1992), Jimmy Cliff (*The Harder They Come* 1972), Bjork (*Dancer in the Dark* 2000), Eminem (*8 Mile* 2002) and countless more. It utilises the performer's primary skill, but also helps tickets sales and marketing potential by tapping into an already established fan base.

Surprisingly, Sakamoto rarely appeared again in front of the camera, restricting himself to appearances for Bernardo Bertolucci (*The Last Emperor* 1987) and a small cameo for Abel Ferrara (*New Rose Hotel* 1998). Perhaps there was a realisation that with *Merry Christmas, Mr. Lawrence* he had already delivered a crowning achievement, working with an internationally renowned director opposite one of the biggest musical stars in the world and alongside a fellow Japanese cultural icon. A comment on contrasting attitudes to issues regarding morals and morality, it also reflects Sakamoto's position as an artist and a human being helping Japan to make the sometimes-difficult transition from one epoch to another and to accept compromise not as an act of weakness or failure but of growth and positive change.

Yonoi: If you didn't do it, who did? We must punish someone!
Col.: John Lawrence : But why? Would you rather punish the wrong man, than see the crime itself go unsolved? And unpunished!
Yonoi: Yes.
Col.: John Lawrence : You mean I'm to die because you think if there's a crime then it must be punished? And it doesn't matter who is punished?
Yonoi: Yes.

[10] Ibid.

References

Rayns, T. (2014), 'Ôshima Nagisa, 1932–2013'. 7 February. Available online: https://www2.bfi.org.uk/news-opinion/sight-sound-magazine/comment/obituaries/oshima-nagisa-1932-2013.

Wong T., A. Jones and Y. Kato (2016), 'David Bowie's Love Affair with Japanese Style'. Available online: https://www.bbc.co.uk/news/world-asia-35278488.

Filmography

8 Mile (2002), [Film] Dir. Curtis Hanson, USA: Imagine Entertainment, Mikona Productions GmbH & Co. KG.

A Scene at the Sea (1991), [Film] Dir. Takeshi Kitano, Japan: Office Kitano.

A Town of Love and Hope [*Ai to kibô no machi*] (1959), [Film] Dir. Nagisa Ôshima, Japan: Shochiku.

Absolute Beginners (1986), [Film] Dir. Julien Temple, UK: Goldcrest Films International, Palace Pictures, Virgin.

Boiling Point (1990), [Film] Dir. Takeshi Kitano, Japan: Office Kitano.

Brother (2000), [Film] Dir. Takeshi Kitano, Japan: Office Kitano.

Dancer in the Dark (2000), [Film] Dir. Lars von Trier, Denmark: Zentropa.

Death by Hanging [*Kôshikei*] (1968), [Film] Dir. Nagisa Ôshima, Japan: Sozosha.

Dolls (2002), [Film] Dir. Takeshi Kitano, Japan: Office Kitano.

Empire of Passion [*Ai no bôrei*] (1978), [Film] Dir. Nagisa Ôshima, Japan: Argos Films, Oshima Productions, Toho-Towa.

Eureka (1983), [Film] Dir. Nicolas Roeg, UK: Recorded Picture Company.

Getting Any (1994), [Film] Dir. Takeshi Kitano, Japan: Office Kitano.

Gohatto (1999), [Film] Dir. Nagisa Ôshima, Japan: Oshima Productions.

Hana-Bi (1997), [Film] Dir. Takeshi Kitano, Japan: Office Kitano.

In the Realm of the Senses [*Ai no corrida*] (1976), [Film] Dir. Nagisa Ôshima, Japan: Argos Films, Oshima Productions, Shibata Organisation.

Kid's Return (1996), [Film] Dir. Takeshi Kitano, Japan: Office Kitano.

Kikujiro (1999), [Film] Dir. Takeshi Kitano, Japan: Office Kitano.

Labyrinth (1986), [Film] Dir. Jim Henson, UK/USA: The Jim Henson Company.

Love Is the Devil (1998), [Film] Dir. John Maybury, UK: British Film Institute.

Merry Christmas, Mr. Lawrence (1983), [Film] Dir. Nagisa Ôshima, UK/Japan: Recorded Picture Company.

Naked Youth (AKA *Cruel Story of Youth*) [*Seishun zankoku monogatari*] (1960), [Film] Dir. Nagisa Ôshima, Japan: Shochiku.

New Rose Hotel (1998), [Film] Dir. Abel Ferrara, USA: Pressman Film, Quadra Entertainment.
Night and Fog in Japan [Nihon no yoru to kiri] (1960), [Film] Dir. Nagisa Ôshima, Japan: Shochiku.
Outrage Coda (2017), [Film] Dir. Takeshi Kitano, Japan: Office Kitano.
Pleasures of the Flesh [Etsuraku] (1965), [Film] Dir. Nagisa Ôshima, Japan: Sozosha.
Ryuichi Sakamoto: Coda (2017), [Film] Dir. Stephen Nomura Schibl, Japan: Dentsu Music and Entertainment.
Takeshis (2005), [Film] Dir. Takeshi Kitano, Japan: Office Kitano.
The Bodyguard (1992), [Film] Dir. Mick Jackson, USA: Warner Bros.
The Catch [Shiiku] (1961), [Film] Dir. Nagisa Ôshima, Japan: Palace Productions, Taiho.
The Ceremony [Gishiki] (1971), [Film] Dir. Nagisa Ôshima, Japan: Sozosha.
The Harder They Come (1972), [Film] Dir. Perry Henzell, Jamaica: International Films.
The Last Emperor (1987), [Film] Dir. Bernardo Bertolucci, UK: Recorded Picture Company.
The Man Who Fell to Earth (1976), [Film] Dir. Nicolas Roeg, UK: British Lion Film.
The Outrage (2010), [Film] Dir. Takeshi Kitano, Japan: Office Kitano.
The Revenant (2015), [Film] Dir. Alejandro González Iñárritu, USA: Production Company.
The Sheltering Sky (1990), [Film] Dir. Bernardo Bertolucci, UK/Italy: Recorded Picture Company.
The Son's Burial [Taiyo no hakaba, 1960], [Film] Dir. Nagisa Ôshima, Japan: Shochiku.
Tomorrow's Sun (1959), [Film] Dir. Nagisa Ôshima, Japan: Shochiku.
Violent Cop (1989), [Film] Dir. Takeshi Kitano, Japan: Bandai Media Department, Shochiku-Fuji Company.
Zatôichi: The Blind Swordsman (2003), [Film] Dir. Takeshi Kitano, Japan, Office Kitano.

Yellow Magic Orchestra Album Discography

Yellow Magic Orchestra, 1978
Solid State Survivor, 1979
Public Pressure, 1980
Xoo Multiplies, 1980
BGM, 1981
Technodelic, 1981
Naughty Boys, 1983
Service, 1983
Naughty Boys Instrumental, 1983
After Service, 1984

Technodon, 1993
One More YMO, 2007
Londonymo: Live in London 15 June 2008
Gijónymo: Live in Gijón 19 June 2008
Encore, 2009

Ryuichi Sakamoto Solo Album Discography

Disappointment-Hateruma, 1976
Thousand Knives of, 1978
Tokyo Joe, 1978
B-2 Unit, 1980
Left-Handed Dream, 1981
Merry Christmas, Mr. Lawrence [Original Soundtrack], 1983
Esperanto, 1985
Miraiha Yaro, 1985
Adventures of Chatran [Original Soundtrack], 1986
Ballet Mécanique, 1986
Koneko Monogatari, 1986
Media Bahn Live, 1986
The Last Emperor [Original Soundtrack], 1987
Neo Geo, 1987
Behind the Mask, 1987
The End of Asia, 1987
Plays Sakamoto, 1989
The Handmaid's Tale [Original Soundtrack], 1990
Beauty, 1990
The Sheltering Sky [Original Soundtrack], 1990
Heartbeat, 1991
Peachboy, 1991
High Heels [Original Soundtrack], 1992
Aile de Honneamise/Royal Space Force, 1993
Little Buddha [Original Soundtrack], 1993
Sweet Revenge, 1994
Hard to Get, 1995
Music for Yohji Yamamoto: Collection, 1995, 1997
Smoochy, 1997
Discord, 1998
Snake Eyes [Music from the Motion Picture], 1998

Love Is the Devil [Original Soundtrack], 1998
BTTB, 1999
Pre-Life in Progress, 1999
Sampled Life, 1999
Gohatto [Original Soundtrack], 1999
Raw Life: Live in Osaka, 1999
Intimate, 1999
Space, 1999
Monogatari No Youni Furusato Wa Toi, 2000
Audio Life, 2000
Discord [Remixes], 2000
Music Encyclopaedia, 2000
Eien No Ko (Eternal Child), 2000
Taboo [Original Soundtrack], 2000
L.O.L.: Lack of Love [Original Soundtrack], 2000
In the Lobby: At G.E.H. in London, 2001
Live in Tokyo, 2001
Comica, 2002
Futurista, 2002
Opera: Classical Works, 2002
Elephantism, 2002
Henkaku No Seiki: Century of Reform, 2002
Femme Fatale [Original Soundtrack], 2002
Vrioon, 2002
Love, 2003
Alexei and the Spring [Original Soundtrack], 2003
Derrida [Original Soundtrack], 2003
Summer Nerves, 2005
Chasm, 2005
Shining Boy and Little Randy, 2005
Chanconette Tedesche, 2005
Insen, 2005
Cendre, 2007
Silk [Original Soundtrack], 2007
Ocean Fire, 2007
*Utp_*, 2008
Out of Noise, 2009
Tokyo 031809, 2009
Sapporo 041909, 2009
Tokyo 042909, 2009
Playing the Piano, 2009

Ryuichi Sakamoto: Playing the Piano, 2009
UTAU, 2010
Flumina, 2011
Summvs, 2011
Ancient Future, 2012
Three, 2013
Disappearance, 2013
Playing the Orchestra, 2013
Perpetual, 2015
Playing the Orchestra, 2014
Mirukuyugafu: Undercooled, 2015
Live, 2015
The Revenant [Original Soundtrack], 2015
Nagasaki: Memories of My Son [Original Soundtrack], 2015
Ikari (Rage) [Original Soundtrack], 2016
Plankton: Music for an Installation by Christian Sardet and Shiro Takatani, 2016
Ryuichi Sakamoto: Music for Film, 2016
Async, 2017
Glass, 2018
Black Mirror: Smithereens [Original Series Soundtrack], 2019
Live in London, 2019
Two: Live at the Sydney Opera House, 2019
Proxima [Original Motion Picture Soundtrack], 2020
The Staggering Girl [Original Soundtrack], 2020

12

Reframing time and space in *Dogs in Space*

Kristy Matheson

Less than a decade after the actual events, Richard Lowenstein embarked on a feature film that eulogised subcultural Melbourne of the late 1970s, communal living and youthful excess. Drawn from his own memories of living in a large, chaotic, inner-city shared house, *Dogs in Space* charts the lives of the housemates and the broader post-punk scene. Taking inspiration from the ensemble casts and cross-cutting dialogue of Robert Altman, the film doesn't chart a linear plot, opting instead for multiple viewpoints with the camera in constant motion, roaming the house, parties, gigs – dropping the audience into random conversations and hilarious escapades. However, if *Dogs in Space* does have a central core, it's the romantic but doomed love affair between Sam (Michael Hutchence), the lead singer in a punk band called *Dogs in Space*, and his devoted girlfriend Anna (Saskia Post).

Released within months of the blockbuster comedy *Crocodile Dundee* (1986), Richard Lowenstein's *Dogs in Space* (1986) posited an entirely different vision of Australia. Without an outback vista or kangaroo in sight, the film ran counter to the preoccupations of mainstream national cinema which was still largely enthralled with promoting egalitarian tricksters like Paul Hogan's Mick Dundee or sweeping historical tales that celebrated white Australia's misguided affinity with the outback (*Man from Snowy River* 1982). But in casting the nation's biggest teen rock idol in the leading role, *Dogs in Space* was looking to sell a countercultural story to mainstream youth audiences, most of whom had more in common with the suburban banality that Lowenstein's characters were fighting against.

Lowenstein cast actors in some key roles – Tony Helou as Luccio, Saskia Post as Anna, the legendary Australian performer, Chris Haywood in a show-stopping cameo as Chainsaw Man and Nique Needles as Tim. Nique had grown up in the Melbourne scene and in the intervening years became a professional actor in Sydney. On returning to Melbourne in 1985 to star in the film he said, 'We were all hanging around at a party in 1980 and then six years later we're getting paid to recreate the same party'. For the most part, Lowenstein drew his cast from non-professionals; teens found at gigs, launderettes, and schools and many who'd been part of the actual Melbourne post-punk scene. In a 2017 interview Lowenstein recalled, 'I had people in costume playing my best friends, and in some cases, the real people were working on my crew and were dressed in the same clothes as the actors in front of them. It was pretty chaotic, but it was also pretty funny'. Another friend at the centre of Lowenstein's anti-establishment drama was Australia's most recognisable and mainstream rock star, Michael Hutchence. Since the early 1980s, Lowenstein had been making chart-topping videos for his band INXS, and they developed a lasting friendship. Casting Hutchence in the lead role of Sam puzzled many from Melbourne's original post-punk scene but elevated *Dogs in Space* out of its natural indie film habitat. With Hutchence in the leading role, *Dogs in Space* generated a huge amount of buzz during production, with interviews in mainstream entertainment press and feverish INXS fans hanging around the set. In a quote attributed to the young director ahead of the film's release, he'd made the 'youth market Crocodile Dundee of the summer of '86'. Or had he …

We're living on dog food, so what! Iggy Pop

The opening scenes of *Dogs in Space* brim with technical bravado, plunging the audience immediately into the world of the film. Cinematographer Andrew de Groot's slick camerawork and editor Jill Billcock's expert cutting offer only fragmented glimpses of the characters but firmly establish the oppositional position that this 'Blank Generation' held within Australian youth culture. Iggy Pop's provocation, 'We're living on dog food, so what!' is writ large on the screen before cutting to the rattling exhaust of an Australian muscle car. The camera glides along the exterior revealing a suburban Aussie skinhead; flat cap, cut-off tee, framed by the window and the fluffy dice hanging from the rear-view mirror. He glares out the window, takes a drag from his cigarette, swigs from his 'tinnie' of Victorian Bitter beer and screams out the window, 'Hey dogface, show us your snatch!' Manically laughing the car screeches off, and in a scene reminiscent of *Mad Max* (1979), the camera ascends and we're tearing through inner-city Melbourne as Iggy Pop's Dog Food blasts out on the soundtrack.

A title card, 'Melbourne, Australia 1978' situates the action. As the camera cranes down, we catch a glimpse of Sam and Anna, beautiful young punks, entangled, giggling, oblivious to their peers, also camped out on the footpath to secure tickets to the David Bowie concert. The muscle car screeches around the corner, the skinhead leaps out shouting to Sam: 'Ey!, you ... Prick-face!! Yeah, you ... Are you from the Planet Poofter, of the Planet Stupider ...?' This is our first real glimpse of (the) Michael Hutchence as Sam; he stares blankly, ruffles his sexy trademark curly locks and nonchalantly crawls back under his blanket. This is not the Hutchence we know, or the environs we expect to find him; after all its 1986 and his band INXS are number two on the Australian charts and number three on the US Billboard chart with their song 'What You Need', but there's simply not enough dirt in the world to make him look unattractive. Anna faces up to the aggressor, 'Why don't you just fuck off!' The skinhead shoves her aside as another punk girl enters the frame, smashing a bottle over the skinhead. Distant screams of, 'Ya fuckin' mole' can be heard as the car hoons off with a hip young punk played by Hugo Race (Nick Cave and the Bad Seeds, The Wreckery) riding the bonnet. As Hugo tumbles onto the road, the glistening chrome title *Dogs in Space* fills the screen before flying off to reveal a ramshackle weatherboard house, washed out in the blazing Australian summer sun.

The sounds of a nation

Ears frontman Sam Sejavka (on whom the lead character of Sam was based) remembers Melbourne in the late 1970s as

> a smaller, greyer, far more conservative city. The only alternative scenes were the sluggish festering hippies in Carlton and Fitzroy, a gaggle of Maori drag-queens in Fitzroy St (St Kilda), and the tribes of skinheads and sharpies in Holmesglen and Bayswater. Musical offerings included pub rock, more pub rock and maybe a bit of flaccid folk rock. Into this dead zone stepped a new generation inspired by the punk movement in London, New York and Detroit. Because the city was smaller, there was a tendency for the weirdos to find each other and congregate for safety. The David Bowie queue portrayed in *Dogs in Space* was one catalyst for this, we made a lot of friends and a lot of people decided to form bands there.

With cheap rents in shared houses, free university education and access to unemployment benefits, DIY music flourished in capital cities across Australia during the 1970:. The Saints and The Go-Betweens in Brisbane, Radio Birdman in Sydney, the Scientists in Perth and most famously in Melbourne, Nick Cave's, The Boys Next Door. Stuart Grant, singer and guitarist from the Primitive Calculators whose band delivers one of the most arresting musical set pieces in the film recalls, 'What made that scene possible in Melbourne in the late 1970s more than anything else was the legacy of the Whitlam government and the way they made the dole liveable. There were just thousands of people all over Australia living on the dole making up bands, it was like an arts grant. The State paid us to reject it.'

The fictionalised world of the film charts an intensely localised history of punk, with Lowenstein's former housemate Sam Sejavka's band The Ears as the inspiration for the central musical act. Refashioned as *Dogs in Space*, Hutchence (as Sam), Nicque Needles (Tim) and Chuck Meo (the band's actual drummer) perform versions of their songs throughout the film. Ollie Olsen, a pivotal member of the Melbourne scene with bands such as The Young Charlatans (with Rowland S. Howard) and Whirlywirld, was the film's musical director. The time lapse between 1978 and the film's production allowed Olsen to present a musical representation of the time rather than be slavish to the true chronology of the film, which roughly spans 1978 to 1981. It also allowed him to showcase the absolute specificity of the scene with bands such as The Primitive Calculators, Thrush & the C*nts, Too Fat to Fit Through the Door all performing in the film alongside Marie Hoy & Friends' show-stopping rendition of The Boys Next Door classic, 'Shivers' in one of the more seriously dramatic moments of the film. Lowenstein said, 'Within that subculture we were depicting, there was a year or so of really crazed energy, very productive; there were a lot of independent records coming out with a lot of energy and excitement.'

Music plays a central role in *Dogs in Space* as Lowenstein's characters hurtle to gigs in overcrowded Volkswagens, play at house parties, have impromptu early morning rehearsals at home and never miss an episode of Australian TV pop show Countdown. But in all of this activity, there's no talk of stardom, managers or a record man anywhere in sight. 'No one was really searching for anything except fun', said Nique Needles. 'Fun was the key word.'

Meanwhile, in the glittering coastal metropolis of Sydney, for Michael Hutchence and his middle-class school friends – guitarist and saxophonist

Kirk Pengilly; bassist Garry Gary Beers; the Farriss brothers, guitarist Tim, keyboardist and guitarist Andrew and drummer Jon – 1978 looked markedly different. 'We all made a pact. It was a Friday, the last day of school. I left home, I left school, and I got into a panel van and drove Mad Max style to Perth across the desert with Kirk. That was it. We just put our hands together and said, "Let's do it."' Michael Hutchence

Geographically isolated from the populous music scene on Australia's East Coast, the Farris Brothers band performed relentlessly, honing their craft with a repertoire of originals and party covers in church halls and remote mining town pubs. Intent on stardom, they returned to Sydney at the end of the 1970s, changed their name to INXS and alongside acts such as Cold Chisel, The Divinyls, The Angels and Midnight Oil took the emerging Oz Rock scene by storm. 'It was an explosive mixture of teenagers, alcohol, cigarettes, and rock music', said the youngest member of the group, Jon Farris. 'Everywhere you'd go you'd find sex, fights, and great bands.' With cover charges as little as $4 and bands playing across suburban beer barns, pubs and working men's clubs, youth audiences grew exponentially. In his biography on Hutchence, *Shine Like It Does*, Toby Creswell highlights how unprecedented the pub rock scene was in Australia, attributing the phenomenon to the 'showmanship' but most importantly that 'these bands were unapologetically Australian. People could see the music evolving in their lives and they could relate to the artists making the music'.

In contrast to Lowenstein's fictional *Dogs in Space*, INXS were tight, cohesive and united in their drive to succeed. In 1979, they met an equally ambitious soul in Chris Murphy, who started managing the band with steely eyed aggression. 'Australia is a matey society, and I didn't play mates with promoters and record companies. I was at home planning INXS's strategy when everybody else in the industry was out at Benny's or wherever snorting coke off the toilet seats. Nobody in the local industry believed "INXS" could be an international band. So my attitude was, "Fuck you."' Unlike their Oz Rock compatriots, whose music was intensely masculine, hard-edged rock in the tradition of AC/DC, INXS brought something new to the scene. Hutchence explained to VH-1 in 1994, 'We were trying to go into pubs and do something that nobody had ever really seen before and that was make people dance and not just throw beer cans at you and pick fights.' The formula was a success, and by the end of the decade, they had their first recording deal and were on a path to rock and roll stardom.

The young bohemians

Born within a year of each other, Richard Lowenstein and Michael Hutchence enjoyed childhoods which – each in their different ways – exposed them to an internationalism well beyond that of most of their suburban peers in 1960s Australia, a factor which surely infused their friendship and creative collaborations.

Hutchence's father Kell was a businessman whose work saw the family adopting a somewhat nomadic existence between different Australian cities and Hong Kong. His mother Patricia Glassop was a make-up artist, regularly taking Michael and his brother Rhett on film and TV sets while she worked. When his parents' marriage dissolved, Michael and his mother decamped to Los Angeles for a spell where he attended Hollywood High before returning to Sydney to finish his schooling. In Melbourne, Lowenstein grew up in a socially progressive household, attending a state school that encouraged an alternative form of education. The Lowensteins didn't have a television, but his father Werner engendered a love of films in his son, taking him to see arthouse fare like Akira Kurosawa's *Seven Samurai* (1954). They also watched films by Ingmar Bergman and Jean Renoir and many other classics from Europe, where Werner had fled Nazi Germany as a child. Lowenstein's mother Wendy was a social activist and historian. Her book *Weevils in the Flour* (1978) on Depression era living in Melbourne and the unpublished manuscript *Dead Men Don't Dig Coal* were the basis for Richard Lowenstein's award-winning short film *Evictions* (1979) and his debut feature *Strikebound* (1984), respectively.

By the start of the 1980s, Lowenstein and his creative collaborators, Lynn Maree Milburn and Troy Davies, were becoming known for their film clips with local acts, and on Hutchence's insistence, INXS came calling. Lowenstein took the job of directing *Burn for You* (1983) entirely on a whim and departed the gloomy climes of Melbourne for the tropical north where INXS were on another of their relentless tours, gigging in every tiny town and pitstop across Australia. 'We were Melbourne punks', said Lowenstein 'wondering who the hell were all these sunbathing types, because we didn't really like the sun, we were children of Nick Cave.' However, in a refrain that's recounted endlessly in relation to anyone who met Michael Hutchence, his openness, magnetism and charisma were utterly disarming. 'Within 24 hours we were all snorkelling off the Barrier Reef and doing very un-Melbourne-like things' recalls Lowenstein. Hutchence was equally enamoured with his new friends from the South, and over the next decade and sixteen clips, they became a creative and emotional backstop for the singer: a second family away from his INXS 'brothers'.

The relaxed, homespun feel of *Burn for You* (1983) belies the level of sophisticated image-making that this team and Hutchence would achieve together across the 1980s. But long before they were MTV darlings, this clip captures the essence of what made Hutchence such a star. Towards the end of the song, Hutchence, framed against a grey London sky, flashes his trademark half smile; without an instrument to hide behind, he works the camera as if it were an extension of himself. With each clip growing in artistic ambition and scale, by the time INXS released their global hit, 'Kick' in 1987, the videos became events in themselves, played on endless rotation on television. The wistful romance of 'Never Tear Us Apart' (1988), the slick cosmopolitan vibe of 'New Sensation' (1987) and the hip, sexy image of Hutchence in 'Need you Tonight' (1987) are ingrained in the popular consciousness of anyone who lived through the 1980s, 1990s or holds an Australian passport.

Long before the rock star and director shared global success in the 1980's, Lowenstein encountered Hutchence at the legendary underground Melbourne music venue, the Crystal Ballroom where an early incarnation of INXS were playing upstairs while The Ears played downstairs. Lowenstein recalls, "As a devoted fan watching The Ears play, some friends came in and said: "You need to go and watch this band playing upstairs, the singer is imitating (Ears frontman) Sam. This guy was throwing himself around on stage in a very similar way to Sam. INXS were from Sydney, so we sneered at them, but that similarity was always there."

After the explosive opening sequence of *Dogs in Space*, the camera comes to settle on 'The Girl' a teenage runaway played by Deanna Bond, who would later serve as the inspiration for the Nick Cave and the Bad Seeds song, 'Deanna' (1988). Camped out on the front stairs, she meets Grant (Adam Briscomb) and Anna, the only housemates who seemingly have gainful employment or study to get to. 'The Girl' maintains her post as the camera tracks into the house to find Sam waking from his sleep on the stairs. Wrapped in a blanket, shaking debris from his hair, he descends into the kitchen to find Tim, cheerfully eating breakfast. 'Yes, little fella. It's food! It's been a long time since we've seen any of that, hasn't it?' 'You're ... weird', replies Sam in a gravelled whisper. As he growls at the TV and lopes down the hallway to inspect the new arrival, Hutchence is almost unrecognisable. Instead of the supremely cool, relaxed, sexy rock star, he's transformed into a strangely comic, six-foot Gollum. The camera then settles on a sleeping housemate, Luchio. Off camera, 'check, check, 1, 2, 3, … "mind explodes, out come dogs, they shoot off into space" sings Sam through a wall of discordant sounds that blast the remaining housemates awake. And in the cramped room where the band are rehearsing, Hutchence's Sam comes alive, channelling the performative qualities Lowenstein and his friends had observed in the late 1970s at the Crystal Ballroom.

During his days living with Sam and fellow film-school students Andrew De Groot and Tim McLaughlan in the Berry Street house (where the actual film was shot), Lowenstein sensed that the unique patchwork of characters and happenings were ripe for narrative exploration. 'Somehow there was always this thought that people wouldn't believe what's going on here,' said Lowenstein on the 2009 DVD director's commentary. 'It wasn't so much the extremities but just the strange groups, the mixtures of characters coming and going and all the overlapping dialogue and all the completely nonsensical stuff mixing with the real emotional stuff.' During the scriptwriting process, Lowenstein brought Tim McLaughlan onboard, drawing on his natural wit and energy to flesh out the vignettes that feature in the final script. But in mining his memories of the house, a notable omission from the script is the film-maker himself. There's some camera and projection equipment to be seen in the layers of detritus strewn all over the house, but it's the only clue of the existence of a film student in the midst. In later years, Lowenstein said he worked elements of himself (and incidents) into the character of Tim.

Developing narratives from reality had proved successful for Lowenstein's debut feature, *Strikebound* (1984), which combined documentary and fictional elements to tell the story of a 1930s coal miners' strike. Born from oral histories that his mother, Wendy Lowenstein and later, Richard, had recorded, *Strikebound* was well received in Australian cinemas, selected internationally at major festivals, including Venice, garnering several nominations and a win for Production Design at the 1984 Australian Film Institute awards.

After the success of his debut, Lowenstein had an idea for a political thriller, but on tour at the Cannes Film Festival with *Strikebound*, his narrative fortunes took a different turn. As legend has it, he met up with Michael Hutchence who was also in the South of France playing shows with INXS. After a wild night of partying, the young, dishevelled Aussies found themselves on their way to a pitch meeting. In his witty and insightful shoot diary called *Telexes in Space* Lowenstein recounts, while moaning artistically and collapsing into our $10 orange juices, I explain the plot of my political thriller. The response is minimal. I am then hit by a bolt of lightning, sit up and suddenly say, 'And of course there's the film that me and Michael are doing!' Michael looks up in a vague stupor and says, 'We are …?' 'Yeah, It's all about this young girl who comes into a household full of hippies and punks and other assorted weirdos in the late seventies …' Michael and I ad-lib the storyline, which wasn't bad since we hadn't discussed it at all up to the moment. The producer is delighted. We promise to get in touch with her as soon as we get back to Australia. We never do … I leave a rather bedraggled Michael lying on the pavement in the sun waiting for his tour bus to pick him up, something I'm not sure they will know how to do since they don't have the slightest inkling where we are. As I leave, I notice Australian film critic David Stratton drop a coin into Michael's out-stretched hand. Michael smiles and says thanks. A few weeks earlier an INXS song had been number one in France. I guess they understand how the tide can turn.

This story offers some insight into how Lowenstein and Hutchence's creative relationship functioned but perhaps more telling is the fun they shared as young people; far from Australia exploring the world and living in the moment. By 1984, the serious commitments that Hutchence and his bandmates had made to INXS since they were teenagers were paying dividends, with international number one singles and their album *The Swing* (1984) propelling them into the top five recording artists in Australian music history.

Fish in Space

As INXS's fame grew, so too did Chris Murphy's determination to manage the band to even greater heights, which likely didn't include their major asset running back home to star in a film where he plays an obnoxious junkie. But for Hutchence, the pull of stardom was in constant dialogue with his desire to explore life as an artist. 'I had had offers before to do movies, but I didn't want to make some cliched, easy, safe, cutesy movie where I looked good on the screen for the sake of my fans and my management. I had to convince a lot of people that I wanted to do this film. It was no whim of mine.' Michael Hutchence

In January of 1985, as production commenced, Lowenstein received a frantic call from Murphy, 'he yells at me about having to protect Michael and himself in case we decide to have a shot of "Michael dragging his dick along the floor."

I mention that if Michael doesn't want to drag his dick along the floor he doesn't have to and, anyway, would it be long enough?' In the end, the production conceded that INXS management could control the portrayal of any drug and sex scenes involving Hutchence. Lowenstein's shoot diary is full of this sardonic back and forth with management, but through this and more contemporary interviews, he alludes to the larger artistic struggles plaguing Hutchence. 'He always felt compromised in having to be the "rock star" which part of him really wanted but also part of him wanted to be this underground creative artist, a-la Nick Cave.'

The camaraderie that Hutchence and Lowenstein developed in the short period from 1983 to 1985 was immense and, no doubt, a huge comfort to the notoriously shy and anxious front man. Since their beginnings, INXS were always sold as a band of brothers, so for Hutchence to step out of the group exposed him artistically in an entirely new way. During the making of *Dogs in Space*, Troy Davies (who did make-up on the film and played two memorable cameos, as the skin head and Leanne's inbred country brother) also played host, filming interviews with cast and crew. Many of these can be seen in Richard Lowenstein's documentary, *We're Living on Dog Food* (2009), and his exchanges with Hutchence are some of the more memorable. Troy asks Hutchence if he wishes his band mates from INXS were in the film? Clearly nervous about the loaded nature of the question but without missing a beat, Hutchence clicks into diplomatic mode, 'getting away from music has been the best thing about it, I'm discovering things about our (INXS) music by being away, it's the first time I've done anything else for a long time.' For the band itself, this dalliance into Melbourne's underground scene was a puzzling departure from their more mainstream ambitions. Combing through the pages of *INXS: Story to Story: The Official Autobiography*, the only mention of *Dogs in Space* alludes to a game-fishing boat, called 'King Kong' that guitarist Tim Farris purchased in the late 1980s. He hired a documentary crew to film his aquatic conquests titled, *Fish in Space*, 'in honor of and as a piss take on his bandmate Michael Hutchence's acting debut.' 'I don't think he ever got the credit he deserved for that role, because he was a pop singer playing a pop singer' Richard Lowenstein

During his time making music videos for INXS, Lowenstein had observed Michael to be a natural mimic, forever doing impersonations for laughs, like a stand-up comic. Convinced of his ability to act, he was surprised and delighted by his friend's genuine interest in doing the film. It also helped enormously that he bore a striking natural resemblance to the real Sam and with his legions of fans, made for a 'bankable' star in anyone's estimation. Three days into production, Lowenstein noted in his shoot diary, 'Michael is doing incredibly well at portraying the character. I keep getting very strange feelings of déjà vu as I catch glimpses of him out of the corner of my eye. He's doing it so well that I am scared no one will realise that the self-conscious posing is part of the character. I think this is the character most people would like to imagine Michael to have and won't want to believe otherwise.'

Amongst the cacophonous action of *Dogs In Space*, Lowenstein inserts moments of dramatic calm for his lead characters in the film. At the midpoint, Sam and Anna retreat to the house to take heroin. The scene cuts to the pub where Tim's smarting after being kicked out of the band. Lowenstein links the action through sound with Marie Hoy & Friends version of 'Shivers' playing over both spaces. Lit in warm red hues, it's intimate, and Hutchence brings a quiet sensitivity and playfulness to the scene. For all his posing and pouting, seeing him like this, it's finally clear to us why Anna is so enamoured with him. In the following scenes, Hutchence is magnetically sexy. Draped over Anna, he reads her a strangely childlike story about a green monster who keeps eating trains before seducing her in an extended sex scene which – obviously – Hutchence handles with aplomb.

By all accounts, Hutchence's dedication to the role was unwavering, and while Lowenstein's strict adherence to the physicality of Sam's character makes for an exceedingly heightened performance, there's a definite sense that Hutchence is inhabiting the role. The real break in this illusion comes with the final scene of the film. Anna is dead, time has passed and now Sam is on a big stage, a professional stage, dressed in a sharp 1980s suit singing Ollie Olsen's 'Rooms for the Memories'. The performance is pure (INXS) Hutchence, the vocal style and movement entirely returned to his own. This performative break delivers a jarring narrative effect; is this still Sam or is this Hutchence? In the 2009 DVD director's commentary, Lowenstein frames the scene in relation to the death of the era but that

> life and life goes on, and ambition goes on – historically it's supposed to lead into a much more commercial time. I also think Michael was undergoing a similar dilemma himself like his emotional life was being compromised by his career and his band and everything … and I think you sort of see all of that in that abyss he goes into at the end there.

A *Star Wars* of punk cinema

Dogs in Space broke with all the conventions of how the Australian film industry perceived a film about grotty punks and drugs should be made. The ambition of casting Australia's most famous rock star in the lead was matched only by Lowenstein's technical expectations, opting to shoot in anamorphic Cinemascope 35-mm film, with Dolby stereo sound. My agenda was, 'We're going to create a Star Wars of punk cinema, and we're going to light it beautifully and have dream sequences. We're going make this like a drug trip.' Opting to shoot in the real house they had lived in as students rather than a studio, meant extensive use of speciality-built cranes and steady-cam, both of which were reserved for big-budget, mainstream Australian films. And because Lowenstein insisted that the spaces had to feel real to enhance the performance of the cast, he convinced the current owners of Berry Street to move out, so they could de-renovate the house to a bombed-out student pad. With the enormous amounts of extras recreating parties, gigs and mayhem, the production reflected the story. Producer Glenys Rowe recalled having to put up signs on set saying, 'Please Do Not Take Drugs' – suffice to say, it didn't work. However, for all of the technical finesse and the huge pop star at its centre, *Dogs in Space* was a wild chaotic ride dropped into a decade when Australian society was embracing a new sense of individualism, corporatisation and materialism. Not to mention a newfound fear of drugs.

In excess!

In his book, *The Eighties: The Decade that Transformed Australia*, Frank Bongiorno highlights the obsession that politicians, media and middle Australia shared about drugs. In one study, 'nineteen out of twenty Australians had never tried either heroin or cocaine … But in 1985, more than one in six Australians saw illicit drugs as the country's greatest problem.' With so much mainstream hysteria surrounding drugs and a major teen heart-throb in the leading role, it's little wonder the Australian Classification Board savaged the broad commercial prospects of *Dogs in Space* by slapping an R18+ Adults Only certificate on the film. 'The Board was of the opinion that, notwithstanding the final element of tragedy, this realistic depiction of the youth drug/music sub-culture glamorised the lifestyle sufficiently to make it appear not only acceptable but also "trendy" and attractive with money readily available despite a casual approach to work, drugs and sex freely accessible and parental and police condonation demonstrated.'

Producer Glenys Rowe was an experienced film marketeer and had devised an extensive strategy for teen and youth audiences that capitalised on their star. During pre-production, she took the (financial) backers to see INXS play: 'There was 2500 kids screaming for Michael and I said, "There's your audience."' Originally slated to release for the Australian summer holidays, their plans to hand out flyers on the last day of the school term and numerous other teen-orientated pitches had to be shelved. After several appeals (including the offer to re-cut particular scenes in the film), the rating was upheld. The mainstream cinema chain Hoyts kept their commitment to screening the film, but as a 'specialised' release on much fewer screens the following year. In *Cinema Papers*, Tony Malone of Hoyts Distribution, came out in public support of the film, 'there's a chance that it will be the Easy Rider of the eighties' – how right he was.

In Lowenstein's shoot diary in November 1986, he notes, 'he (Michael) seems very depressed when I speak to him. He thinks he is too prominent on the poster. He seems very worried about the possibility of being crucified critically for his first attempt at acting. I am unable to console him as I have no idea how the critics will respond, especially the mainstream ones.' With the exception of tabloid papers beating up the 18+ rating for additional Hutchence-related column inches, the film was well received by Australia's daily newspaper critics. Neil Jillett in the Melbourne broadsheet *The Age* proclaimed it 'dazzling in its technical assurance and mature handling of controversial themes.' In the *Sydney Morning Herald*, David Stratton (who dropped that coin in Hutchence's hand in Cannes) said, 'One of the extraordinary achievements of this immensely impressive film is the ensemble acting. As Sam, Hutchence – lead singer of the group INXS – is most effective.' Rob Lowing in the *Melbourne Herald Sun* noted, 'If a film's function is to take an audience into a different experience, then there's little doubt that innovative *Dogs in Space* has accomplished this.' Almost all were universal in their condemnation of the R18+, citing it as a death knell for the film's chances of mainstream box office success. However, those closest to the events depicted in the film were less kind in their reception, with many being critical of Hutchence's performance and Lowenstein's 1980s 'fantasy version' of the scene. While it didn't become the youth market *Crocodile Dundee* of the summer of 1986, *Dogs in Space* returned a respectable box office, playing in select cinemas for months and gaining official selection at international festivals, including the Berlinale, Edinburgh, London and New York Film Festivals.

As predicted, *Dogs in Space* did become something of an Australian *Easy Rider*. And following Hutchence's years in the wilderness, out of step with popular music as it moved from stadium rock to grunge, tawdry tabloid custody battles and a series of (post-death) trashy telemovies, he now holds the place of beloved fallen soldier – his death at the young age of thirty-seven – preserving him as an artist of note in the nation's mind.

Ahead of the film's re-release in 2009, Lowenstein commented that 'the punk scene was an embarrassment to the Australian music industry back then. In a similar way, *Dogs in Space* was a total embarrassment to the Australian film industry'. Twenty years later, this beloved cult film was accompanied by a flurry of new critical writing, and a spotlight program at the 2009 Melbourne International Film Festival, 'Punk Becomes Pop: The Australian Post-Punk Underground', celebrated the city's post-punk scene and simultaneously introduced the film to a new generation of fans. Distanced from the real events, many in Melbourne's underground scene who were originally critical of the film, now saw it as a historical marker of an important but largely undocumented moment in Australian music. Hutchence was equally transformed by this temporal shift, with contemporary audiences able to access his performance rather than simply grappling with the contradiction of a bona fide star 'slumming' it on screen as an anti-establishment punk.

'The whole point of acting is to lose yourself. That's why people in music want to become actors, because you can become anything'38 – Michael Hutchence

As an actor, Hutchence starred in *Frankenstein Unbound* (1990) and *Limp* (1999, unreleased), but *Dogs in Space* was his only leading role. And for all of his personal desire to navigate the world as a Bowie-esque chameleon through his work as an actor, and musical side projects such as Max Q (with Ollie Olsen), the frontman never managed to break from his INXS band of brothers and straddle both sides of the fame equation. However, through his artistic collaborations with Lowenstein and, in particular, their work on *Dogs in Space*, we're offered a unique glimpse of Hutchence: on the cusp of mega stardom, exploring life as an artist and allowing himself to become anything.

References

Bongiorno, F. (2015), *The Eighties the Decade that Transformed Australia*, Melbourne: Black Inc.

Caputo, R. and P. Tapp (2009), 'Interview with Richard Lowenstein', *Senses of Cinema*, July 2009, Available online: https://www.sensesofcinema.com/2009/miff-premiere-fund-post-punk-dossier/richard-lowenstein-interview/.
Chandra, S. (2020), 'Michael Hutchence's Space Dog Days', *Monster Children*, February 2020, Available online: https://www.monsterchildren.com/michael-hutchences-space-dog-days/.
Creswell, T. (2017), *Shine Like It Does: The Life of Michael Hutchence*, Australia: Echo, Bonnier Publishing.
Decurtis, A. (1988), 'INXS: New Sensation, Coming up from Down under, INXS Enjoys Life at the Top', *Rolling Stone Magazine*, 16 June.
Dogs in Space (1986), [DVD Directors Commentary] Dir. Richard Lowenstein, Australia: Umbrella Entertainment.
Donavan, P. (2009), 'At the Scene of the Grime', *The Age*, July 2009, Available online: https://www.theage.com.au/entertainment/movies/at-the-scene-of-the-grime-20090724-ge8062.html.
Galvin, P. (2009), 'We're Living on Dog Food. So What?', *SBS Movies*, September 2009, Available online: https://www.sbs.com.au/movies/article/2009/09/07/were-living-dog-food-so-what.
INXS and A. Bozza (2005), *INXS: Story to Story: The Official Autobiography*, New York: Atria/Simon & Schuster, Inc Pg 60.
Jillett, N. (1987), *The Age Newspaper*, 1 January 1987.
Levy, Jo (1989), '20th Century Fox', *Spin Magazine*, November: 64–6.
Lowenstein, R., A. Standish and H. Bandis (2019), Dogs in Space *a Film Archive*, Melbourne: Melbourne Books.
Lowing, R. (1987), 'Saved by a Sense of Fun', *Sun-Herald Newspaper*, 11 January.
Nichols, D., and S. Perillo, eds (2020), *Urban Australia and Post-Punk Exploring* Dogs in Space, London: Palgrave Macmillan.
Pape, S. (2019), 'He Changed My Life – Richard Lowenstein on Michael Hutchence doc Mystify', *The Hot Corn*, October 2019, Available online: https://hotcorn.com/en/movies/news/richard-lowenstein-interview-mystify-michael-hutchence/.
Roddick, N. (1987), 'Putting the Bite into *Dogs in Space*', *Cinema Papers #61*, 14–17 January.
Rowlands, P. (2020), 'Richard Lowenstein on 'Mystify – Michael Hutchence', *Money into Light*, Available online: http://www.money-into-light.com/2020/04/richard-lowenstein-on-mystify-michael.html.
Sejavka, S. (2009), 'The Resurrection of *Dogs in Space*', *Sails of Oblivion*, May 2009, Available online: https://sailsofoblivion.blogspot.com/search?q=dogs+in+space.
Simic, Z. (2020), 'Rock Star in Space', in D. Nichols and S. Perillo (eds), *Urban Australia and Post-Punk Exploring* Dogs in Space, 105–22, London: Palgrave Macmillan.
Stanton, G. (2017), 'Dog Days: The Making of *Dogs in Space*', *Filmink*, 22 November. Available online: https://www.filmink.com.au/dog-days-making-dogs-space/.

Stratton, David (1987), 'The Drug World: An Ugly Life on the Periphery', *Sydney Morning Herald Newspaper*, 1 January.

Strickland, C. (2001), 'The Naked Gun Meets Jean Luc Godard?', *Metro Magazine: Media and Education Magazine*, January 2001: 37–45.

The Michael Hutchence Memorial, [Blog] '*Dogs in Space* – Sam and Anna', Interview with Richard Lowenstein. Available online: https://michaelhutchence.org/dogs-in-space-sam-and-anna/?highlight=sam%20and%20anna.

Tofts, Darren (2009), 'Chronicles of the Blank Generation', *RealTime Arts*, 93 (Oct–Nov): 21.

We're Livin' on Dog Food (2009), [Film] Dir. Richard Lowenstein, Australia: Ghost Pictures.

Index

Aap Jaisa Koi song (Someone Like You) 132
Abe, Sada 187
Abhimaan (1973) 3
Absolute Beginners (1986) 2, 70, 189
Adamson, Barry 4
Adu, Sade 2
Advocate, The magazine 33
Ae Oh Aa Zara Mudke song 135
African American women 13
Afro-American solidarity 150
Afrofuturism 7
Age, The 207
AIDS 33
Akhtar, Zoya 131, 140
Ali, Zaheer 56
Allen, Lewis 3
All That Heaven Allows (1955) 155–6
Almodóvar, Pedro 42, 44
Alphabet St.' music video (1988a) 55
Altman, Robert 195
Alvarez, Luis 52
American Bandstand (1964) 16
amoral Aryan zombie 63
And God Created Woman (*Et Dieu ... créa la femme* 1956) 101
Angel and the Snake, The 84
Angels, The 199
Anna (1967) 101
Ant, Adam 113, 127–8
   acting 116–18
   Cyber Bandits (1995) 119
   Dirk Wears White Sox (1979) 115
   Equalizer, The 117
   Friend or Foe album 117
   Jubilee (1978) 115–16, 120
   Love Bites (1993) 119–20
   media, relationship with 116
   music career 117
   Nomads (1985) 117–18, 126
   Northern Exposure 118
   pop persona 119–20
   Prince Charming 116, 118
   songs 119
   Spellcaster (1988) 118
   stardom 115–16
Anthony, Richard 99
Ants, The 111, 115
Apna Time Aayega song 143–4
ArchAndroid, The (2010) 7
Armstrong, Louis 168
Armstrong, Michael 64
Arquette, Roseanna 72
Arsenio Hall Show, The (1990) 16
Asanuma, Inejirō 186
Ashraf, Ajaz 137
As Time Goes By 173
A Team, The (1986) 117
Audio Sponge (2002) 184
Austin, Guy 96–7
Awaara (The Vagabond 1951) 133
'Awop-Bop-A-Loo-Mop-Alop-Bam-Boom' 18
Ayler, Albert 169

B. B. (1964) 101
Baal (1982) 67–8
Baar Baar Dekho 131
Baby I'm a Star (Prince 1984a) 49
Bachchan, Amitabh 3, 132
Bacon, Francis 76
Badalamenti, Angelo 74
Baker, Chet 178
Bambaata, Afrika 184
Bamboo Houses/Bamboo Music 183
Banana Cop (1984) 3
Banderas, Antonio 44
Bandslam (2009) 72
Bardot, Brigitte 100–2
   B. B. (1964) 101
   Bonnie and Clyde (1968) 102

And God Created Woman (Et Dieu … créa la femme 1956) 101
Barthes, Roland 58
Basquiat (1996) 72
Basquiat, Jean-Michel 41
Batdance (1989b) 48, 50, 56, 58
Batman film 48, 51, 58
Batman symbol 47–8, 50, 56–7
Baudelaire, Charles 53
Baywatch (1985) 16
Beatles, The 6, 104, 184
Beers, Garry Gary 199
Behind The Mask 184
Belafonte, Harry 3
bell hooks 35–7
Benton, Jerome 51
Berger, Helmut 42
Bergman, Ingmar 200
Bergman, Ingrid 153
Berlin Trilogy 67
Bertolucci, Bernardo 181, 189
Besson, Luc 4
Beyoncé 4
Bhatt, Alia 140–1
Billcock, Jill 196
Bird (1988) 174
Birkin, Andrew 3
bisexuality 13
Bjork 4, 189
Black African American culture 7
Blackboard Jungle (1955) 4
black comedy 66
Black Dandyism 53–4
black gay life 36
Black Lives Matter movement 178
Black Looks 36
Black male homosexuality 13
Black Panther (2018) 7
Black performance stereotypes 12
Black performers, cultural characters available to 5, 12
Black Power 149–50, 163
Black Skin, White Masks (Fanon) 147–8
Black to the Future (1994) 7
Blade of the Immortal (2017) 4
Blade Runner (1981) 68–9
Blade Runner (1982) 119
Bland, Michael 51

Bless This House 151, 162
Blond Ambition World Tour 32, 35
Blondie band 82, 84–7
blouson noirs 99–101
Blue (1993) 113
Bodyguard, The (1992) 8
Body of Evidence (1993) 32
Bogle, Donald 12
Bohemian Rhapsody (2018) 7
Bolan, Marc 64
Bond, Deanna 201
Bonnette, Lakeyta M. 141
Bonnie and Clyde (1968) 102
Book of Life, The (2000) 4
Bowie, David 2–3, 183, 185, 189, 197
  acting 64
  anisocoria 64
  Baal (1982) 67–8
  Bandslam (2009) 72
  Basquiat (1996) 72
  Blade Runner (1981) 68–9
  cinematic career 64
  cocaine addiction 63, 65, 67
  Everybody Loves Sunshine (1999) 72
  Hunger, The 68
  Il Mio West (1998) 72
  Image, The (1969) 64
  Just a Gigolo 66
  Labyrinth 70–2
  Linguini Incident, The (1991) 72
  Man Who Fell to Earth, The (1976) 65–6, 69, 78, 88, 95
  Merry Christmas, Mr. Lawrence 68–70
  Mr. Rice's Secret (2000) 72
  Prestige, The 72–3, 78
  Rutles 2: Can't Buy Me Lunch, The (2002) 72
  supporting roles 70
  theatrical personas 63–4
  as trickster showman 73
  Twin Peaks: Fire Walk with Me (1992) 72–8
  We Children from Zoo Station 67
  Zoolander (2001) 72
BowieNet 63
Boyer, Charles 97
Boys Next Door, The 198
Boyz n the Hood (1991) 7

Brady, Sara 15
Brando, Marlon 6, 99, 116
Breaking Glass (1980) 3
Breathless (1960) 89
Brecht, Bertolt 67
Briggs, Jonathyne 99–100
Bronson, Charles 108
Brooks, Richard 4
Bros, Coen 4
Brosnan, Pierce 118
Brown, James 50
Brunckhorst, Natja 67
Bryant, Carolyn 14
Bucheit, Liz 57
Buddy Holly Story, The (1978) 6
Bullet Boy (2004) 4
Burgoyne, Martin 41
Burle, Milton 97
Burn for You (1983) 200–1
Burton, Tim 47, 49–50
Butler, Judith 34

Cage, Nicolas 73
Calloway, Cab 3
Camacho, Luis Xtravaganza 32
Cammell, Donald 2
Campbell, Virginia 65–6
Candy Mountain (1988) 4
Cannes 33
Cannes Film Festival 73, 202
Carax, Leos 4, 82–4, 86, 89–90, 92
Cardiff, Jack 3
Carey, Dorien 36
Carey, Mariah 2, 153
Carmichael, Stokely 149, 163–4
Carné, Marcel 96
Carpenter, John 3
Casares, Ingrid 42
Cash, Johnny 3
casting couch culture 153
Catch, The (*Shiiku* 1961) 186
Cateforis, Theo 88
Cave, Nick 4, 83
Celliers, Jack 183
celluloid jukebox tradition 4
Cement Garden, The (1983) 3
Ceremony, The (*Gishiki* 1971) 187
Certain Sacrifice, A (1979) 31

Chakraborty, Mithun 133
Channel V 144
Cheng, Sammi 4
Cher 1–2, 81
Chinai, Alisha 144
Chinatown (1962) 131
Christiane F. (1981) 67
Christopher 33
Chungking Express (1994) 4
cinema and jazz
   avant-garde jazz 169
   Bird (1988) 174
   costs 168–9
   Hollywood 168
   movie-making 171–2
   Round Midnight 168, 170–1, 173–9
   unskilled newcomers 169
Cinema Papers 207
Clark, Candy 65
Clarke, Alan 64, 67
Cliff, Jimmy 2, 189
Cluzet, François 176–7
Coal Miner's Daughter (1980) 6
Cohn, Harry 171
Cold Chisel 199
Coleman, Ornette 169
Collins, Phil 117
colonialism 147–8
Coltrane, John 169
Columbo (1991) 16
Come Back to the 5 and Dime, Jimmy Dean,
   Jimmy Dean (1982) 2
Commedia Dell'Arte 51, 64
Computer Game 184
Condon, Bill 4
Confession, The (1970) 96
Connelly, Jennifer 70
Conseil de famille (1985) 105
Control (2007) 7
Coogler, Ryan 7
Cook, Paul 119
Cooper, Alice 3, 116
copains
   Bardot, Brigitte 101–2
   culture 100
   emergence of 99
   Goya, Chantal 102
   and stars 100

Yé-Yé girls 99–103
Coppola, Sofia 42
Cording, Henry 99
Cornelius 185
Costa-Gavras 96, 105
Costello, Elvis 123
Cotton Club Orchestra 5
counterculture communities 52
Country-Folk-Rock (1972) 104
Coward, Noël 155
Cowboy George 117
Crenshaw, Kimberlé 34, 37–8
Creswell, Toby 199
Crimes of the Future (1970) 84
Crip Theory (McRuer) 39–40
Critters (1986) 120
Crocodile Dundee (1986) 195, 207
Cronenberg, David 82, 84–90, 92
  Crimes of the Future (1970) 84
  Rabid (1977) 84
  Shivers (1975) 84
  Stereo (1969) 84
  Videodrome (1983) 82, 84–8, 90–2
Crosby, Bing 3, 5, 97
Crosland, Alan 3
cross-dressing 13
Crowe, Melissa 33
Crown Trout Jewelers 57
Crumes, Oliver 33
Cyber Bandits (1995) 119

Damned, The (*La caduta degli dei* 1969) 42
Dance of the Infidels (Paudras) 171
Dancer in the Dark (2000) 4
Dando, Evan 4
Dandyism 53
Daniels, Phil 123
Dark Shadows 120
Datta, Jayanti 141–2
Daubny, Sarah 51
Davies, Ray 2
Davies, Troy 200, 204
Davis, Miles 117, 162, 170–1, 176
Dead Man (1995) 4
Dead Men Don't Dig Coal 200
Deanna (1988) 201
Death by Hanging (*Kôshikei* 1968) 187
deconstructivism 6

Deeper and Deeper 41–2
Deewaar (The Wall 1975) 132
Def, Mos 4
de Groot, Andrew 196
de Lempicka, Tamara 41
Delinquents, The (1989) 83
Delon, Alain 107
DeLory, Donna 33, 36
DeMille, Cecil B. 13
Deneuve, Catherine 68–9
Denis, Claire 83
Der Himmel über Berlin 43
Dern, Laura 73
Dery, Mark 7
De Santis, Giuseppe 96
Desperately Seeking Susan (1985) 1, 8, 31–2, 41, 81, 95, 117
Détective (1985) 105
deus ex machina 151
'Dharavi Rap' 141
Diamonds and Pearls (1991) 52
Dibb, Saul 4
Dick Cavett Show, The (1970) 16
Dick Tracy (1990) 32
Die Hard (1988) 118
Dietrich, Marlene 13, 42, 66
Dirk Wears White Sox (1979) 115
Dirty Mind (1980) 48
Disco Dancer (1982) 139, 141
  commercial success 132–3
  dancing 133–4
  disco 134–6
  eroticism 135
  music 132–3
  Soviet audiences 133, 135
Divinyls, The 199
Dogs in Space (1986) 3
  cast 195–6
  final scene 205
  Melbourne, late 1970s 197–9
  music 198
  Olsen, Ollie 198
  opening scenes 196
  R18+ Adults Only certificate 206–7
  re-release 208
  shoot 204, 206
  teen and youth audiences 207
  young bohemians 200–3

youth drug/music sub-culture 206
Dollars Trilogy 116
Donny & Marie (1976, 1998, 2000) 16
Donovan, Jason 92
Don't Knock the Rock (1956) 16, 24
Don't Look Now (1973) 64
Dors, Diana 116
Douglas, Emory 150
D'où viens-tu Johnny? (Where Are You from, Johnny? 1963) 105
Down and Out in Beverley Hills (1986) 11
Dreamgirls (2006) 4
Drop Dead Rock (1995) 119
Duff, DeAngela 51
Dulfer, Candy 51
Dutronc, Jacques 4
Dutta, Nandita 138–9
Dyer, Richard 36, 41, 135
Dylan, Bob 3, 7

Ears, The 201
Eastwood, Clint 116, 118, 174
Ebert, Roger 108
Edel, Ulrich 67
Edwards, Altevia 171
effeminacy 13
Eighties: The Decade that Transformed Australia, The (Bongiorno) 206
8 Mile (2002) 4
Elephant Man, The 67
Elephants and Flowers (Prince 1990a) 50, 57
Ellington, Duke 168
Ellison, Joy 56
Eminem 4, 189
Empire of Passion (*Ai no bôrei* 1978) 187
Empty Arms song 157–8, 160
Entertaining Mr Sloane 117
Equalizer, The 117
eroticism
  and disco 135
  proletarian 132–6
Essex, David 3
Étoile sans lumière (Star Without Light 1946) 96
Eureka (1983) 188
Evans, Bill 178
Evans, Herschel 173

Everybody Loves Sunshine (1999) 2, 72
Evictions (1979) 200
Evita (1996) 32
Ewell, Tom 20
Expresso Bongo (1959) 3
Express Yourself (1989) 31, 35
Eyes Without a Face (1960) 89

Faenza, Roberto 3, 120–1, 123–4, 128
Faithful, Marianne 3
Fanon, Frantz 147–51, 155–6
Farris, Jon 199
Farris, Tim 204
Farris Brothers, the 199
feminism 32, 34, 43
Fennesz, Christian 185
Ferrara, Abel 189
Fifth Element, The (1997) 4
Fight Club 4
film grammar 5
Fincher, David 4, 32
Fitzgerald, Ella 3
Fleetwood, Hugh 121, 123, 126–7
Flesh (1968) 42
Flynn, Christopher 41
For a Few Dollars More (1965) 118
Forbidden Colours 183
Fox, William 168
Franju, Georges 89
Frank, Robert 4
Frankenstein Unbound (1990) 208
French popular music star
  Hallyday, Johnny 103–8
  Montand, Yves 95–8
  Yé-Yé girls 99–103
Friend or Foe album 117
Frost, Mark 73–4
Furie, Sidney J. 3

Gainsbourg, Charlotte 3
Gainsbourg, Serge 3, 101
Ganga Jumuna (1961) 132
Garcia, Mayte 58
Gault, Sharon 33–4
Gauwloos, Salim 33
gay pornographic films 42
gender and muslimness 136–9

gender performativity 17
Gender Trouble 35
Gentlemen Take Polaroids (1980) 183
Gérard, Danyel 99
Get on Up (2014) 7
Getz, Stan 178
Ghosts of the Civil Dead (1988) 4
Gibson, Brian 3
Gilbey, Ryan 44
Gillespie, Dizzy 168
Girl Can't Help It (1956) 11, 15, 20–6
Girl on a Motorcycle (1968) 3
Girl on the Bridge, The (1999) 4
Glam Slam night club 56
Glassop, Patricia 200
Go-Betweens, The 198
Godard, Jean-Luc 89, 101–2, 105
Goddard, Stuart 115
Gohatto (1999) 187
Golden Exits (2017) 4
Gold Experience 57
Gomez, Selina 4
Gone with the Wind (1939) 150
Goodbye Again (1961) 97–8
Good Golly Miss Molly 18
Gordon, Dexter 6, 8, 172–3
Gordon, Kim 4
Goth, Andrew 72
Goya, Chantel 102–3, 108
Graff, Todd 72
Graffiti Bridge (1990) 47, 50, 55, 57
Grant, Stuart 198
Gray, F. Gary 7
Great Balls of Fire! (1989) 6
Griffin, Johnny 171
Guardian, The 44
Guest, Val 3
Gully Boy (2019) 131, 136
  Apna Time Aayega song 143–4
  hostility, Muslims 143–4
  marginalised community 140–1
  Meri Gully Mein song 141–3
  Muslim patriarch 140
  political resistance 142
  rap, means of protest 141
  social and economic deprivation 139–40
Gunfight, A (1971) 3

hagiography 160
Hahn, Alex 47
Hairspray (1988) 2, 91
Haley, Bill 4
Hall, Stuart 43
Hallyday, Johnny 4
  L'homme du train (Man on a Train, 2002) 106–8
  rebellious image 103–4
  rock 'n' roll image 104
  Specialists, The (1969) 105–6, 108
  star persona 104–7
  Vengeance (*Fuk sau* 2009) 107–8
Hamilton, Charles V. 14, 149, 163–4
Hammersmith Apollo 63
Hampton, Howard 85
Hancock, Herbie 8, 172, 176
Hanging on the Telephone 84
Hanson, Curtis 4
Hard Day's Night, A (1964) 6
Harder They Come, The (1972) 2
Hardy, Françoise 100–1
  Château en Suède (*Nutty, Naughty Chateau* 1963) 101
  What's New Pussycat (1965) 101
Haring, Keith 41
Haris, Niki 33, 36
Harlem renaissance 13
Harry, Debbie 2, 4
  Union City (1980) 82–3, 91
  Videodrome 82, 84–8, 90–2
Harry, Deborah 119
Hartley, Hal 4
Harvey, P. J. 4
Hassan, Nazia 3, 132
Hawkins, Coleman 168
Hawks, Howard 3
Haywood, Chris 195
Head (1968) 6
Heart of Glass 84, 86
Heavy (1995) 4
Hebden, Kieran 185
Hebdige, Dick 52, 54
Hellman, Monte 3
Helou, Tony 195
Hemmings, David 66
Henson, Jim 64, 70, 72
Heroes (1977) 67, 185

Her-Story (2017) 43
heterosexuality 39
Hiatt, Helen 50, 52
Higgins, Billy 172, 176
Hill, Walter 4
Hillcoat, John 4
hip-hop 7, 140, 143, 181, 183, 185
History and Sociology of Clothing, Some Methodological Observations' (Barthes) 58
Hitler 63
Holiday Inn (1942) 3
Holy Motors (2012) 4, 82, 89–92
homophobia 12
homosexuality 13–14, 33, 187
Honeycutt, Kirk 107–8
Hooked on You (2007) 4
Hopper, Dennis 72
Horatio, Helen 51
Horne, Lena 5
Horovitz, Adam 4
Hosono, Haruomi 181, 183–4
House of Xtravaganza 33, 41
Houston, Whitney 81, 189
How I Won the War (1967) 3, 6
Hoyts Distribution 207
Hubbard, Freddie 8, 172
Hudson, Jennifer 4
Hui, Michael 3
Hui, Sam 3
Human Audio Sponge (HAS) 184
Human Stain, The (2000) 153
Humfress, Paul 112
Hunger, The 68
Hurt, William 176
Hustler White (1996) 42
Hutchence, Michael 3, 196–200
Hutcherson, Bobby 8, 172, 176

Ice Cube 4, 7
Ice T 4
identity politics 37–8
Idle, Eric 72
If I Was Your Girlfriend (1987a) 49, 55
Il Mio West (1998) 72
Image, The (1969) 64
Imitation of Life
    African American 'house servant' 150

Annie's funeral service 158–60
Annie's story 154–5
crowd shots, newsreel 162, *163*
deus ex machina 151
Empty Arms song 157, *158*, 160
Jackson, Mahalia 151, 158–61
Moore, Juanita 151, 162
opening credit titles 151, *152*
passing (Sarah Jane) 153–4
rags-to-riches story 153
romance 154
Trouble of the World song 151, 160, *161*, 164
Iñárritu, Alejandro González 181
In Bed with Madonna 32–4
Independent, The (2000) 120
Indian cinema, pop stars in
    Disco Dancer (1982) 131–6
    gender and muslimness 136–9
    Gully Boy (2019) 131, 136, 139–44
    political ambiguities 139–44
    proletarian eroticism 132–6
    Secret Superstar (2017) 136–9
In Fabric (2018) 4
influential international performances 1
Inside Llewyn Davies (2013) 4
Insolitudes (1973) 104
intersectionality 34
In the Realm of the Senses (ai no corrida) 187
Into the Night 70
INXS 196–7, 199–205, 207–8
Islam, Maidul 138
Islamophobia 137
It's Little Richard (1964) 16

Jackman, Hugh 73
Jackson, Mahalia 151, 158–61
Jackson, O' Shea 7
Jagger, Mick 2, 7, 64, 124
Jamaican music industry 2
Jarman, Derek 112–13, 115–16, 122, 128
Jarmusch, Jim 3–4
Jarrett, Keith 170
jazz music 5, 134, 162
    American 170, 174–5
    avant-garde 169
    Baker, Chet 178

Black Americans 178
Coleman, Ornette 169
collaboration 171
cost 168
Evans, Bill 178
Getz, Stan 178
Griffin, Johnny 171
Hancock, Herbie 176
Hutcherson, Bobby 176
integrity of 169
Mulligan, Gerry 178
Parker, Charlie 168–9, 171–2
Pepper, Art 178
pioneers 168
Powell, Bud 171–3, 176, 178–9
Roach, Max 173–4
Round Midnight 168, 170–1, 173–9
Shorter, Wayne 176
Tavernier, Bertrand 168, 170–4, 176, 179
Jazz Singer, The (1927) 3
Jenkins, Barry 4
Jillett, Neil 207
Jiya, Femi 47
Johannson, David 4
Johnny Au Palais Des Sports (1967) 104
Johnson, Lamont 3
Jolson, Al 3
Jones, Allen 115
Jones, Grace 3, 119
Jones, Steve 119
Jordan 127
  ballet performance 114
  Jordan's Dance 113
  Jubilee (1978) 113–14, 127
  Nightshift (1981) 113
  punk style 112
  Rule Britannia 113–14
  Sebastiane (1976) 112–13
  self-expression 111–12
Jordan, Louis 97
Jordan's Dance 113
J-Pop phenomenon 183
Jubilee (1978) 113–16, 120, 127–8
Juice (1992) 1
Juilliard School, The 170–1
Just a Gigolo (1978) 6, 66
Justify My Love (1990) 31, 35, 42

Kapoor, Raj 133
Kapoor, Shammi 131
Karina, Anna 100–1
Karlen, Neal 54
Kassell, Nicole 4
Keaton, Michael 50
Keitel, Harvey 120, 126
Kelly, Gene 97
Kemp, Lindsay 63, 70, 185
Kemp, Martin 119
Kendall, Nicholas 72
Kensit, Patsy 2
Keshishian, Alek 33
Khan, Aamir 136
Kick (1987) 201
Kier, Udo 42
Kimura, Takuya 4
King Creole (1958) 2
King of Comedy, The (1982) 123
Kiss music video (1986b) 48–9
Kiss Napoleon Goodbye (1990) 4
Kitano, Takeshi 187
Klotz, Claude 106
Knight, Nick 112
Knots (Laing 1972) 148
Korine, Harmony 4
Koyama, Akiko 186
Kravitz, Lenny 2
Kristofferson, Kris 3, 7
Kulkarni, Damini 142
Kurosawa, Akira 200

Labyrinth (1986) 70–2, 189
Ladies and Gentlemen, the Fabulous Stains (1982) 119
Lady Gaga 81
Lady Gaga: Five Foot Two 44
Lady Sings the Blues (1972) 3, 6, 8
Laemmle, Carl 168
La Guerre est Finie (The War is Over 1965) 96
Lahiri, Bappi 133
Laing, R.D. 148
Lam, George 3
Lamé song 119
Lancaster, Burt 176
Landis, John 70
Land of 10,000 Loves (Van Cleve) 55

Lang, Fritz 119
Lang, Stacia 52
LaRue, Chi Chi 42
Last Days (2005) 4
Last Emperor, The (1988) 181
Last Temptation of Christ, The (1988) 2, 70
Late Late Show with Tom Snyder, The (1997) 16
Late Night Line Up (1972) 16
Late Night with David Letterman 98
Lau, Andy 4
Lavant, Denis 84, 89
Lawrence, Tim 134
Le Cercle rouge (1970) 107
Leconte, Patrice 4, 106–7
Le Golf Drouot dance hall 103
Le Joli Mai (The Lovely Month of May) 96
Lennon, John 3
Leong, Po Chih 3
le prolo chantant 96
Le Samurai (1967) 107
lesbianism 13
Les Portes de la nuit (Gates of the Night) 96
Lester, Richard 3, 6
Let's Go Crazy 8
Let's Make Love (1960) 97–8
Letterman (1982, 1984) 16
Let the Good Times Roll (1973) 16
Letts, Don 113
Le Voleur De Tibidabo (The Thief of Tibidabo 1964) 101
LGBTQ+ community 34, 40, 55, 89
L'homme du train (Man on a Train, 2002) 106–8
LIFE (1999) 181
Life magazine 98
Like A Virgin 31
Limp (1999, unreleased) 208
Lindsay, Arto 4
Linguini Incident, The (1991) 2, 72
'Little-Richard-ness' 18
Little Richard (Richard Wayne Penniman) 5, 11–14
  American Bandstand (1964) 16
  Arsenio Hall Show, The (1990) 16
  Baywatch (1985) 16
  Black performers, cultural characters available to 12
  characters 15, 26
  Columbo (1991) 16
  cultural impact of 11
  death 26
  Dick Cavett Show, The (1970) 16
  documentary presentation 16
  Donny & Marie (1976, 1998, 2000) 16
  Don't Knock the Rock (1956) 16
  dramatic production 16
  expressive coherence 20
  Girl Can't Help It (1956) 11, 20–6
  homosexuality and 13–14
  It's Little Richard (1964) 16
  Late Night Line Up (1972) 16
  Letterman (1982, 1984) 16
  Let the Good Times Roll (1973) 16
  London Rock and Roll Show, The (1973) 16
  Mister Rock and Roll (1957) 16
  multimedia stylistic originator 11
  musical performance 16
  performance modes 16
  performative legacy 12
  performativity 17–19
  playing himself 15
  screen performance 11
  Simpsons, The (2003) 16
  stardom 12, 19
  Three Angels Broadcasting Network (2017) 16
  Tonight Show Starring Johnny Carson, The (1986) 16
Livi, Ivo 96
Livingston, Jennie 35–6
Lodger (1979) 67, 185
London Film Festival 187
London Rock and Roll Show, The (1973) 16
Long Tall Sally 24
Loophole (2003) 184
Looseley, David 99, 101, 103, 105–6
Lopez, Jennifer 2, 81
Los Rancheros 116
Love and Mercy (2014) 7
Love Bites (1993) 119–20
Love is the Devil (1998) 181
Love/Lovesexy symbol 48, 55–7, 59
Love me Tender (1956) 5
Lovesexy tour and album 48–50, 54–6

Love Symbol (1992) 52
Low (1977) 67
Lowenstein, Richard 3, 195–6, 198–208
Luce, Liz 56
Lucille 24
Lunch, Lydia 4
Lurie, John 3
Lydon, John 3, 128
    acting role 124
    Independent, The (2000) 120
    international profile and reputation 123
    Order of Death (1983) 120–1, 123–4, 126
    punk identity 122
    punk persona 127
    Sons of Norway (2011) 120
    star persona 121, 125
    vocal delivery 125
Lynch, David 2, 64, 72–4, 77

Madden, Emma 37
Mad Max (1979) 196
Madonna 1, 8
    activism 43
    AIDS/HIV awareness 39–40
    ballroom culture 35–6, 39
    In Bed with Madonna 32–4
    Body of Evidence (1993) 32
    Certain Sacrifice, A (1979) 31
    cultural studies 32, 34, 43–4
    Desperately Seeking Susan (1985) 31–2, 41, 81, 95, 117
    Dick Tracy (1990) 32
    Evita (1996) 32
    Express Yourself (1989) 31, 35
    flak 35
    identity politics 37–8
    Justify My Love (1990) 31, 35
    Like A Virgin 31
    as maternal figure 36
    New York years 41–3
    Paris is Burning (1990) 35–7
    screen presence 32
    Shanghai Surprise (1986) 32
    Truth or Dare (1991) 32, 34–5, 38–9, 41–2, 44
    Vogue video 32, 35, 41
    Who's That Girl? (1987) 32

Madonna Connection: Representational Politics, Subcultural Identities, and Cultural Theory, The (Schwichtenberg) 32, 34
Madonna Connection, The 34
'Madonna Studies' 31
magical negro 13
Magnani, Anna 176
Magnoli, Albert 51
Main Kaun Hoon song 138
Malone, Tony 207
Manchester Royal Exchange Theatre 117
Maness, Fred 162
Mangold, James 4
Man on the Train, The (2002) 4
Mansfield, Jayne 20, 88
Man Who Fell to Earth, The (1976) 3, 64–6, 69, 78, 88, 95, 188
Marker, Chris 96
Marsalis, Wynton 170
Marsh, Calum 74
Mars–Venus symbol 55–6
Martin, Dean 3
Masculin-Feminin (1966) 102
Matsutake, Hideki 184
Maybury, John 181
Mayersberg, Paul 69, 188
Mazar, Debi 42
Mbembe, Achille 155–6
McGowan, Todd 74
McKee, Lonette 176
McLaren, Malcolm 115
McLaren's King's Road clothes shop 112
McLaughlan, Tim 202
McLaughlin, John 172, 176
McLean, Jackie 172
McQueen, Steve 118
McRuer, Robert 39
McTiernan, John 118
Meat Loaf 4
Mehndi, Daler 144
Melbourne International Film Festival, 2009 208
Melehy, Hassan 102–3
Melville, Jean-Pierre 107
Memo from Turner song 124
Meo, Chuck 198

Meri Gully Mein song 141–3
Merrick, John 67
Merry Christmas, Mr. Lawrence (1983) 2, 6, 68–70, 181, 183, 185–7, 189
Metropolis (1927) 119
Miami Vice 117
Michelot, Pierre 172
micro celebrities 137–8
Midnight Oil 199
Miike, Takashi 4
Milburn, Lynn Maree 200
Miles Ahead (2015) 7
Miller, Monica 53–4
Mingus, Charles 174
Minneapolis Pride March 55
Minogue, Kylie 4, 82–4, 86–92
  Delinquents, The (1989) 83
  Holy Motors (2012) 82, 89–92
minority identity 40
Mishima, Yukio 185
Mister Rock and Roll (1957) 16, 24
Mitchell, Elvis 106–7
Mitchum, Robert 176
Modi, Narendra 131, 137, 140–4
Monáe, Janelle 4, 7
Monk, Thelonious 168
Monroe, Marilyn 88, 97–8, 153
Monson, Mitch 56
Montand, Yves 103, 108
  blue-collar persona 97
  On a Clear Day You Can See Forever (1970) 98
  Confession, The (1970) 96
  Étoile sans lumière (Star Without Light 1946) 96
  Goodbye Again (1961) 97–8
  La Guerre est Finie (The War is Over 1965) 96
  left-wing politics 96
  Le Joli Mai (The Lovely Month of May) 96
  Les Portes de la nuit (Gates of the Night) 96
  Let's Make Love (1960) 97–8
  as music-hall singer 95
  My Geisha (1962) 97–8
  Paris chante toujours (Paris Still Sings 1951) 96
  Paris est toujours Paris (Paris is Always Paris 1951) 96
  romantic image 98
  Saluti e baci (1953) 96
  Souvenirs perdus (Lost Souvenirs 1950) 96
  star persona 96–7
  Unominie e lupi (The Wolves 1956) 96
  Wide Blue Road, The (1957) 96
  Z (1969) 96–7
Monty Python 70
Moon, Chris 48
Moonage Daydream 64
Moonlight (2016) 4
Moore, Juanita 151, 162
Moores, Pamela M. 95
More Trees project 182
Morin, Edgar 105
Moroder, Giorgio 119, 184
Morricone, Ennio 124
Moschen, Michael 71
Moulin Rouge! (2001) 83
Mountains video (1986c) 54
Movieline 65
Mr. Rice's Secret (2000) 72
MTV 31, 39, 144, 201
Mukherjee, Hrishikesh 3
Mulligan, Gerry 178
Multiples (1980) 184
Mumbai rap 141–2
Murphy, Chris 199, 203
Murphy, Dudley 3, 5
My Geisha (1962) 97–8

Naked Youth (*Seishun zankoku monogatari* 1960) 186
Naremore, James 20
Needing You (2000) 4
Needles, Nique 195, 198
Need you Tonight (1987) 201
Négritude 147, 150, 161, 164
Nell, Little 115
Nelson, Ricky 3
neo-feminist warrior 141
Never Tear Us Apart (1988) 201
Newley, Anthony 2
Newman, Paul 176
New Power Generation, the 58

New Sensation (1987) 201
New Yorker, The 97
New York Times 32, 43, 106
Nicholson, Jack 49–51
Nigam, Sonu 144
Night and Fog in Japan (*Nihon no yoru to kiri* 1960) 186
Night of the New Moon, The (1970) 69
Nightshift (1981) 113
nihilism 115
1999 song (Prince) 49
Nolan, Christopher 2, 64, 72
Nomads (1985) 117–18, 126
Northern Exposure 118
Nouvelle Vague 101
Novak, Kim 66, 88
nuberu bagu (new wave) movement 186
Nude Tour (June to September 1990) 48, 50, 54–8
Nutty, Naughty Chateau (1963) 100–1

O'Brien, Edmond 20
O'Connor, Hazel 3
Odds Against Tomorrow (1959) 3
Oe, Kenzaburo 186
O'Hagan, Andrew 35
O'Hara, Mary Margaret 4
Oldham, Will 4
Old Joy (2006) 4
Olsen, Ollie 198
On a Clear Day You Can See Forever (1970) 98
Order of Death (1983) 3, 120–1, 123–4, 126, 128
Ôshima, Nagisa 64, 68–9, 181–2, 185
  Catch, The (*Shiiku* 1961) 186
  Ceremony, The (*Gishiki* 1971) 187
  Death by Hanging (*Kôshikei* 1968) 187
  Empire of Passion (*Ai no bôrei* 1978) 187
  Gohatto (1999) 187
  Merry Christmas, Mr. Lawrence 188–9
  Naked Youth (*Seishun zankoku monogatari* 1960) 186
  Night and Fog in Japan (*Nihon no yoru to kiri* 1960) 186
  Pleasures of the Flesh (*Etsuraku* 1965) 187
  In the Realm of the Senses (*ai no corrida*) 187
  Sozosha 186
  Sun's Burial, The (*Taiyô no hakaba* 1960) 186
  Tomorrow's Sun (1959) 186
  A Town of Love and Hope (*Ai to kibô no machi*, 1959) 186
Out of Africa 172
Out of Sight (1998) 2
Oz Rock 199

Paglia, Camilla 43
Paik, Nam June 181
Pal, Anuvab 132
Palmer, R. Barton 97
Palmer, Robert 23
Pande, Vinod 3
Paradis, Vanessa 4
Parallel Cinema 132
Parallel Lines (1978) 82, 84
Paramount Pictures 64
Paris chante toujours (Paris Still Sings 1951) 96
Paris est toujours Paris (Paris is Always Paris 1951) 96
Paris is Burning (1990) 35–7
Parker, Charlie 168–9, 171–2, 174
Partyman music video 49
pastiche 41
Pat Garrett and Billy the Kid (1973) 3
Pathak, Ankur 140
patriarchal violence 138
Patsy Valida 13
Paudras, Francis 171–2, 176–9
Peckinpah, Sam 3
Pengilly, Kirk 199
Pennebaker, D.A. 63
Penniman, Richard Wayne *see* Little Richard
Pepper, Art 178
Performance (1970) 2, 64, 124
performativity 17–19
Permanent Vacation (1980) 3
Perry, Alex Ross 4
Pete Kelly's Blues (1955) 3
Petit, Chris 3
Pettibone, Shep 42

Piaf, Édith 96
Pialat, Maurice 4
Pierrot Le Fou (1965) 101
Pirroni, Marco 119
plagiarism 133
Plastic Surgery 115
Platinum Blonde, Blondie song 88
Pleasures of the Flesh (*Etsuraku* 1965) 187
Pointrenaud, Jacques 3
Pollack, Sydney 172
Pomerance, Bernard 67
Pontecorvo, Gillo 96
Pop, Iggy 4
Pop Stars on Film 1
Pose 38
Post, Saskia 195
Powell, Bud 171–3, 176, 178–9
Power of the Zoot: Youth Culture and Resistance during World War II, The (2008) 52
Precious (2009) 2
Presley, Elvis 1–2, 5, 99, 108, 131
Prestige, The (2006) 2, 72–3, 78
Prévert, Jacques 96
Primitive Calculators, the 198
Prince Charming video 116, 118
Prince of Darkness (1987) 3
Prince (Prince Rogers Nelson) 1, 8–9, 18–19, 95
  aesthetic and personal branding 48
  Batdance (1989b) 48, 50, 56
  Batman music video 50–1, 56
  Batman symbol 56–7
  branding, celebrity identity 58
  Under the Cherry Moon (1986) 47, 49, 51, 54
  Dandyism 53–4
  Elephants and Flowers (Prince 1990a) 50, 57
  Gemini costume 50, 52, 54, 56–7
  Gemini/Partyman character 47–50
  Graffiti Bridge (1990) 47, 50, 55
  heart mirrors, bracelet 54–5
  If I Was Your Girlfriend (1987a) 49, 55
  as international superstar 48
  Joker character 49
  Kiss music video (1986b) 48–9
  Love/Lovesexy symbol 48, 55–7, 59

Lovesexy tour and album 48–50, 54–6
Mountains video (1986c) 54
New Power Generation, the 58
Nude Tour (June to September 1990) 48, 50, 54–6, 58
Partyman suit 51–2, 54
purple image 48–9, 51, 54, 59
Purple Rain (1984) 47, 49–51, 55, 117
semiotics, fashion 54
Sign O' the Times (1987) 47, 49–50, 54
split-design look 50
U Got the Look (1987b) 49
Private Eyes, The (1976) 3
proletarian eroticism 132–6
Prothero, David 121, 125
Public Image Limited (PiL) 120–1, 124
Public Pressure (1980) 184
pub rock scene, Australia 199
punk cinema 206
Punk Rock Movie, The (1978) 113
punk stars
  Ant, Adam 115–20
  Jordan 111–14
  Lydon, John 120–8
Purple Rain (1984) 1, 8, 47, 49–51, 55, 117

Quadrophenia (1979) 123
Queen Latifah 1
Queen Sonya 13
Qurbani (Sacrifice 1980) 132

Ra, Sun 7
Rabid (1977) 84
Race, Hugo 197
race and on-screen representation 5
racism 5–6, 12, 170, 175, 179, 188
Radio Birdman 198
Radio On (1979) 3
Rainey, Gertrude 'Ma' 13
Ramones, the 118
Rayfiel, David 172–3
Ready Teddy (1956) 23
Reaves-Phillips, Sandra 176
Reichardt, Kelly 4
Renais, Alain 96
Renoir, Jean 200
Revenant, The (2015) 181
Ribowsky, Mark 23

Richard, Cliff 3
Richard III, Laurence Olivier (Sir) 122
Ringwood, Bob 49–50, 52
Rio Bravo (1959) 3
Ritchie, Casci 52
Roach, Max 173–4
Robinson, Bill 5
Rochefort, Jean 106
Rock a Memphis (1975) 104
rock and roll 5, 11–12, 21–3, 25, 27, 99, 103, 199
Rock Around the Clock 99
rock biopics 6
Rocketman (2019) 7
Rock 'n' Roll High School 118
rock 'n' roll performers 100
Rock'n Slow (1974) 104
Rodin, Teddy 3
Roeg, Nic 64–5
Roeg, Nicolas 2–3, 88, 188
Rolling Stone magazine 31
Rollins, Henry 4
Rome, Open City 176
Rome, Sydne 66
Romero, Cesar 49
Rooke, Pamela 111
Rose, Robina 113–14
Ross, Diana 3, 6, 8
Rossellini, Roberto 153
Roth, Philip 153
Rotten, Johnny 121–5
'Round Midnight (1986) 8, 168, 170–1, 173–9
Rowe, Glenys 207
Rule Britannia 113–14
Russell, Ken 3
Rutles 2: Can't Buy Me Lunch, The (2002) 72
Rylance, Mark 123
Ryuichi Sakamoto: Coda 181

Sadler's Wells 63
sadomasochistic homoeroticism 122
Saints, The 198
Saint Sebastian 122
Sakamoto, Ryuichi 7, 182
  environmental and activism work 182
  Last Emperor, The (1988) 181
  Love is the Devil (1998) 181
  Merry Christmas, Mr. Lawrence (1983) 181, 183
  polymath status 181
  Revenant, The (2015) 181
  Sheltering Sky, The (1990) 181
  Sketch Show 184
  stardom 182
  synthpop 181
  YMO 181–3
Saldaña, Zoe 178
Saluti e baci (1953) 96
Salut les Copains 100
Sandrich, Mark 3
Sant, Gus Van 4
Saturday Night Live (1989c) 56
Schechner, Richard 15
Schible, Stephen Nomura 181
Schnabel, Julian 64, 72
Scientists, the 198
Scob, Édith 89
Scorsese, Martin 2, 64, 177
Scott, Tony 64, 68
Seacer, Levi Jr. 51
Sebastiane (1976) 112–13, 122
Seberg, Jean 89
Secret Superstar (2017) 141
  Chinese film audiences 136
  micro celebrity 137–8
  Muslims, India 137, 139
  patriarchal violence 138
  women, repression of 136, 138
Sedgwick, Edie 42
Seed and the Sower, The (1963) 69, 182
Seft, Theresa 137
Sejavka, Sam 197
semiotic radicalism 52
Set It Off (1996) 1
Seven Samurai (1954) 200
Sex Pistols 111, 115, 119–23
Shakur, Tupac 1
Shanghai Surprise (1986) 32
Sheila 100
Sheltering Sky, The (1990) 181
Shepard, Rich 72
Sherman, Cindy 42
Sherrin, Jim 49
She's Got It (1956) 23

Shine Like It Does 199
Shivers (1975) 84
Shorter, Wayne 172, 176
'shut up' 18
Sid and Nancy (1986) 6
Signoret, Simone 97
Sign O' the Times (1987) 47, 49–50, 54
Simmons, Gene 117
Simpsons, The (2003) 11, 16
Sinatra, Frank 3, 5, 7
Singh, Ranveer 140, 143
Singleton, John 7
Sirk, Douglas 150–8, 160, 162
Si Tu Gagnes Au Flipper (1965) 102
Sketch Show 184
Slade in Flame (1975) 6
Slam Dance (1987) 120
Small World of Sammy Lee, The (1963) 2
Smash Hits magazine 116
Smet, Jean-Phillipe 103
Smiley Culture 2
Smith, Bessie 3, 5, 13
Solid State Survivor (1979) 183–5
Sonar Festival 184
Song of the South (1946) 150
Son's Burial, The (Taiyo no hakaba 1960) 189
Sons of Norway (2011) 120
Soul Train 184
Souvenirs perdus (Lost Souvenirs 1950) 96
Space Oddity 64
Specialists, The (1969) 105–6, 108
Spellcaster (1988) 118
Spring Breakers (2012) 4
St. Louis Blues (1928) 3, 5
Stahl, John M. 150, 154
Stamp, Terence 117
Stanley, Bob 2
Star (1982) 3
stardom
  ant, Adam 115–16
  Little Richard 19
  Minogue, Kylie 83
  Sakamoto, Ryuichi 182
Starr, Ringo 3
Stea, Kevin 33, 37
Stella, Susan 50, 52

Stereo (1969) 84
Stilettos, The 84
Stiller, Ben 72
Sting 3, 123
Stone, Andrew 3, 5
Stone, Sly 50
Stormy Weather (1943) 3, 5
Straight Outta Compton (2015) 7
Stratton, David 207
Street Fighter (1994) 83, 91
Streisand, Barbara 7
Streitz, Michelle Kasimor 50, 54
Strickland, Peter 4
Strike a Pose (2017) 34
Strikebound (1984) 200, 202
Strip-Tease (1963) 3
Strummer, Joe 4
Subculture: The Meaning of Style (Hebdige) 52
Suddenly (1954) 3
Sun's Burial, The (Taiyô no hakaba 1960) 186
Swing, The (1984) 203
sycophantic political sympathies, Bollywood elite 140
Sydney Morning Herald 207
Sylvian, David 183
synecdochic responsibility 20
synthpop 181

Takahashi, Yukihiro 183–4
Takatani, Shiro 181
Tashlin, Frank 20
Tavernier, Bertrand 168, 170–4, 176, 179
Taylor, James 3
Taylor, Lisa 95
Tchaikovski's Destruction 124
technopop 184
Telexes in Space 202
Temple, Julien 64, 70
Tevis, Walter 64
Thatcher, Margaret 63
That'll Be the Day (1973) 3
Theatre 625, BBC drama series 64
Thieves in the Temple (1990b) 57
Thin White Duke 63
Thomas, Jeremy 69, 187
Thompson, Ben 81, 91

Three Angels Broadcasting Network (2017) 16
Three Days of the Condor 172
Till, Emmett 14
Timberlake, Justin 4
To, Johnnie 4
Tom Horn 118
Tomita, Isao 184
Tommy (1975) 3
Tomorrow's Sun (1959) 186
Tonight Show Starring Johnny Carson, The (1986) 16
Too Fat to Fit Through the Door 198
Toop, David 184
Town of Love and Hope, A (*Ai to kibô no machi,* 1959) 186
Toyah 114
Trespass (1992) 4
Tricky 4
Trouble of the World song 151, 160, *161*, 164
Trupin, Gabriel 33
Truth or Dare (1991) 32, 34–5, 38–9, 41–2, 44
Tschetter, Sotera 56
Tucker, Ken 85
Turner, Tina 3
'Tutti Frutti' 14, 23–4
Twin Peaks: Fire Walk with Me (1992) 2, 64, 72–8
Twin Peaks: The Return (2017) 74
Two-Lane Blacktop (1971) 3
Tyrannosaurus Rex rock duo 64

U Got the Look (1987b) 49
Under the Cherry Moon (1986) 47, 49, 51, 54
Underwood, George 65
Union City (1980) 82–3, 91
Unominie e lupi/The Wolves (1956) 96
Untitled Film Stills exhibition 42

Valentino, Rudolph 116
Vales, Vicky 50
Vamp (1986) 3
Van Cleve, Stewart 55
Van Damme, Jean-Claude 83
Van der Post 188

van der Post, Laurens (Sir) 69
Van Gogh (1991) 4
Vartan, Sylvie 100, 105
Vaughn, Frankie 98
Vengeance (*Fuk sau* 2009) 107–8
Veronesi, Giovanni 72
Videodrome (1983) 2, 82, 84–8, 90–2
Village Voice 74
Visconti, Luchino 42
Vogue House of Xtravaganza 33, 41
Vogue magazine 38
Vogue video 32, 35, 41
von Trier, Lars 4
Von Tussle, Velma 91

W. E. (2008) 31
Wai, Wong Kar 4
Waits, Tom 2, 4, 81
Walk the Line (2005) 7
Walters, Ashley 4
Walton, Cedar 8, 170–1
Wang, Wayne 120
Ward, Tony 42
Warhol, Andy 41–2, 72
Warner Bros. 51, 57, 172
Waters, John 91
Watham, Claude 3
Watts, Richard Jr. 97
Weaver, Miko 51
Webb, Jack 3
Webb, Robert D. 5
We Children from Zoo Station 67
Weevils in the Flour (Wendy) 200
Wells, Sadler 67
Wenders, Wim 42–3
Wenk, Richard 3
We're Living on Dog Food (2009) 204
What's Love Got to Do with It (1993) 6
What's New Pussycat? (1965) 100–1
When Doves Cry (1984b) 8, 55
Where the Wild Roses Grow 83
Whirlywirld 198
white female star worship 36
white male homosexuality 13
white performers 5
Who's That Girl? (1987) 32
'Who Were We' 83
Wide Blue Road, The (1957) 96

Wilborn, Carlton 33
Wild at Heart (1990) 73
Wild One, The (1953) 99
Williams, Tony 172
Wilson, Dennis 3
Wind in the Willows, The 84
Wings of Desire (1987) 42
Wise, Robert 3
Wojcik, Pamela Robertson 19
Wong, Faye 4
Woodlawn, Holly 42
Woods, Bobby 42
Woods, James 84–5, 88, 92
Woodsman, The (2004) 4
World Gone Wild (1988) 119
Woronov, Mary 118
Wretched of the Earth, The (Fanon) 149

Xtravaganza, Jose Gutierez 32

Yamamoto, Kansai 185
Yellowbeard (1983) 70

Yellow Magic Orchestra (YMO) 181–3
   Solid State Survivor (1979) 183–5
   technopop 184
Yeung, Miriam 4
Yé-Yé girls
   Bardot, Brigitte 100–2
   French-ness 99
   Goya, Chantel 102–3
   Hardy, Françoise 100–1
   Karina, Anna 100–1
Young, Lester 162, 172, 174
Young Charlatans, The 198
YouTube 136–7

Z (1969) 96–7
Ziggy Stardust 63–4, 71
Ziggy Stardust and the Spiders from Mars (1979) 63
Zoolander (2001) 72
zoot suit 52–4
Zukor, Adolph 168

www.ingramcontent.com/pod-product-compliance
Lightning Source LLC
Chambersburg PA
CBHW062215300426
44115CB00012BA/2069